Dorothy Yim

descriptive Ilg. continuum (Reinecke)

popular

PGP (subj. matter know)

Da Kine Talk

DA KINE TALK

From Pidgin to Standard English in Hawaii

ELIZABETH BALL CARR

with a chapter by
DONG JAE LEE

THE UNIVERSITY PRESS OF HAWAII

for Jane

Contents

Foreword

It is fitting that the first descriptive book on Hawaiian Island English should be written by Elizabeth B. Carr, the person who has done the most to stimulate in Island people, and particularly in Island teachers, a scientific outlook toward our formerly despised and denigrated "pidgin English."

Scholarly attention to local English began in 1933 with sociologist William C. Smith's article in *American Speech*. But that article and my own articles in 1934 and 1938 had at the time no impact whatever upon the school system, whose interest in a scientific examination of "pidgin English" could not have been less. The most advanced step of which Island educators then were capable was compilation of the most frequent "errors" committed by their students. Psychologist Madorah E. Smith and her students at the University of Hawaii, over a long span of years (1931–1961), produced a number of published and unpublished studies of local English. But this work was motivated by Dr. Smith's debatable thesis that early bilingualism—unavoidable here in any event —was detrimental to children, and the studies concentrated upon the speech of young children. Their essential outlook is indicated by a remark in a 1957 article, that preschool children's speech was "still contaminated by pidgin English." Sociologists Bernhard L. Hormann and Andrew W. Lind made sensible observations on the "pidgin English" situation, but in the key areas of speech instruction and general education their voices were little noticed. Before the creation of the university's

large and technically sophisticated departments of linguistics and
TESOL (teaching of English as a second language) the speech department was crucial, and it was there that Dr. Carr played an essential
role.

Almost from the day of her arrival in Hawaii in 1935 Dr. Carr has
been concerned with the speech of Island students—and that of their
elders. Her training as a speech teacher and in linguistics gave her an
outlook which combined appreciation of linguistic principles and their
practical application in education. After four years in the Territorial
Department of Public Instruction, Dr. Carr's twenty-three years at the
University of Hawaii (1943–1966), first in the Department of English,
and from 1947 in the new Department of Speech (which she headed for
seven years), gave her the opportunity to impress upon a whole generation the need to treat "pidgin" as worthy of serious and objective study.
To some extent her influence was felt through her papers and articles
and her training of students in research techniques. (See Bibliography
entries under Carr, Hayes, Kindig, Morimoto, Shun, and Vanderslice
and Pierson.) But to a much greater extent she left her mark through her
teaching, particularly of students who brought a new outlook into the
public school system, and through her lectures and her continual contacts with educators and organizations concerned with education.

The reaction that a scientifically based examination of "pidgin"
aroused in many people, only ten years ago, is illustrated by a letter to
the editor of the *Honolulu Advertiser* of August 30, 1961. The writer took
issue with one of Dr. Carr's addresses, declaring that pidgin has "no
grammatical structure, no order." But Dr. Carr's views, pressed year
after year, had their effect in the public school system. She laid the
groundwork for acceptance by the State Department of Education of
the federally funded Keaukaha Oral Language Program at Hilo (1965–
1969), for the study of effective ways of teaching standard English to
"pidgin"-speaking children, which has had a notable, and salutary, impact on local educational thinking. The Department's official attitude
now, as stated in its 1971 report on the Keaukaha project, is that "Hawaii Islands Dialect is a respectable, useful tool of communication for
its speakers."

This book, intended primarily for residents of Hawaii and written
with a minimum of technical language, continues the author's career as
an educator of a wide public. Its illustrations and grammatical descriptions of five types of Hawaiian English should make it clear that even
the true pidgin of the early immigrants does indeed have order and grammatical structure. Order and grammatical structure are still more apparent in the creole English of contemporary youth (Dr. Carr's Type

III), the type of speech that still disturbs some educators emotionally. The lexical section of the book is an introduction to the rich and picturesque nature of local speech.

More technical studies of our local English can be, and are being, written, but technicality is not the aim of this work. As I see it, its aim is to induce the average Islander to see and appreciate, and not to scorn, the rich variety of our daily speech. Such a book was long overdue.

JOHN E. REINECKE

Preface

[handwritten notes:]

Lgs in Contact
Eng & Fr.
Norman Conquest 1066
cow · beef
pig pork)
sheep mutton

In Hawaii we get many lg. bkgrnds.
eg What ethnicities are you?
(shes.)

All languages and dialects change, and one of the chief causes of this change is intensive contact with other languages. The best known example in the history of the English language is its prolonged contact with French in the centuries following the Norman Conquest. Our language emerged from that long period of eclipse still basically *English*, but profoundly altered, by the influence of French, in both vocabulary and structure. That was a relatively simple instance of contact: only two languages were involved and both were of the same group—the Indo-European family.

In Hawaii, the contacts of English with other languages have been far more complicated, involving not only Indo-European languages (Portuguese, Spanish), but also several of the Malayo-Polynesian group (Hawaiian, Ilocano, Visayan, Tagalog) and several Asian languages (Chinese, Japanese, Korean). At a point of high intensity in this contact, around the year 1900, the number of native speakers of English (then all, or nearly all, Caucasians), was only a little more than 5 percent. Yet, because English was the language of the government and the language of instruction in the schools, it kept the ascendency. The great majority of the people, however, spoke forms of English that showed the influence of the impinging foreign languages heard so widely in everyday life.

The twentieth century has seen a long, and often uphill, pull toward the standard form of the English language. Today a large number of people born in Hawaii (and subject in varying degrees to this language

interference) have moved into the standardized language—the form
called Type V in this book. Great numbers of nonstandard speakers remain, however, and their forms of speech show the many points at which
our language has been touched, altered, and crystallized into slightly
different molds by the influence of the foreign languages so long in com-
petition in the Islands. The myriad small results of the interchange will
provide fascinating language study for future years.

Unfortunately we are without records of the many intermediate stages
in this change. Although the simplest plant in Hawaii's soil was described, sketched, and carefully recorded long ago, no such scientific
records have been kept of the languages spoken. The speech forms of the
early Hawaiians as they learned English, and those of the immigrants as
they responded to orders in pidgin on the plantations are forever lost.
Such utterances, until recently, have been considered too unimportant
and too substandard to warrant observation. A quarter of a century ago
antipidgin campaigns were conducted in the Islands with such puritani-
cal zeal as to affect the attitudes of children and to inhibit the flow of
communication between people of all ages. Fortunately, the recent
growth of descriptive linguistics and the concurrent interest in human
communication have produced a gentler climate for the study of dialect
in Hawaii.

Acknowledgments

This book has drawn heavily upon the knowledge and generosity of a number of consultants and assistants. Pualani (Alberta) P. Anthony, University of Hawaii, accompanied the author on field trips to the outer islands of the Hawaiian chain, recorded on tape the interview used in chapter 5, and furnished examples of loanblends and of glossary terms. O. A. Bushnell, University of Hawaii, a *kama'aina* whose memory of Island terms and inflections is long and trustworthy, served as a sounding board for many glossary items. Denzel Carr, Department of Oriental Languages, University of California at Berkeley, from his knowledge of more than forty languages of the East and West, was able to contribute parallel forms for many items in the glossary and to assist with loanwords. Samuel H. Elbert, compiler (with Mary K. Pukui) of the standard Hawaiian-English and English-Hawaiian dictionaries, checked all parts of the book dealing with the Hawaiian language and gave advice about the presentation of material in other sections. Dong Jae Lee, University of Hawaii, wrote the greater part of chapter 2, contributed to the section on Korean loanwords and to many of the glossary entries, and acted as a patient general assistant.

Many other persons have had a hand in the various stages of development of this book. Dozens of students, graduate assistants, and colleagues have shared in the work and pleasure of gathering the material. Edgar C. Knowlton, Jr., a colleague who is familiar with a score of languages (including Tagalog, Mandarin, Japanese, Korean, Portuguese, and Spanish), has patiently checked a variety of items. He has been especially helpful with the Portuguese. Other colleagues at the University of Hawaii who have assisted include Stefan Baciu, Janet Bell, Kathleen Bourcier, A. Grove Day, Bernhard L. Hormann, Beatrice Krauss, Nobleza Landé, Amos P. Leib, Andrew W. Lind, Thomas Nickerson, Albert J. Schütz, Gregg M. Sinclair, Frederick Y. Smith, Lorinda W. Thomas, and Helene H. Wong. Willard Wilson has given pleasant assistance and wise advice for more than a decade. Kenneth P. Emory and Eleanor Williamson of the Bernice P. Bishop Museum have been enthusiastic and cooperative. The staff members of the Hawaiian and Pacific Collections at the Sinclair Library, University of Hawaii, have taken a special interest in the book through all its stages.

It is especially pleasant to be able to acknowledge the assistance of many former students, including Ethel Aotani, Connie Hall, Nancy Hiu, Donna Ikeda, Melba Kop, Elizabeth Kunimoto, Jean Sato Motokane, Laura Shun Pierson, Pat Morimoto Segura, and Rose Yasuhara.

Congresswoman Patsy T. Mink delighted the author by consenting to make a tape recording in her office. Shunzo Sakamaki was similarly generous with a tape recording of his recollections of the first public appearance of the University of Hawaii's debate team.

Among the residents of Honolulu who have given aid and advice are John E. Reinecke, one of the earliest investigators in the field of Hawaii's English dialects, and Fancey B. Opiopio, daughter of Annie Loo Akana, whose interview is studied in chapter 3.

During 1968 and earlier, the Department of Speech at the University of Hawaii and its chairmen, Bower Aly and Richard L. Rider, gave shelter and encouragement to the growing manuscript. At that time, Jasmine Miyamoto and Velma Francisco furnished careful secretarial work and assistance extending beyond the keyboard of the typewriter.

The scholar who most influenced the book during its early stages was the late Claude M. Wise of Louisiana State University, who devoted his life to a lively pursuit of dialects, drawing his spellbound students along the trails with him. Several other scholars who live beyond the boundaries of Hawaii have added generously with material and with suggestions for organization. Among them are Frederic G. Cassidy of the University of Wisconsin; Ernesto Constantino of the University of the Philippines; S. I. Hayakawa of San Francisco State College; Robert A. Hall, Jr., and Charles F. Hockett of Cornell University; and Susumu Nagara of the University of Michigan.

The local and Mainland foundations that have graciously supported this research on several occasions deserve and receive the author's appreciation in full measure, not only for financial assistance but also for confidence in the project.

For the shortcomings of the book and for all inadvertent omissions, the author is solely responsible. Comments from readers and, most especially, examples of Island expressions which have escaped the author's attention will be gratefully received.

Part I Varieties of Speech in Hawaii

1886-1900 61T ᵗʰ Japanese < Hiroshime & Yamaguchi

　　1901　6T Puerto Ricans

　　1904-5　8T Koreans

1907-13　　8T Spaniards
1907-31　　Philipines < Ilocano
　　　　　　　　　　　　Visayan
　　　　　　　　　　　　Tagalog

P.lANTATION ∧ PIDGIN　　　　← ↙

① *Chapter 1* **Introduction**

The English language was first heard in the Hawaiian Islands in 1778, in
the British accents of Captain James Cook and his men when they
touched land on Kauai. Not long after this time, as the Pacific fur trade
became profitable, trading vessels began making frequent voyages between the northwest coast of America and the commercial ports of
China, with brief stops in Hawaii. This flourishing trade took the English language to the China ports, where, to make bargaining possible
between traders and merchants, a much reduced form of English (with
borrowings from Portuguese and Cantonese) was evolved into a dialect
soon to be called *pidgin*—probably a Cantonese pronunciation of the
word *business*. The term and the dialect held prestige in Canton because,
wherever pidgin was spoken, activity, excitement, and contact with the
Western world could be found.

In these early days pidgin was written down only in word lists published for the use of servants in Canton applying for work with foreign
firms and families. One of these early lists was a booklet of a dozen or
more pages called "A Vocabulary of Words in Use among the Red-Haired
People [Caucasians]." Pidgin of several varieties spread with incredible
speed in the China ports. There was *joss pidgin*, the language of religion;
sword pidgin, special terms used in fencing; *chowchow pidgin*, the vocabulary of eating and cookery; *love pidgin*, auspicious phrases for love and
courtship; and *larn pidgin*, the term used for those apprentices who
bound themselves out to work in a foreign household and learned pidgin

3

in the process (Leland 1904:4,131). Thus the word *pidgin* had only good connotations in China, with the promise of excitement and promotion for young people who learned it.

It is little wonder that young Hawaiian men, signing on trading ships as sailors for the Alaska-Hawaii-Canton run, should have brought back to Hawaii (probably with pride) words from the new international language they had heard in China. By 1791, at least two words from Cantonese pidgin had arrived in Hawaii and were in use here. Lieutenant Manuel Quimper, a young Spaniard collecting information about the Islands in that year, compiled a word list from the Hawaiian language as he heard it spoken. Included in his list was the term *caucao*, his own spelling for what he believed to be a true Hawaiian word. What he had heard was the Hawaiians' pronunciation of the Chinese pidgin *chowchow* 'food', which had arrived in Hawaii before him. As *kaukau*, the word is still widely used in Hawaii where it passes for a Hawaiian term to those who do not know its origin. Another word listed by Quimper that gave further evidence of contact between Hawaii and Canton was the Portuguese-derived *pickaninny*, a term used in Chinese pidgin (Quimper 1822). Thus, within a little more than a decade after the discovery of Hawaii, bits of pidgin English were coming in from Asia.

Soon after the first group of New England missionaries arrived in the Islands in 1820, they began, as a regular part of their work, to teach English to the Hawaiians. Encouraged by members of the royal family, who were themselves the first eager pupils, the learning of English acquired great prestige, and, as Kuykendall noted, by the end of 1821 about two hundred Hawaiian people had received instruction (1938:106). Although for several decades major efforts in education were directed toward making the people literate in their own language, the desire to learn English remained and increased. By the middle of the century, nearly all the native people were able to read and write in Hawaiian (Kuykendall 1938:344 fn), and they could therefore learn a second language with greater facility. Kuykendall further recorded: "During the later 1840's and the early 1850's, the craze among the Hawaiians for learning English led to the establishment of a number of small schools . . . whose sole or principal object was to teach the English language to natives" (1938:365). By the end of 1854, ten English-language schools were in operation, among them the famous Royal School for the education of the children of the higher chiefs (1938:113, 361–362). As a culmination of this steady rise in the use of English, it was made the official language of the Hawaiian government and the medium of instruction in the public schools during the last decade of the century (Wist 1940:130).

The structure of a student's native language has a profound influence upon the ease with which he can learn a second one. Pronunciation alone may be a serious obstacle. A few examples will show the major differences between Hawaiian and English in phonology, and will suggest the many problems in pronunciation that faced the Island learners of the new language. Hawaiian has only eight consonants, compared with the twenty-four consonant sounds of English (Pukui and Elbert 1957:xix); Hawaiian has no consonant clusters, whereas English contains numerous initial and final clusters; Hawaiian has no words ending in consonants, in contrast to the vast numbers of English words that end with one, two, three, or even more consonants. The early pronunciation of English words by Hawaiians is illustrated by the Hawaiian forms of four English proper names: Bruce, Frank, Fred, and Frances, pronounced, respectively, Puluke, Palani, Peleke, and Palakika. In attempting to master the unfamiliar sounds, the Hawaiians (1) separated English clusters by the insertion of a vowel, (2) substituted consonants contained in their own language for English consonants lacking in Hawaiian, and (3) attached a final vowel to each name to make it conform to the word pattern of Hawaiian. The fact is that even during the decades when the major linguistic contact in the Islands was confined to two languages, Hawaiian and English, the learning problems were formidable, and the indigenous language had a marked effect upon the spoken English.

Adding to the complexity of the linguistic situation, thousands of foreign laborers from Asia and Europe were brought to Hawaii to work on the sugar plantations and, as their families grew and their children entered the public schools, the English language, so recently established as the medium of instruction, suffered a kind of "linguistic swamping." The ratio of *haoles* (Caucasians) dropped at the turn of the century to about 5.4 percent of the population (Lind 1967:32). Ideally, the English teachers should have been drawn from this small group of *native* speakers of the language, but very few of them, of course, were interested in teaching. In fact, at the moment when Hawaii most needed excellent English teachers, they were in short supply. Many an Island classroom was presided over by a teacher who was able to speak only very nonstandard English for the pupils to imitate. Dialectal patterns, once established in a community, persist for a very long time.

Key dates of the great influx of foreign peoples may well be reviewed here. In two periods, between 1876 and 1885 and again between 1890 and 1897, the government of Hawaii brought in a total of 46,000 Chinese laborers from South China; between 1878 and 1887 and again between 1906 and 1913, about 17,500 Portuguese workers came from Madeira and the Azores. An important difference between the two immigrant groups was that the Portuguese brought their families and planned to remain, while the Chinese were single men expecting to return to China. Between 1886 and 1900, about 61,000 Japanese workers were brought to the Islands, most of them from Hiroshima and Yamaguchi and nearby prefectures in the west of Japan. In 1901, nearly 6,000 Puerto Ricans arrived, and in 1904 and 1905, about 8,000 Koreans. Nearly 8,000 Spaniards were recruited between 1907 and 1913. The largest mass importation of workers—more than 120,000 from the Philippines, most of them speakers of Ilocano, Visayan, and Tagalog—took place between 1907 and 1931 (Lind 1967:26-31). Careful, thorough studies of the sociological and linguistic backgrounds of these immigrants, particularly those from Japan, have been made by Reinecke (1969) and Nagara (1969).

As the few English-language schools continued to teach the language to Hawaiian pupils in an orderly way during the last quarter of the century, a far different variety of English was being taught and learned on the sugar plantations. There, pressed by daily necessity, plantation overseers gave instructions to the newly arrived laborers in a condensed, minimal form of English (content words, very few function words, no inflections). This telegraphic speech was interlarded with terms from the Cantonese pidgin that the laborers already knew (or had learned during the voyage to the Islands)—*can do, no can, bumbye, savvy*, and the like. Certain plantation terms from the Hawaiian scene were included, as well as a few colorful or expressive words from the tongues of the laborers themselves (see chapter 7). The laborers imitated their foremen—the *lunas*—and a new pidgin was developed in Island surroundings for Island circumstances.

As time went on and as single laborers who had intended to return to Asia married and settled down in Hawaii, the vocabulary of the home and the playground was added to the plantation jargon, and the language moved into its creole stage. As the children studied and used English regularly in school they began to progress from the simplest forms of the language toward the more fully developed forms—along that path which Reinecke has aptly termed the *language continuum* of the Islands. To this day, individuals can be identified at various spots on the progression. Although Hawaii's pidgin era has long since passed, in isolated cases of communication with elderly immigrants we can still find examples of conversations in which the pidgin situation is partially re-created, as in the case of the granddaughter who reduces her own language structure to meet the broken English of her grandmother (chapter 2). As we listen today to the conversations of some Hawaii-born youngsters, we are keenly aware, almost a century after the time of the plantation immigrations, that some forms of English in the Islands are still roughly at the creole stage—sharply reduced in structure, as shown in chapter 4.

The labor recruits from China, Portugal, Japan, Puerto Rico, Spain, Korea, and the Philippines still constitute, with their children and their grandchildren, well over half of Hawaii's population (Lind 1967:9). They and their ancestral languages have had a profound effect upon the forms of English in Hawaii. The purpose of this book is to take a careful look at the kinds of English to be found in Hawaii today and to study these diverse dialects in the light of the influences brought to bear upon them.

As we have seen, only about 5 percent of the people of the Islands at the turn of the century were *native* speakers of English. Therefore, probably less than 5 percent of the population (including Hawaiians) could have spoken a type of English well enough developed to have been called standard. Today, even though all degrees of language development can be found, from the simplest to the most accomplished, thousands of individuals from all of Hawaii's ethnic groups are speakers of standard English. Other thousands, from almost all the ethnic groups, have been caught in one type of nonstandard dialect or another. It will be interesting, therefore, to examine some of the types of spoken English heard in the Islands, considering always the factors that have made them what they are.

TYPES OF SPEECH

Degrees of proficiency in English speech in Hawaii today form a continuous broad spectrum, ranging from the most rudimentary, broken English at one end to the norms of standard American speech at the other. No two individual speakers are at exactly the same point in this drift toward the form called standard, and of course there are no sharp dividing lines separating groups according to their mastery of the language.

For practical purposes of identifying stages on this spectrum, however, we can mark off segments as theoretical types and attempt to describe the characteristics of speakers at the midpoints of these artificial segments. Although any number of divisions might be made, for the present study five types are arbitrarily set up corresponding to five "stations" along the sweep of the spectrum. So that characteristics of speech at each station may be noted by the reader, transcriptions from the tape recordings of actual speakers representing each group will be presented.

It is important to make one point clear. In studying each type of speech in turn, from the simplest to the most developed, the aim will not be to show what the speakers lack as compared with the ideal, but what they *have* in their particular forms of speech to make communication possible, and what devices they use to make themselves understood. The developments they have made, in comparison with the preceding simpler type, will be of primary concern. Thus the descriptions will not be in terms of "errors," but in terms of growth from the simplest speech of the plantation toward the most complex forms of the language.

PHONETIC NOTATION

Phonetic symbols used to transcribe the interviews in the following chapters are based on those of the International Phonetic Alphabet, a system of notation devised in 1888 for the study of languages of Western Europe and published, with revisions from time to time, by the International Phonetic Association of London. This notation was chosen because it has been learned as a required subject by great numbers of high school and university graduates who now form a part of the community in Hawaii. Additional symbols have been added to the IPA by the Association, for the transcription of American English.* Because no true phonemicization can be attempted on the basis of the limited material in the interviews, the Trager-Smith phonemic symbols for consonants and vowels have not been introduced here.

For the convenience of the reader, a list of phonetic symbols for English consonants and vowels is given in table 1, with key words and parallel pronunciation symbols from *Webster's Third New International Dictionary*. Modifying diacritics and additional symbols for stress and intonation are explained on the pages following the table. Additional symbols needed for the transcription of the speech of Type I, an immigrant whose English is heavily influenced by the Korean language, will be introduced in chapter 2.

MODIFYING MARKS FOR PHONETIC SYMBOLS

$(C = consonant; V = vowel)$

C^h	aspirated	$\tilde{C}$	palatalized
C	dentalized	$V:$	given extra length
$C>$	unreleased	$\tilde{V}$	nasalized
C	syllabic (forming a syllable without an accompanying vowel)		

---

* The chart of the International Phonetic Alphabet may be obtained from the office of the secretary of the International Phonetic Association, Department of Phonetics, University College, London. This chart, revised to 1951, is reproduced and explained by Bronstein (1960:28–32; 298–299).

TABLE 1　Phonetic Notation Used in the Transcriptions

IPA PHONETIC SYMBOLS	WEBSTER'S THIRD PRONUN-CIATION SYMBOLS	KEY WORDS	IPA PHONETIC SYMBOLS	WEBSTER'S THIRD PRONUN-CIATION SYMBOLS	KEY WORDS
			CONSONANTS		
[p]	p	pat, tap	[š] or [ʃ]	sh	shed, dash
[b]	b	bat, tab	[ž] or [ʒ]	zh	azure, rouge
[t]	t	top, pot	[m]	m	main, name
[d]	d	dot, Tod	[n]	n	net, ten
[k]	k	keep, peek	[ŋ]	ŋ	ink, ring
[g]	g	got, dog	[l]	[l]	lane, nail
[č] or [tʃ]	ch	chin, each	[r]	r	red, wear
[ǰ] or [dʒ]	j	joy, urge	[w]	w	will, always
[f]	f	fall, off	[y] or [j]	y	yes, million
[v]	v	van, have	[h]	h	had, ahead
[θ]	th	thin, myth	[hw]	hw	whale, awhile
[ð]	*th*	then, breathe	[ſ][1]	d·	letter
[s]	s	set, bus	[ʔ][2]	ʔ	Oh⸲ oh!
[z]	z	zoo, ooze			
		VOWELS AND DIPHTHONGS			
[i]	ē	each, bee	[u]	ü	ooze, zoo
[ɪ]	i	it, bit	[ʊ]	u̇	book, put
[e][3]	ā	bait, date	[o][3]	ō	obey, boat
[ɛ]	e	ebb, bet	[ɔ]	ȯ	audit, saw
[æ]	a	fat, tab	[ɒ][7]	—	on, doll
[a][4]	a̍	ask, path	[ɑ]	ä	calm, father
[ɨ][5]	ə̇	roses, rented	[eɪ]	ā	aid, pay
[ɝ] or [ɜ][6]	ür	urn, her	[oʊ]	ō	old, go
[ɚ] or [ə][6]	ēr	river, actor	[aɪ]	ī	item, tie
[ʌ]	u	up, son	[aʊ]	au̇	out, cow
[ə]	ə	away, soda	[ɔɪ]	ȯi	oil, boy
			[yu] or [ɪu]	yü	use, cue

[1] The sound [ſ], called a flap, is heard in much of America for the medial /t/ of words like *letter* and *butter*; it is heard also in the British pronunciation of the /r/ in *very*.

[2] The glottal stop, heard only incidentally in English, is a consonant phoneme in Hawaiian. In spelling words containing this sound, it is indicated by a reversed apostrophe.

[3] The sounds [e] and [o], as in *date* and *obey*, are written with one symbol when they are not diphthongized, although in standard American speech they are usually heard as diphthongs.

[4] The vowel [a] is a sound between [æ] and [ɑ], heard in some English dialects in words like *ask* and *path*.

[5] The "barred i" is described by Gleason (1955:35) as the highest central vowel and by Webster's Third as an unstressed vowel intermediate between the [ɪ] and the [ə].

[6] These are alternate pronunciations, depending on whether the [r] is pronounced or not pronounced.

[7] The sound [ɒ] is intermediate between [ɔ] and [ɑ]. It is very commonly heard in Hawaii in words like *doll*, *not*, and *on*.

NOTATION FOR STRESS AND INTONATION

Descriptive linguists have developed a set of symbols that are extremely useful in the study of spoken English. The representation of stress and intonation in this book follows the notation of Gleason (1961:40–50). Bronstein (1960:242–279) and many other phoneticians who employ the IPA for segmental phonemes (vowels and consonants), make use of the notation explained below for the suprasegmentals (stress, pitch, and clause terminals).

Stress. The relative force or loudness of syllables is more finely marked in a linguistic description than it is in standard English dictionaries. Four degrees of stress are differentiated as follows:

1. *Primary*, or strongest, stress is indicated by a mark slanting from right to left placed over the vowel of the syllable which receives it. Example: *dél ta*.

2. *Secondary* stress, a new feature for many readers, is a reduced loud stress, not used extensively in single words but often needed in compound words and clauses. It is represented by the symbol /^/. Example: *él e và tor - ôp er à tor*. If the first syllables of the two words are compared, it will be clear that *el-* is stronger than *op-*, yet within the separate words each has strongest stress. In comparison with each other, *el-* takes precedence over *op-* because of the habits of compounding in English.

3. *Tertiary* stress is marked by the symbol [`] placed above the vowel of the syllable to receive it. This corresponds to the secondary stress of American dictionaries. Example: *àr bi trá tion*.

4. *Weak* stress is left unmarked. Examples are to be seen in the second syllable of the word *dél ta* and in the second and fourth syllables of *àr bi trá tion*.

Intonation. Gleason describes intonation as follows: "Every clause is marked and held together by two, three, or four pitch phonemes and one clause terminal" (1961:48). For the reader, much depends on an understanding of the four levels of *pitch*—the relative position of a syllable on an up-and-down scale, as in musical notation. The speaking voice in English has four pitch levels. The base line, from which the voice most often begins an utterance, is called *mid*, or *level 2*. In a typical sentence in standard English the voice may remain on level 2 for several syllables, then rise to *level 3*, called *high*, for the most prominent syllable of the clause. For example:

²He's at the ³store. ¹\

At the end of this sentence, the voice drops to a level lower than 2, called *low*, or *level 1*. If the last word of the sentence had contained more than one syllable, however, the entire final syllable would have been spoken on level 1. Example:

²She's in the ³kit¹chen.

Or, as it is more commonly written, with the final number at the end of the clause:

²She's in the ³kit chen.¹

An additional visual aid is given by the following method of marking the same sentences, with horizontal lines at the different levels:

²He's at the ³|sto|re.¹   ²She's in the ³|kit|chen.¹

In animated conversation and in exclamations, a fourth level is heard; this is called *level 4* or *extra high*. Example:

⁴Oh!¹   ²that's a ³|ter|ri ble thing!¹

The direction of the voice at a pause is marked by an arrow and is referred to as the *clause terminal*. There are three possibilities. If the voice falls and is reduced in volume at the end of a clause (as in a statement, a command, and certain questions), a downward-pointing arrow is used. This is called a *falling* or *fading* terminal:

²He's at the ³store.¹↘

If the voice rises (as at the end of a simple question or between members of a series), a rising arrow is used, indicating a quick but short rise in pitch:

²Is he at the ³store?³↗

The same question, with pitch lines added, is as follows:

²Is he at the ³|store?³

If the voice neither rises nor falls but is held at a steady pitch during a pause, a horizontal arrow is used. An example, shown with and without horizontal lines, is the following:

³That's ²right²→ ²I ³knew that.¹↘

³That's|²right²   ² I ³|knew|that.¹

This example serves to show that the horizontal lines at the pitch levels are not actually necessary. A reader soon learns to follow the numbers without them.

The features of stress and intonation are not used at random by native speakers of English, but follow certain patterns inherent in the language. Some American patterns are slightly different from British ones. This will be touched upon in chapter 4. The most commonly used intonation pattern is "2–3–1 falling," used in statements, commands, and questions beginning with a question word such as *who*. This was illustrated in the sentence *I knew that*, above, but it is further shown in the following example:

^{2}It's a good day to go on a ^{3}picnic.$^1\searrow$

This example shows the tendency of the voice to remain at level 2 for a space of time before rising to level 3 for the emphasized word. The pitch-level number is assumed to be the same until a change comes; that is, level 2 is not rewritten before each of the syllables in the sequence. Of course, the speaker may choose to emphasize some other word, such as *day*, and the pattern might then become:

^{2}It's a good ^{3}day for a picnic.$^1\searrow$

(or)

^{2}It's such a ^{3}good day for a picnic!$^1\searrow$

Another extremely common intonation pattern is "2–3–3 rising," illustrated by the simple questions:

^{2}Are you ^{3}sleepy?$^3\nearrow$ ^{2}Do you think we should ^{3}go now?$^3\nearrow$

A third pattern is "3–2 sustained" or "2–3 sustained," as in the sentence fragments:

^{3}Johnny$^2\rightarrow$ (and) ^{2}get some ^{3}rice,$\rightarrow^3$bread,$\rightarrow^3$milk,$\rightarrow$

Both fragments might be completed by a "2–3–1 falling" final clause, as follows:

^{3}Johnny$^2\rightarrow^2$go to the ^{3}store.$^1\searrow$ ^{2}Get some ^{3}rice,$\rightarrow^3$milk,$\rightarrow^2$ and ^{3}meat.$^1\searrow$

The members of a series of items are often separated from each other by a rising rather than by a sustained terminal. Many speakers might say:

^{2}Get some ^{3}rice$^3\nearrow^2$some ^{3}milk$^3\nearrow^2$and some ^{3}meat. $^1\searrow$

The intonation pattern of a public speaker may be 3–2–2 rising between items in a series, as shown in the second transcription in chapter 6.

These basic patterns, and others, are combined in a wide variety of sequences in a normal English conversation. They make up the characteristic "tune" of English. They are in stress-timed rhythm, a pattern in which the primary stress in each group of words falls on the word emphasized for the meaning. This kind of rhythm is in sharp contrast to a non-English type, such as syllable-timed rhythm, characteristic of the languages of Spain, the Philippines, and Japan. In the latter type, each syllable is given the same minute portion of strong stress. That, with the absence of weak stress, gives a staccato effect to the speech, which the English listener sometimes describes as "choppy." Speakers of Type III illustrate this difference in the application of stress.

It should be kept in mind that the basic intonation patterns described above are those of standard English. The persons chosen to represent the first four types of Island speech attempt these patterns but do not always complete them successfully.

Because the readers anticipated are teachers and laymen, the transcriptions in this book are not "close" ones. Modifying marks have been kept to a minimum. The plus mark used by descriptive linguists for open juncture has been deliberately omitted, and other simplifications have been made, especially in regard to problems inherent in a partially interlingual analysis, as between the speech of Types I and II.

Chapter 2

**Speech
of the
Immigrants:
Type I**

The speech of this group includes the "pidgin-talk" of the plantations
and the speech of immigrants who came to Hawaii with native languages
different from English. These people are the relatively unschooled speakers and not, of course, those foreign visitors or immigrants who have
come to Hawaii after a period of formal education in English.

Speakers of Type I carry over characteristics of their native languages
into their English speech—characteristics of phonology, grammar, and
vocabulary. Frequently they omit function words: articles, prepositions,
auxiliaries, conjunctions, the *to* of the infinitive, and so forth. These are
the words which are usually unstressed in standard spoken English and
are not perceived by many persons who have had no formal training in
English and have learned the language entirely by ear. Speakers of Type
I use skeletal sentences consisting mainly of content words: nouns, main
verbs, adjectives, and adverbs. In place of the inflections of the English
verb, which they do not attempt, they use a number of other devices.
Although they have not yet acquired the pluralizing inflection of English, they indicate plurality by devices borrowed from their native languages or by methods peculiar to pidgin English. Similarly, methods
employed by Type I speakers to express degree, manner, and place are
simpler than those of standard English, and methods of indicating questions also are different. The effect of the native language upon the English speech of a person at this stage can be assessed adequately only by
one who knows both English and the native language of the speaker.

The speaker who will represent Type I is Mrs. Susanna Kim, a woman seventy years of age. As a young girl she immigrated to Hawaii from Korea to marry a plantation worker who had preceded her to the Islands. Mrs. Kim is interviewed by her granddaughter—a third-generation citizen of Hawaii, a graduate of the University of Hawaii, and a speaker of standard American English. As the interview gets under way, the granddaughter simplifies and "pidginizes" her own English to effect understanding. Such a conversation is probably as near as we can come today to the original pidgin used by the plantation foreman and worker.

The analysis of the speech of Mrs. Kim has been undertaken by Dong Jae Lee, who is a native speaker of Korean, a teacher of English and of Korean, and an advanced student in linguistics. Because the speech of Mrs. Kim includes phonological elements from the Korean language, Mr. Lee's analysis requires the phonetic symbols shown in table 2 in addition to those given in table 1.

In table 1, the symbols [p t k] represent the stops of English and the symbol [č] is used for the affricate, even though these sounds are usually aspirated. It is not necessary to mark aspiration in English, since its presence or absence is not a factor that can change the meaning of words. In Korean, the difference must be indicated because the meanings of words can change according to the presence or absence of aspiration. The aspirated stops and affricate are represented by [pʰ tʰ kʰ čʰ], and those not aspirated by [p t k č].

In the following transcription, then, [p t k] represent sounds similar to the initial consonants of *police, tobacco,* and *kinetics,* respectively. The stops [p t k], however, are much more weakly aspirated than the [p], [t], and [k] of the words cited. On the other hand, [pʰ tʰ kʰ] represent the sounds which have stronger aspiration than the initial [p], [t], and [k] of the words *pat, top,* and *keep.* The fortis (tense) stops [pp tt kk] are similar

TABLE 2 Additional Symbols Used in Chapter 2

	BILABIAL	DENTAL	ALVEO-PALATAL	VELAR
Stops				
Aspirated	pʰ	tʰ		kʰ
Fortis (tense)	pp	tt		kk
Affricates				
Aspirated			čʰ	
Fortis (tense)			čč	
Fricatives	ø		ṣ	
Flapped lateral		l̆		
Flap		ř		

to the English [p], [t], and [k] in *spy*, *sty*, and *sky*. These sounds are pronounced with the muscles of the throat and mouth tense and the breath
released abruptly without aspiration. The differences between the
affricates [č], [čʰ], and [čč] are the same as those between, for example,
[p], [pʰ], and [pp]. The bilabial fricative [ø] is similar to the first sound in
who; the lips, however, are much more rounded and protruded. The
flapped consonants [l] and [ř] are similar to the pronunciation of the
spelling "tt" in the word *letter* in northern, midland, or western American
English. The [l] is more like the English [l] in *light*, and the [ř] is closer to
the English [r] in *right*.

In addition to tables 1 and 2, showing the phonetic symbols used for
consonants and vowels, the reader is referred to chapter 1 for an explanation of the notation used for stress and intonation. Only primary stress
is shown in this transcription.

RECOLLECTIONS OF KOREA AND OF EARLY DAYS IN HAWAII

Speaker of Type I: Mrs. Susanna Kim. Transcribed and analyzed by
Dong Jae Lee. Questions asked by the interviewer are in parentheses.

(I would like to introduce my grandmother, Mrs. Susanna Hew Kim.
Gramma, when were you born?)

1   December twenty-four.
     ²tisémbə²→ ²tʰweniǿɔ́²↘

(What year?)

2   1892.
     ²ʔeɪtʰin na¹ɪntʰi ³tʰú³↗

(Where were you born?)

3   Katsa.
     ³kʰǽtsə²↘

(Katha? Where is that?)

4   Korea.
     ²kʰo³říə¹↘

(Korea. When did you come to Hawaii?)

5   1916.
     ²naɪntʰin ṣik>s²ttí¹→

(1916? And why—why did you come?)

6 Mm. Me Grandpa marry.

²im²→ ²mi kȓæmppə ³méȓi¹↘

(When you come to Hawaii, what island you live on?)

7 Hm?

³įm³↗

(When you come to Hawaii, what island you live?)

8 O-o-oh, yeah. Koloa, Kauai.

³o: ³hijá²→ ²kʰo lówa kʰa³wáɪ¹↘

(When did you learn to speak English?)

9 Yeah, citizen, yeah, night— night school.

²hijá²→ ²şidişin ²ijá²↗ ²náɪt>²→ ²naɪt> ²skkúl²→
Two year me go.
²tʰu ija mi ²kó²↘

(Before that you speak English.)

10 No.

²no²↘

(I thought you speak English before that.)

11 No-o.

³no:¹↘

(You no learn English in Korea?)

12 Only Korean school study. Korea. Korea school three,

²oñi kʰo³ȓíəl²→ ²skkúl sttədi¹↘ ³kʰoȓíə ³kʰoȓíə skkul²→ ²tʰȓi²→
no, four year graduate yeah. Three year teacher—
²áɪ²→ ³pʰó ija²→ ²kȓeǰueɪ ³jéɲ³↗ ²tʰȓi ³ijá²→ ²tʰíčʰə²→
school teacher.
²skkúl tʰičʰə¹↘

(And when you come to Hawaii, what? You teach school?)

13 No, yeah, country, yeah— school, only three year

²no²→ ²ja²→ ²kʰóntʰȓi ja²↗ ²skkul²→ ²oñi tʰȓi ija
country, yeah. Then, yeah, hospital nurse one year.
²kʰóntʰȓi ja²↗ ²ten ²já²→ ²hasppitʰəl ³nó:s¹↘ ²wón ija²↘

(Oh.)

14   Bumbye, yeah, Hawaii come.
      ²pambáɪ ja²→ ²ha³wáɪ kʰəm¹↘

      (And then you come Hawaii. Ah, when you in Korea, your name
      Susanna?)

15   Yeah. Baptize.
      ²ijá¹↘ ²pap>ttáɪčʰ¹↘

      (When you baptize?)

16   O-oh. Eighteen year I think baptize. The Methodist
      ²oʔ:²→ ²eɪtʰin ³ijá²↗ ²aɪ diŋ bap>²ttáɪs¹↘ ²ča médədis
      Church.
      čʰə:čʰ¹↘

      (Oh, I see. But born-time not Susanna?)

17   Susanna.
      ²su³sénnə¹↘

      (Born-time?)

18   No. Born-time, yeah, two kind name— ah—
      ³no²↘ ³pó:n tʰaɪm²→ ²hiɟa²→ ³tʰu kʰaɪn neɪmə́²→
      three-kind name, yeah. Small-time Myungju. Me inside
      ²sři kʰaɪn³ném ije²↘ ³smó:l²tʰaɪm²→ ²mjə́ŋju²→ ³mi insaɪ
      Myungju all same yeah. Bumbye me school go, graduate,
      ³mjə́ŋju²→ ²o:l sem ³jé²↗ ²pambaɪ mi ³skkúl go²→ ²křéjueɪ²→
      Youngok.
      ²jə́ŋok>¹↘

      (And then Susanna?)

19   Um-hum.
      ²im²→

      (How come name change from small-time, school-time? How come
      change?)

20   Name?
      ³ne¹ɪm³↗

21   Yeah. School-time, baby name me no like. That's why
      ²hijá²→ ²skkúlə tʰaɪm²→ ²pebi³néɪm²→ ²mi no³láɪ²→ ²etsaɪ
      change.
      čʰéɪnji¹↘

(Oh, you change? Oh! When you first come Hawaii, you live Kauai?)

22   Yeah. Grandpa Kauai live.
²ijá¹↘ ²kræmppə kʰawaɪ lipʰi²↘

(What did Grandpa do?)

23   Cut cane, *hanawai* [irrigation].
²kʰɔ́t> kʰeɪn²→ ²hana³wáɪ²→

(What was Kauai like when you first come? Different from Korea?)

24   That time me, yeah, Korea, yeah, school get,
²hija ³tʰáɪm²→ ²mi²→ ²hijá²→ ²kʰoř̌ɩə²→ ²hijá²→ ²skkúl get>²→
you know. I think one year me school teacher.
²ju nó¹↘ ²aɪ díŋ²→ ²wən ³ijá mi²→ ²skkúl tʰi:čʰə²↘

(On Kauai? Korean school?)

25   Kauai nihi.
²kʰawaɪ ³níhi¹↘

(Kauai what?)

26   Nihi.
³níhi¹↘

27   Now me Catholic.
³náo mi kʰe¹tʰilik³→

(How long you live Kauai?)

28   Five year.
²ǿaɪb ija¹↗

(And then where you move?)

29   Honolulu.
²honəlúř̌u²↗

(And how long you stay Honolulu?)

30   A-a-m. Honolulu stop, no more— one month. Ewa.
²ã:²→ ²honəlú: sttap>²→ ²nó moə²→ ²wən mə́ns¹↘ ³ɛ́wa²↘
Ewa I think ten year over live. That's why, you
³ɛ́wa aɪ diŋ²→ ²tʰen ³ijá obəs lip>¹↘ ²ɛtsaɪ ju
mother Kauai born. Yeah. Uncle Albert, yeah,
³mádə²→ ²kʰawaɪ bó:n¹↘ ²hijá²→ ²əŋkʰl ²álbe²→ ²hijá²→
Margie, Ella, Adeline, are all Ewa.
²máji²↗ ²ɛ́llə²↗ ²adəláɪn²→ ²a: o:l ³ɛ́wa¹↘

(Ewa. And you live Molokai. I visit you Molokai.)

31   Um, Molokai. Me like yeah—
²ɨm mořə³kkáɪ²→ ²mi laɪk> hijá²→

(From Ewa you move to Molokai?)

32   Yeah.
³ja³→

(How long you stay Molokai?)

33   Molokai? I don't know— nine year— Me get them
³mořəkkáɪ³↗ ²aɪ³ don no³↘ ²naɪn i¹já²↗ ²mi get>ttem
high blood pressure. I think seven year. I think work.
haɪ blət> ³pʰiřéšə²↘ ²aɪ diŋ sebɨn ³ijá²→ ²aɪ diŋ wə́:k>¹↘
All auntie, uncle, all small, yeah. Grow old.
²o:l ǽntʰi²→ ²əŋkʰl²→ ²o:l smó:l ja²↗ ²křó o:l¹↘

(You went Mainland visit Auntie Adeline for long time.)

34   Three year.
²tʰři ijá²↘

(Three year. How you like Mainland?)

35   Good.
³kúdi²↘

(You have hard time understand them talk on Mainland?)

36   Some me— some can understand.
³sə́m mi³→ ²səm kʰæn əndə³sttén¹↘

(Some can? But Auntie— Auntie used to talk for you?)

37   Uh-hm. Richie, Stephen— he teach me.
²ɨm¹↘ ²ríčʰe²↗ ²sttébin²→ ²hi tʰičʰ mi:²→

(Oh. You want to go back Mainland?)

38   I cannot. Too much money. Now here what-time
²aɪ kʰǽnnət>²→ ²tʰu məčč ³méni¹↘ ²nao hijá²→ ²wətʰáɪm
die I don't know.
daɪ²→ ²aɪ don ³nó¹↘

(You say school go for citizenship. Where?)

39   Kaimuki High School.
kʰaɪmukkí²→ ²háɪ skkul¹↘

(What they teach you in citizenship school?)

40 Mrs. Young.

²misi ³ján²↘

(Hm?)

41 Mrs. Young, Sato—

²misi ³ján²↗ ²sát>tto³↗

(No, *what* they teach? English?)

42 English.

²íŋgiřiš²↘

(And what else?)

43 English, yeah, history.

²íŋgiřiš²→ ²hijá²→ ²hístʰiři¹↘

(American history. When you citizenship get?)

44 May— May fifteen, yeah.

²méɪ²→ ²meɪ øiøtí:n je²↗

(May fifteenth, when? What year?)

45 Nineteen fifty-five. About fifty-five, I think. Fifty-five.

²naɪntʰi:n øiøtʰi²øáɪ²→ ²paʊt> øiøtʰi³øáɪ aɪ diŋ¹↘ ²øiøtʰi øáɪ¹→

(And then go Mainland?)

46 Yeah.

²ijé²↘

(And how long you stay Mainland?)

47 Three years.

²tʰři ijəs¹↘

(What was, ah, Korea like when you live there?)

48 Korea like?

²kʰořiə ³láɪ³↗

(Um-huh.)

49 Good.

³kud>³→

(But how was it— nice place?)

50 Hm?

³im³↗

(Nice place?)

51   Nice place.

³náɪs pʰr̃eɪs²↘

PHONOLOGY

The English consonants Mrs. Kim uses in the interview are [pʰ tʰ kʰ b d g čʰ ǰ s š l m n ŋ w j h ʔ]. The English consonants not used in her speech are [f v θ ð z ž r], all of which are non-Korean. She used ten typically Korean, non-English sounds: [p t k pp tt kk čč l r̃ ṣ].

The speaker's simple vowels are [i e ɛ æ ɨ ə a u o]. The English vowels she does not use in the interview are [ɜ ɝ ɚ ʌ ɔ]. Mrs. Kim's diphthongs are [eɪ aɪ au ao iə oə]. The common English diphthongs [ou] and [ɔɪ] are absent in the corpus.*

PHONOLOGICAL DISTORTIONS

Frequent transfer of Korean sounds into the informant's pidgin English occurs because (1) some English sounds are not used, (2) some Korean sounds are used in lieu of English sounds, and (3) the arrangement of sounds is different even when she uses English ones. The instances of such transfer of sounds are discussed below (the numbers in parentheses refer to the numbered sentences in the transcription).

The Korean lenis stops /p t k/ are used in lieu of the English voiced stops /b d g/. The Korean lenis stops have the voiced allophones [b d g] between voiced phonemes, and the voiceless allophones [p t k] elsewhere. The English /b d g/ which are not between voiced phonemes are, therefore, pronounced [p t k] by the informant:

[po:n] born (18)   [pebi] baby (21)
[tisɛmbə] December (1)   [sttədi] study (12)
[kr̃eǰueɪ] graduate (12)   [iŋgir̃iš] English (42)

In several instances, however, we find that Mrs. Kim uses the voiceless allophones [p t k] rather than the expected voiced allophones [b d g] in intervocalic positions:

[mi kr̃æmppə mer̃i] Me Grandpa marry (6)
[tʰu ija mi ko] Two year me go (9)

This could be accounted for by the fact that her speech is a concatenation of words at a rather slow speed and phonetically there is a short pause before those stops; consequently they are not influenced by the

---

* The word *corpus*, as used here, means the entire transcribed interview of the informant. For this and other technical terms, the reader is referred to the appendix.

preceding voiced sounds. In a narrow transcription, such short pauses, which are called *plus junctures*, would have been represented.

The English /f/ is represented by [ø], which is an allophone of the Korean phoneme /h/, or by [b], an allophone of the Korean /p/, or by [pʰ], an allophone of the Korean /pʰ/:

[øə] four (1)   [øiøtʰiːn] fifteen (44)
[sttɛbin] Stephen (37)   [pʰo] four (12)

In place of English /v/, Mrs. Kim uses the Korean /pʰ/ or /p/ which has the allophones [p] and [b]:

[lipʰɨ] live (22)   [sebɨn] seven (33)
[lip⁾] live (30)

The English /ɵ/ is represented by Korean /s/, /t/, and /tʰ/:

[sři] three (18)   [diŋ] think (16)
[tʰři] three (13)

/ð/ is replaced by Korean /t/:

[madə] mother (30)   [ten] then (13)

It is also represented by Korean /tt/ after an unreleased consonant:

[get⁾ ttem] get them (33)

Tensing of an obstruent after an unreleased consonant is a regular phonological phenomenon in Korean:

[pap⁾ ttaɪčʰ] baptize (15)   [sat⁾ tto] Sato (41)

/ð/ is deleted in the phrase *that's why* (21), which is pronounced [ɛtsaɪ].

/z/ is replaced by either Korean /čʰ/ or /s/; for example:

[pap⁾ ttaɪčʰ] baptize (15)   [şidişin] citizen (9)

As the last example shows, English /s/ is realized as [ş] before [i]. This is a reflection of Korean /s/ which becomes [ş] before /i/ or /wi/.

The English /l/ and /r/ (excluding the final and preconsonantal /r/) are not distinct in Korean. These phonemes are phonetically similar to the Korean liquid, which has three main allophones—a flapped lateral [l], an alveolar flap [ř], and an alveolar lateral [l]. The distribution of these allophones is such that [l] occurs after a pause, [ř] between vowels, and [l] elsewhere:

[kʰořiə] Korea (4)   [iŋgiřiš] English (42)
[mořəkkaɪ] Molokai (31)   [skkul] school (9)
[albe] Albert (30)   [ɛllə] Ella (30)

In the interview with Mrs. Kim, the English /l/ or /r/ does not occur after a pause. The transcription, however, shows several occurrences of [l], which is an after-a-pause phonetic form.

[kʰolowa] Koloa (8)   [honəluřu] Honolulu (29)
[kʰořiəlaɪ] Korea like (48)   [kʰetʰilik] Catholic (27)

This seemingly contradictory phenomenon can be accounted for again by the presence of a plus juncture. As has been mentioned, the informant's speech is a concatenation of syllables or words at a rather slow speed. The data could, therefore, be analyzed as having a plus juncture in front of [l] in these examples. This plus juncture causes the liquid to be pronounced like an initial sound, which is [l] rather than [ř].

In the case of [o:lɛwa] 'all Ewa' (30), even though the liquid is between vowels, it is pronounced [l] rather than the expected [ř] or [l] as in the above examples. This is because there is a juncture between the liquid and [ɛwa], causing the liquid to be pronounced like a final sound. In [obəslip⁼] 'over live' (30) the expected allophone [l] does not occur, and [l] is used instead because of the presence of a plus juncture between the preceding sound and the liquid itself. As in the case of the occurrence of the voiceless allophones of the lenis consonants in the position where the voiced allophones are expected, the plus juncture would have been represented if a narrow transcription had been used here.

It is noteworthy that the informant uses the English /r/ in the proper name [rič̔ʰe] 'Richie' (37) when it is initial and [l] is expected.

The final and preconsonantal /r/ is either completely omitted or replaced by the lengthening of the preceding vowel in the informant's speech. This is also a reflection of the Korean phonological pattern.

[tisɛmbə] December (1)   [ija] year (9)
[øə] four (1)   [nə:s] nurse (13)

The Korean /i/ is used in place of English /i/ and /ɪ/. The Korean /i/, a high front vowel, is not as high as the English /i/ nor as low as /ɪ/. The English /ɪ/, which occurs as the second vowel in English diphthongs, is correctly pronounced. The Korean /i/ is often lengthened when it represents the English /i/:

[insaɪ] inside (18)   [naɪntʰin] nineteen (5)
[ʔeɪtʰin] eighteen (2)   [naɪntʰi:n] nineteen (45)
[øiøtʰi:n] fifteen (44)

In lieu of /u/ and /ʊ/, the Korean /u/ is used, a high back vowel that is not as high as /u/ nor as low as /ʊ/. The English /ʊ/, which occurs as the second vowel in diphthongs, is correctly pronounced:

[skkul] school (13)   [tʰu] two (18)
[susɛnnə] Susanna (17)   [kudɨ] good (35)
[paʊt>] about (45)

The Korean /æ/ is phonetically [æ] or [ɛ], and the English /æ/ is often represented by [ɛ], as in:

[mɛři] marry (6)   [susɛnnə] Susanna (17)

Koreans often do not distinguish /æ/ from /e/, which is phonetically [e]. This trait is transferred into the informant's speech. The English /e/ is always replaced by [ɛ] when stressed.

[křeǰueɪ] graduate (12)   [kʰetʰɨlik>] Catholic (27)
[mɛdədis] Methodist (16)   [křæmppə] Grandpa (6)

The Korean /o/ and /e/ are used in place of /oʊ/ and /eɪ/ respectively—/oʊ/ always and /eɪ/ occasionally:

[no] no (21)   [go] go (18)
[sem] same (18)   [pebi] baby (21)
[křeǰueɪ] graduate (12)

/ɔ/ is replaced by /o:/ as shown in:

[o:l] all (18)   [smo:l] small (18)

Some other phonological distortions found in the informant's speech are the following:

Assimilation.

[křæmppa] Grandpa (6)   [oñi] only (13)

Two interpretations are possible in accounting for the pronunciation of *only* as [oñi]. One is to describe it as having undergone progressive assimilation and other changes in the following sequence of derivations:

/oʊnli/
   ↓   by progressive assimilation
/oʊnni/
   ↓   by replacement of /oʊ/ by /o/
/onni/
   ↓   by loss of /n/
/oni/
   ↓   by palatalization of /n/
[oñi]

The second explanation is that the /l/ is lost from /oʊnli/, and the rest of the changes follow, except the loss of /n/.

Dissimilation.

[honəluřu] Honolulu (29)

Loss of a duplicated syllable and compensatory lengthening of /u/.

[honəlu:] Honolulu (30)

Loss of word-final phonemes.

[křejueɪ] graduate (18)   [laɪ] like (48)
[diŋ] think (24)   [øaɪ] five (45)

Developed consonants.

[susɛnnə] Susanna (17)   [obəs] over (30)
[sat‹tto] Sato (41)

Insertion of extra vowels.

[lipʰɨ] live (22)   [kudɨ] good (35)

Loss of a weak vowel.

[paʊt‹] about (45)

Deletion of a consonant and a semivowel.

[ɛtsaɪ] that's why (21)

Intercalated semivowel.

[kʰolowa] Koloa (8)

INTONATION

The Korean language is characterized by a level intonation and a so-called dip intonation used at the ends of utterances. Mrs. Kim retains much of the level intonation, as shown by the following example:

²Yeáh,²→ ²citizen, ²yeáh,²↗ ²níght² ²night ²schóol²→ (9)

A dip intonation is a typical Korean rising intonation, in which the pitch level of the voice drops immediately before it goes up. An example from Mrs. Kim's speech is the following phrase: ‿

²eightéen ¹ninety │two³ ³↗ (2)

Frequently, however, Mrs. Kim uses the basic English 2–3–1 falling intonation (see chapter 1) as in the following examples:

²Me Grandpa ³márry¹↘ (6)   ²Koloa, Kau ³ái¹↘ (8)

Stress is not phonemic in Korean. In the informant's speech, the primary stress usually coincides with the highest pitch level, for example:

²Ko ³réa¹↘ (4)   ²Bumbye me ³schóol ²go→ (18)

The rhythm of the Korean language is syllable timed; that is, the number of syllables determines the length of time needed to utter a sentence.* Mrs. Kim's rhythm, originally of this type, has shifted in some measure to the stress-timed rhythm of the English language, a fact that agrees with the commonly held theory that a language learner acquires elements of the rhythm of the new language early in his experience with it.

GRAMMAR

"The essential grammatical tenor of a language, and the key differences between the grammatical systems of different languages, lie in what we call the *grammatical core*" (Hockett 1958:265). The grammatical core of Mrs. Kim's English is analyzed here. The available corpus is extremely restricted, and any generalization on the basis of the data is tentative.

THE PART-OF-SPEECH SYSTEM

Eight parts of speech are traditionally recognized in English: noun, pronoun, verb, adverb, adjective, preposition, conjunction, and interjection. Of these, the preposition and conjunction are nonexistent in the informant's interview. The pronouns are limited to *I*, *me*, *he*, and *you*. The article, a subclass of the adjective, is also restricted to the definite article *the;* the indefinite article, *a* or *an*, does not occur.

GRAMMATICAL CATEGORIES

The grammatical categories dealt with by Hockett are gender, number, person, case, allocation or possession, subject and object reference, voice, tense, mode and aspect, predication or finiteness (Hockett 1958:230–239). Of these, only the categories relevant to Mrs. Kim's speech are discussed; these are gender, number, person, case, subject and object reference, voice, and tense.

Gender. English gender is manifested by the choice of pronouns and certain nouns. In Korean, gender is not an important grammatical category. To show that an animate being is male or female, a word indicating the sex is prefixed to the noun, as is done occasionally in English—for

* Syllable-timed and stress-timed rhythm are discussed in chapter 4, in connection with the speech of Type III.

example, *girl scouts*. Neither the English nor the Korean gender system is reflected in the informant's material. She uses the pronoun *he* but not *she*.

Number. Nouns are not inflected for number in Korean. Korean pronouns, however, have different forms for the singular and the plural, as in English. In general, the informant's English does not show the inflection, but there is one exception: She says "three years" (47) where "three year" is expected from the contrastive analysis of Korean and English.

Person. First, second, and third person singular pronouns appear in her speech. In Korean, only first and second person pronouns occur, and the third person is expressed by paraphrasing: *that* plus *man* express the meaning of *he; that* plus *woman*, the meaning of *she*.

Case. Korean pronouns are not inflected for case, unlike their English counterparts. Instead, particles show the case of the nouns and pronouns preceding them. Pronouns are used twenty-three times in the informant's speech. The first person occurs twenty times—nine times in the subject form and eleven in the object form. The second person, used twice, and the first person, used once, occur only in the subject form.

The first person subject *I* is always used correctly. It appears in such familiar phrases as "I don't know" (38), "I cannot" (38), and "I think" (16). In the object form (*me*) the first person is used in nine instances in lieu of the subjective case (6), once instead of the possessive (18), and once in place of the first person plural (24). It is used correctly only once, in "he teach me" (37).

The second person subject *you* is used once correctly, in the familiar expression "you know" (24), and once incorrectly in lieu of the possessive (30). The third person singular pronoun *he* is used only once, and then incorrectly to represent the third person plural pronoun *they* (37).

Subject and Object Reference. Korean verbs are not inflected to show the person and number of either a subject or an object. For subject reference, by contrast, the English *be* has a full inflection and main verbs have limited inflection. In the corpus, the verb *be* is omitted except in the form *are*, which occurs only once (30). The verb *teach*, which is used with the third person singular subject *he* (37), does not inflect for the subject. The corpus, therefore, shows neither subject nor object reference.

Voice. Both the Korean and the English languages have active and passive voice. The informant, however, did not use the passive voice in the interview.

Tense. Only the present tense is found in Mrs. Kim's English. The one apparent exception is the use of the past participle *born* in "you mother Kauai born" (30). The present tense form *bear*, however, is not frequently used in English, and the verb is usually heard in the passive voice, *be born*. This, rather than her awareness of the past tense of the verb, seems to be the reason for her use of *born*, even though both Korean and English have the three basic tenses, past, present, and future.

FUNCTORS

Functors make up a large category that includes function words and also other grammatical forms, not all of which are whole words. According to Hockett's definition, "Functors are . . . all substitutes . . . all markers . . . all inflectional affixes . . . and perhaps . . . abstract governing derivational affixes" (1958:264).

The substitutes found in the material are: personal, *I, me, you, he;* demonstrative, *that;* indefinite, *some;* inclusive, *all.* Relative substitutes and verb substitutes are not found. Markers such as prepositions and conjunctions are not used in the utterances. The only connector found is *are* (30). Auxiliary verbs used are *can* (38) and *do* (33).

The Korean functor [ãi], a variant of /ani/, which means 'no' and has a high frequency of occurrence, is used in Mrs. Kim's speech; for example:

Korea school three [ãi] four year graduate (12) 'I graduated from a three, no, four-year Korean school'.

Inflectional affixes for number and tense are found only in *three years* (47), *are* (30), and *born* (30). Abstract governing derivational affixes (such as *-ness*, which governs the part of speech of the derivative built on it) are not found at all.

CONSTRUCTION TYPES

"Constructions are the . . . smaller pattern out of which the patterns of whole sentences are built" (Hockett 1958:164). Examples of four of Hockett's construction types are found in Mrs. Kim's speech: coordinate, attributive, directive, and connective. Fragments and contractions are also considered here as construction types.

Coordinate constructions. English has coordinate constructions of several types. One, called *additive*, usually involves the word *and*, expressed or implied. Mrs. Kim uses the following additive constructions:

twenty-four (1)
Uncle Albert, Margie, . . . Adeline (30)
English, yeah, history (43) 'English and history'

Another subtype of the coordinate construction is called the *alternative* because it involves the conjunction *or*. An example from the informant's speech is:

two kind name—three kind name (18) 'two or three kinds of names'

A third coordinate construction is the *appositive*, a subtype which Mrs. Kim uses repeatedly, for example:

Uncle Albert (30)   Mrs. Young (40)

Attributive constructions. Very common in English, these constructions contain a head (principal word) and an attribute (modifying word). Examples from the informant's speech are given with the head underscored:

night school (9)   only three (13)
two year me go (9)   Kauai live (22)

The first two (9 and 13) follow the English pattern; the second two (9 and 22) are patterned after the Korean structure. Head-attribute and attribute-head-attribute constructions are not found in the speech of the informant. The only occurrence of the head-attribute-head construction is in the phrase "I don't know" (33).

Directive constructions. As has been mentioned before, prepositions and conjunctions were not used by the informant. Therefore, of the three directive constructions discussed by Hockett (1958:191–196), only the *objective construction* occurs in the informant's utterances. The English objective construction, which consists of a verb plus an object, is replaced by a typical Korean object-plus-verb sequence:

Me Grandpa marry (6) 'I married Grandpa'
Baby name me no like (21) 'I did not like the baby name'
Some can understand (36) 'I could understand some'

The speaker has the English objective construction when her utterances begin with such a familiar phrase as *I think:*

I think one year me school teacher (24) 'I think that I taught school for
     one year'
I think ten year over live (30) 'I think that I lived over ten years'

In the expressions *me get* and *I don't know*, Mrs. Kim has both English and Korean patterns:

Me get them high blood pressure (33) 'I had high blood pressure' (English pattern)

Me, yeah, Korea, yeah, school get (24) 'I had a Korean school' (Korean pattern)

I don't know nine year (33) 'I don't know whether or not it was nine years' (English pattern)

What time die I don't know (38) 'I don't know when I will die' (Korean pattern)

There is one utterance which could be called a genuine English objective construction. It is "He teach me" (37) 'they taught me'. It does not parallel any Korean sentence pattern nor does it begin with one of the familiar phrases such as *I think, me get,* or *I don't know.*

Connective constructions. These involve a so-called connector, and English connectors are verbs. Except in one case in which *are* is used, the commonest English connector, *be,* is omitted and therefore the connective construction is replaced by a subject-plus-predicate attributive construction, which is neither English nor Korean. For example:

Me Catholic (27) 'I am a Catholic'
All auntie, uncle, all small (33) 'All of your aunts and uncles were small'

In Korean, the topic of an English predicative construction is often omitted when it is understood from the context, and the comment alone is used to represent the construction. The informant transfers this linguistic phenomenon into her English:

Bumbye Hawaii come (14) 'Soon [I] came to Hawaii'
Only Korean school study (12) '[I] studied only at a Korean school'

Fragments. As is true in any pidgin (and in standard dialects as well), fragments are found quite frequently in the speech of this informant. Those listed below are completive; that is, they were uttered in response to the quoted sentence:

December twenty-four (1). "When were you born?"
No (11). "I thought you speak English before that."

Contractions. A contraction is the shortening of a word or phrase by the omission of sounds; also the new expression formed by this process may be called a contraction. The form [ɛtsaɪ] is the contraction of 'that's why'. The informant uttered this twice:

Baby name me no like. [ɛtsaɪ] change (21). 'I didn't like the baby name.
That's why I changed it.'

Ewa I think ten year over live. [ɛtsaɪ] your mother Kauai born (30). 'I
think I lived in Ewa more than ten years. That's why your mother was
born on Kauai.'

SUMMARY

Mrs. Kim does not have much difficulty with English stops and affricates.
In lieu of aspirated allophones of the English voiceless stops and affricates, she uses Korean aspirated phonemes, and in place of unaspirated
allophones of the English voiceless stops and affricates, she makes use of
Korean fortis stops and affricates. Instead of English voiced stops and
affricates in intervocalic positions, she uses Korean lenis stops and
affricates, which, in such environments, have phonetically similar allophones to English voiced stops and affricates. These substitutions do
not render the informant's speech unnatural. The informant, however,
uses Korean lenis stops and affricates in lieu of English voiced stops and
affricates even in nonintervocalic positions. Such substitution makes her
speech unnatural because Korean lenis stops and affricates have voiceless allophones in such environments. To English speakers these voiceless
allophones are acoustically similar to English voiceless stops and
affricates.

Other consonants that are present in English but not in Korean are
replaced by a Korean consonant or by several consonants; for example,
/θ/ is replaced by Korean /s/, /t/, or /tʰ/. It is interesting that the informant can produce English /r/ correctly in her son's name *Richie* (37)
but transfers the Korean liquid to represent English /l/ and /r/ elsewhere.

Only those vowels present in both English and Korean are used by the
informant; English /ɔ/ and Korean /ö/ are not found in the corpus. The
distinction between English /ɪ/ and /i/, and between English /ʊ/ and
/u/, is merely a difference of length in Korean, and the informant re-
places these pairs with the Korean /i/ and /u/, respectively, lengthening
the second member of each pair occasionally. The distinction between
/o/ and /ɔ/ is also simply a difference in length, /ɔ/ being a long /o/
both in Korean and in Mrs. Kim's speech.

In many cases the informant retains Korean intonation. Examples of
level intonation and of the Korean "dip" intonation, included in the
interview, are cited in the analysis. Mrs. Kim has mastered elements of
typical English intonation patterns, however, as shown by her use of the
basic 2–3–1 falling pattern of the English language. Stress is not phone-

mic in Korean, and differences in degrees of stress do not play an important part in her speech, primary stress usually coinciding with the highest level of pitch. Although the rhythm of the Korean language is syllable timed, Mrs. Kim's interview shows frequent examples of the stress-timed rhythm of English. This is understandable considering her long period of contact with the English language in Hawaii.

The construction of Mrs. Kim's utterances is predominantly Korean, and a word-for-word translation into Korean from her English is generally possible. English patterns are used in such familiar phrases as *I think, I don't know, me get.* The informant is construed to understand and use these phrases as units rather than as constructions or grammatical patterns. In a few instances she has patterns that are neither Korean nor English; the subject-plus-complement construction *me Catholic* is one of them. In one instance, she uses a genuine English objective construction, "he teach me" (37).

The sentences are generally concatenations of contentives (content words) and a few functors that are existent in both Korean and English. The informant, however, has picked up a handful of functors that are exclusively English—the plural suffix *-s* (47), the connector *are* (30), the definite article *the* (16), and the third person singular pronoun *he* (37).

The vocabulary is extremely limited, and paraphrasing is found frequently. Redundancy, common also in the pidgin of other speakers, is another characteristic of the speech of this informant.

Chapter 3 **The Early Creole Remnant: Type II**

For immigrant laborers and foremen on the plantations, pidgin was the common tongue—a language that was both impersonal and utilitarian. Although the early Chinese immigrants came to Hawaii as single men, they sometimes married Hawaiian women and set up homes in which plantation pidgin served as the language of the household because it was simpler to use than either Chinese or Hawaiian. When children were born into these homes, their first language was the pidgin English that their parents spoke to each other, and to which were soon added new household words and connotations. When the children went to school, the language widened to become the speech of the peer group. The result of this development is known as *creole* English (Lind 1960:44–45).

Although the early creole stage is long past in Hawaii, a speaker may occasionally be found who has grown up in a bilingual family at an isolated spot, with little opportunity for formal schooling in English. Such a person may use a form of speech that is as near to the early creole stage as any speech heard in the Islands today. The speaker chosen to represent Type II is a woman of Hawaiian-Chinese ancestry, Annie Loo Akana of remote Waipio Valley on the island of Hawaii. Her schooling did not extend beyond a few years in the elementary grades. At the time of the recording, she was sixty-nine years old.

(The phonetic notation used in this transcription is explained in chapter 1.)

34

DESCRIPTION OF WAIPIO VALLEY, ISLAND OF HAWAII

Speaker of Type II: Annie Loo Akana. Questions and comments of the interviewer appear in parentheses.

(How many people live down in the valley now?)
Before, thousand— Oh— now— no full one hundred.
²bi³fóa²→ ³táusən ou²→ ²nau²→ ²no ful wàn ³hándɪd¹↘

(Before— one thousand?)
Thousand or what.
³táu²sən ou wàt¹↘

(A thousand? But now?)
Now, ah, no full. No no full two hundred people down there.
²náu²→ ²a²→ ²nòu fúl¹↘ ²no ³nóu ²ful tu handɪd pipəl dau ³dὲ:³→
No much. All Kukuihaele. My family, my brother, all
³nó mač¹↘ ²ɔ̀l kuki³háli¹↘ ²maɪ³ fǽmli²→ ²maɪ ³bráda²→ ³ɔ̀l
Kukuihaele. Kukuihaele, Waimea.
²kukihàli¹↘ ²kukɪhàlɪ wàɪ³mé:a¹↘

(Long ago there was a school there. Did you go to that school?)
Yeah. I went 'at school. Waipio Valley.
³yέə²→ ²aɪ ³wén ²æt skùl²→ ²waɪpìou ³vǽli¹↘

(I've been inside that school.)
Three be— three schoolroom.
³ərí bɛʔ²→ ³ərí ²skûlrùm¹↘

(Now?)
Now, no more. They tear down. The man buy the place.
²nàu nou ³móa²→ ²dɛ ³téə daun¹↘ ²də mæn bàɪ də ³pléɪs¹↘

(Do the children go up the trail to Kukuihaele School?)
Yeah. Yeah. When they been— the water been disturb—
³yέ:²→ ³yέ²→ ²wὲn deɪ bén²→ ²də wàta bɛn ³dístəb²→
'as why they— nobody— all move Kukuihaele. Ah, the
²ǽs waɪ dὲɪ²→ ²no³bádɪ²→ ²ɔ̀l mûf kukɪ³háli¹↘ ²á:²→ ²də
people down leave the valley go Kukuihaele. Nowdays they

pìpəl dâʊn lìf də ³vǽli²→ ²goʊ kuki³háli¹↘ ²nàʊdêɪs deɪ
rent house. They go home all up there now
rènt ³háʊs³→ ²de go hôʊm ɔ̀l ɑp deə ³náʊ²→
for school day. When no school day they all go down the
²foə skùl ³déɪ¹↘ ²wɛn no ³skúl ²dèɪ ²de ɔ̀l goʊ daʊn də
place. Clean taro patch— go catch fish—. Hard to leave that
³pléɪs¹↘ ²klin tɑ̀ro ³pǽč³→ ²go kǽč ³fíš³→ ²hɑ̀ːd tu ³lív ²dǽt
place, very good place. If you lazy, you no more *kaukau*. You
plêɪs²→ ²vérɪ gûd plèɪs¹↘ ²ɪf yu ³léɪsi³→ ²yu no moɑ ³káʊkàʊ¹↘ ²yu
can go beach fishing, you go catch stream fishing, get taro,
kǽn gò ³bîč ³fíšɪŋ³→ ²yu go kǽč strím ³fîšɪŋ³→ ²gèt ³tɑ́ro³→
get *lū'au*, all kind, free.
²gèt ³luʔáʊ³→ ²ɔ̀l ³kɑ́ɪn frî¹↘

(What do they raise besides taro?)
Taro, before, taro and ah, rice. Now, only taro.
²tɑ́roʊ²→ ²bifòʊ ³tɑ́ro²→ ²æn²→ ²ə²→ ³rɑ́ɪs¹↘ ²nâʊ²→ ²ònɪ ³tɑ́roʊ¹↘
Only taro. That taro take all over Hilo. All Kohala,
³ó:ni tɑ̀roʊ¹↘ ²dǽt tɑ̀ro teɪk ³ɔ́l ²ovɑ ³hilo²→ ³ɔ̀l ²ko³hálɑ²→
Waimea, all around.
²wàɪ³méɑ²→ ³ɔ́ːl ²ə³rɑ̀ʊn¹↘

(They've wonderful taro. Did they have pigs long ago?)
Uh?
²ʌʔ²↗

(When you were a little girl, did they raise pigs down there?)
Yeah.
³yéɑ²→

(And *lū'au*?)
Yeah!
⁴yɛːə²→

(*Lū'au* pigs?)
Yeah. We keep pig. We keep chicken. We pick—take
³y⁴ɛ́ː ə¹↘ ²wi kìp ³pfg³→ ²wi kìp ³číkɪn²→ ²wi pɪk²→ ²tèɪk
care ducks, lay eggs plenty. All country living. Not like
kɛə ³dɑ́ks³→ ²leɪ ɛ̀ks²→ ³pléntɪ²→ ²ɔ̀l kʌntri ³lívɪŋ¹↘ ²nɑ̀t laɪk

Honolulu—lazy. No more nothing.
hònolúlu²→ ³léɪsi²→ ²nòʊ moɑ ³nátɪŋ¹↘

(It must have been wonderful living down in the valley.)
It is. Good place, country place, living. Raise taro,
²ɪt ³ís¹↘ ²gʊ̀d ³pléɪs³→ ³kʌn²tri plèɪs²→ ³lívɪŋ¹↘ ²rèɪs ³tárovᵌ³→
raise pig, raise chicken, raise cow, no worry—
²rèɪs ³píg³→ ²rèɪs ³číkɪn³→ ²rèɪs ³káʊ³→ ³nóʊ ²wʌ̀ri²→

(I wish we had a picture of you in those days.)
Oh, yeah. I stay over there long time, since I born.
²ðʊ ³yέ:ɑ¹↘ ³àɪ ²stêɪ owɑ dɛ: lɔ̀ŋ ³táɪm²→ ²sìns aɪ ³bɔ́:n¹↘
I go Kauai ten year old.
²aɪ goʊ kɑwà?i tɛn ?yɪ ³óʊl¹↘

(What was your maiden name—when you were a little girl?)
Annie.
²ǽni¹↘

(Annie?)
Um-hm.
² ḿhm̀²→

(That's a pretty name. Were you *hanai*?)
My grandmother take me *hanai*. My mother, my father,
²maɪ grǽn³mádɑ ²teɪk mi hɑ³nàɪ¹↘ ²maɪ mádɑ²→ ²maɪ ³fádɑ²→
no take care me, but my grandmother take me— take-care.
²nòʊ teɪk kɛɑ ³mí³→ ²bət maɪ ³grǽn²màdɑ teɪk mì²→ ²tek³kéɑ¹↘
That's why I learn Hawaiian.
²ǽs waɪ aɪ lân hɑ³wáɪən¹↘

(Oh, that's how you happened to learn Hawaiian!)
Yeah. I learn from my grandmother. My grandmother is
³yέ:ɑ¹↘ ²aɪ làn fɔ maɪ grǽn³mádɑ¹↘ ²maɪ grǽnmàdɑ ɪs
Hannah. Hawaiian name, Hannah.
³hǽnɑ²→ ²hɑ³wáy²ən nèɪm²→ ³hǽnɑ¹↘

(Your grandmother was pure Hawaiian?)
Yeah. She's pure. My grandmother pure, and my grandfather
²yέ:¹↘ ²šìs ³pyúə¹↘ ²maɪ grǽnmàdɑ ³pyúə²→ ²æn maɪ grǽnfâdɑ

is pure *Pākē*. That's a time he's a *luna* of take-care five
ɪs pyùə pɑ³kéɪ¹↘ ²æs ə tàɪm his ə ³lù²nɑ ɑf teɪkkèɑ ³fâɪ
hundred people for cut cane at the Honokaʻa. My grandfather
³hʌnɪd ³pípəl²→ fɔ kʌt ³kèɪn ²æt də hono³kɑʔɑ¹↘ ²maɪ græn³fádɑ²→
he's the *luna*. I stay with my grandfather, my grandmother.
²hìs dɑ ³lúnɑ¹↘ ²aɪ stèɪ wɪd maɪ græn³fádɑ²→ ²maɪ græn³mádɑ¹↘
When my grandmother die, my grandfather go back China.
²wɛn maɪ græn³mádɑ dàɪ²→ ²maɪ grænfâdɑ gou bæk ³čáɪnɑ¹↘
He did! He went! But he die already.
²hì ³dɪ́d¹↘ ²hi ³wǽ:nt¹↘ ²bɑt hi ³dáɪ ²ɔrèdɪ¹↘

(And where did you go then?)
Ah, I stay with my adopt— ah— my namesake. Um-hm, I
²ɑ: aɪ ³stéɪ wɪd maɪ ədɑ̀p²→ ²ɑ: maɪ ³néɪmsèk¹↘ ²m̋ hm̀²→ ³àɪ
don't want go home with my mother, I don't— I don't raise
don wɑ̀n ²gou hôum wɪd maɪ ³mádɑ²→ ²aɪ don²→ ²àɪ don ³réɪs
from them. I don't feel good. Yeah, and then I stay with my
frɑm dɛ̀m²→ ²aɪ dòn fil ³gúd¹↘ ³yǽ:ə²→ ²æn dɛn aɪ stèɪ wɪd maɪ
namesake because my grandmother take-care her and me.
³néɪmsêk²→ ²bikɔs ²maɪ grænmɑ̀dɑ teɪk kèɑ hɔ̀: æn ³mɪ́¹↘
I like stay with her.
²aɪ làɪk stêɪ wɪd ³hɔ́:¹↘

(Oh, she was older than you?)
Yeah. She more old than me— she marry. Then my grandmother
³yéɑ²→ ²ši mɔ ³ðul dæn mɪ́²→ ²ši ³mǽri¹↘ ²dɛn maɪ grænmɑ̀dɑ
die and I stay with her. 'As why I never go back with my
³dáɪ æn aɪ stèɪ wɪd hɔ̀:¹↘ ²æs waɪ aɪ nèva gou ³bǽk ²wɪd maɪ
mother and father.
mɑ̀dɑ æn fâdɑ¹↘

PHONOLOGY

Mrs. Akana's consonants are [p t̯ k b d g f v ɵ s š č m n ŋ l r w y h].* The
voiceless fricative [ɵ] is produced only occasionally and only in the
initial position. The voiced fricative [ð] is not attempted at all; its place
is taken by a voiced alveolar stop closer to [d] in acoustic effect. The

* No complete phonemicization is implied by these lists of consonants and vowels.

voiced sibilants [z] and [ž] and the voiced affricate [j] are not developed, at least within the limits of this material. The glottal stop does not occur in contrast with any consonant in English words, but it is used in Hawaiian words.

The speaker has seven initial consonant clusters, [br- gr- fr- ɵr- str- pl- kl-], and one final cluster, [-ks], which she uses for both *ducks* and *eggs* because she unvoices the two final sounds in *eggs*. She tends to unvoice all final voiced consonants except [m n ŋ l]. All the initial clusters contain [r] or [l] as the second member; these two sounds are well differentiated in her speech, singly and in clusters. It is well known that Asian immigrants often have great difficulty in keeping the [r] and [l] apart. Mrs. Kim, the Type I speaker interviewed in chapter 2, exhibited this difficulty in her pronunciation of only two words—*Honolulu* [honəluřu] (29) and *place* [p̞ireis] (51). In Hawaii the problem with [r] and [l] has almost always disappeared in the speech of members of the second generation, even though these same speakers may have difficulty with the interdental consonants, the lax vowels, the consonant clusters, and with other features of the phonemic structure of English that are troublesome for learners with a foreign-language background.

The speaker's simple vowels are [i ɪ ɛ æ з ʌ ə u ɔ ɑ]. The lax high back vowel [ʊ] is undeveloped. The diphthongs are [eɪ oʊ aɪ aʊ]. The complex [ɔɪ] does not appear in this interview.

Although she has developed the lax vowel [ɪ], Mrs. Akana substitutes [i] for it in many instances. For [ʊ] she uses an allophone of [u]. She most nearly approaches a production of [ʊ] in the word *good*. She uses [ɑ] with more than weak stress in the final syllables of words such as *mother* and *father*. The mid and low front vowels [ɛ] and [æ] are held distinctly apart in most instances, an exception being the vowel of the word *went* which approaches [æ]. There is an interesting lengthened variety of [ɛ] used in final position in the words *there* [dɛ:] and *yeah* [yɛ:]. For the vowel in the word *her*, the speaker uses either a lengthened [з] or this somewhat unusual final [ɛ:]. In the treatment of pronunciation in *Webster's Third New International Dictionary*, this lengthened [ɛ] is classified as a foreign sound and is given the marking *ee*. Although the central vowel [ʌ] is present in Mrs. Akana's speech, she often uses a variety of [ɑ] instead.

As to stress, pitch, and the other elements of intonation, a marked development is evident in comparison with the patterns found in the speech of Type I. Here the intonations of American English can be heard in different stages of development. Primary stress is usually applied in the stress-timed manner of standard English described in chapter 1. There are no examples of syllable-timed rhythm in Mrs. Akana's speech —a rhythm that we have assumed to be the result of contact with the

Japanese, Korean, or Philippine languages (see chapter 4), which were
not heard in remote Waipio Valley in the earlier days. Many weak syllables in words are overstressed, however, and the clear distinction between the four degrees of English stress has not yet been fully developed.

The pitch range of this speaker is much wider and more flexible than
that found in the speech of immigrants. In some of Mrs. Akana's utterances, her pitch tune describes an interesting little arc. The spelling and
the transcription can do little to indicate this voice curve, as in the exclamation "Yeah!" which sometimes becomes pitch levels 2–3–4–3–2–1.
This peculiar characteristic can readily be heard from the tape. Some of
the sequences of phrases in a series run along at a level a little higher
than the conventional English rendering, yet the handling of members
of the series is basically English. Sequences that should be heard from
the tape are: "Clean taro patch, go catch fish, hard to leave that place,
very good place," and "You can go beach fishing, you can go stream
fishing, get taro, get *lū'au*, all kind, free."

GRAMMAR AND VOCABULARY

Mrs. Akana is at the preinflectional stage in her handling of English.
In the interview, she attempts only two inflectional endings of nouns, in
the words *ducks* and *eggs*, uttering both with a final [-ks] ending. In all,
she uses twenty-three nouns in their singular meanings (not including
place names) and twelve nouns in their plural meanings, but she fails
to use the plural inflectional endings. She has a feeling for pluralization,
however, and is generally successful with the singular-plural concept
when it does not involve inflectional endings. For example, she uses the
words *men* and *people*, and, among the pronouns, she uses the singular
forms *I*, *me*, *my*, and *her* successfully, as well as the plural forms *they* and
them.

Mrs. Akana's speech is interesting also as a study of the developing
verb inflections for tense. In the material presented, she utters a total of
sixty-two verbal phrases. Although for a part of the interview she is
speaking of past times in Waipio Valley, a true preterit form is uttered
only three times, and then only with irregular verbs: "He did," "He
went," "I went." Of the sixty-two verbal expressions, seventeen represent the present or historical present involving no use of inflectional
endings. In the remaining forty-five cases, the speaker attempts the
preterit or present perfect meaning, but produces only the simple present
tense of the verb.

For a particular study of the absence of the copula, or linking verb,
Mrs. Akana's interview is useful when it is compared with that of Mrs.

Kim, who was interviewed in chapter 2. Of twenty-one instances in which the linking verb might be expected, Mrs. Akana produced the verb six times: "It is," "My grandmother is Hannah," "She's pure," "My grandfather is pure *Pākē*," "He's the *luna*," and again, "He's the *luna*." In comparison, Mrs. Kim produced the linking verb only once in her recorded speech, although in eight instances the verb would have been expressed in standard English.

Speakers of Types I and II avoid the negative contractions *doesn't, didn't, hasn't, hadn't, haven't, can't, couldn't, wouldn't, shouldn't*, using instead the full forms *cannot, did not*, and so forth. The speakers explain that they are not able to perceive the contractions clearly and cannot pronounce the endings. As will be shown in chapter 4, contractions are developed in the speech of Type III, but usually in such variant forms as *dint, didint*, and *couldint*. Mrs. Akana has begun to use the contraction *don't* which she consistently pronounces [doun]. She uses many negative expressions in a pidginized form. For example, of seven phrases including the word *no*, six are actually shortened forms of *not: no full one hundred* 'not fully one hundred', *no much* 'not very much', *no more* 'not any', *when no school day* 'when it was not a school day', *no more nothing* 'not anything else', *no take care me* 'didn't take care of me'. She used the fully articulated word *not* only once, in *not like Honolulu*.

A characteristic of the immigrants' speech of Type I is the absence of the function words of English, particularly the articles and prepositions. Speakers at the Type I stage make skeletal sentences with the content words. One indication, then, that Type II is further developed than Type I is the presence of a larger number of the function words of standard English in Type II speech.

In the interview, Mrs. Akana uses the definite article consistently but makes no use at all of the indefinite article. She uses the coordinating conjunctions *and, or*, and *but* and the subordinating conjunctions *because, if*, and *since*. With these subordinating conjunctions she is able to handle dependent clauses to a limited extent; this alone shows an advance over the expression system of Type I. Whereas Mrs. Kim, the representative of Type I makes no use at all of prepositions, Mrs. Akana uses seven prepositions successfully in the short interview: *over, around, from, for, of, at*, and *with*. A preposition which she omits consistently is *to*: "They go Kukuihaele." As for the *to* of the infinitive, the speaker substituted *for* in one instance ("for cut cane at Honoka'a"), omitted the word entirely in two instances, but produced one complete infinitive phrase ("hard to leave this place—very beautiful place").

Thus it seems quite clear that the function words are being developed at this level of speech. Some are still undeveloped, however, as is shown by Mrs. Akana's consistent omission of the preposition *to* and of the indefinite article.

As to types of sentences, the form of the interview limited Mrs. Akana to declarative utterances. She had no opportunity to use interrogative or imperative forms.

In her utterances, the speaker uses several expressions which have identical forms in pidgin English recorded elsewhere. For example, she uses *before* as an indicator of past time in place of a verbal inflection: "Before, tousand, . . . now, no full one hundred." Similarly, she uses *already* to indicate the present perfect tense: "But he die already." The absence of the copula in many of her sentences—for example, "since I born"—and the use of *plenty* as an indicator of pluralization or as a strengthener, as in "lay eggs, plenty," are similar to Cantonese-pidgin usage.* Another instance in which Mrs. Akana employed a word cited in other pidgin glossaries was her use of *catch* for 'get' in "go catch stream fishing." A possible influence of the Hawaiian and Portuguese languages is shown in the use of *get* for 'have': "Get taro, get *lū'au*, all kind, free." She uses *no more* for 'no' in the statement, "If you lazy, you no more *kaukau*." The word *kaukau* is itself a pidgin form.

The difficulty that dialect speakers have with the passive voice is illustrated in three sentences spoken by Mrs. Akana: "That taro take all over Hilo," meaning that taro 'is taken', and "I don't raise from them," meaning 'wasn't raised by them'. In the third case, she seems to be on the way to mastering the passive form when she says, ". . . the water been disturb."

In addition to place names, the speaker used four words from the Hawaiian language in the short interview: *taro, lū'au, luna,* and *hanai* 'adopted'. She also used *Pākē,* the locally coined term for Chinese persons, and a curious compound word, *take-care,* to mean 'custody'.

Students of the structure of the English language may find it interesting to compare the utterances of Mrs. Kim and Mrs. Akana for possible insights concerning the learning process of speakers who approach the intricacies of English from a background of foreign languages—particularly Asian ones. Pointed up is the dependence of grammar upon a mastery of the phonemes, especially the final consonant clusters involved in English inflections. Those whose first language contains no final consonants whatever (not even single consonants as in the word *dog*) have an impressive learning problem—not in mastering the theory but in the actual physical production of the sound. Equally interesting is the slow

---

* Words noted here as parallels to forms in Cantonese pidgin are listed in the Glossary (chapter 9) with references to dictionaries or published articles containing them.

development of function words in a speaker's vocabulary in comparison with content words. For example, Mrs. Kim used no articles at all and Mrs. Akana has developed only the definite one. The indefinite article *a* or *an* is so elusive and difficult for foreign speakers that the word *one* is often used as a substitute: "We get one holiday Monday."

Many other persons would be interested in Mrs. Akana just for herself and would enjoy the skill and charm she shows in handling her own expression system.

Chapter 4 **Talking Da Kine: Type III**

Sociologists and sociolinguists see pidgin in Hawaii as a thing of the past, as a form of communication used on the plantations at the turn of the century and earlier—the speech of a time, a place, and a certain human relationship. These students are vastly outnumbered, however, by the residents of the State who look upon Type III speech (described in this chapter) as present-day pidgin, the "neo-pidgin" of the here and now. They are thinking of the actual structure of the speech itself, and not of its history. Some look upon it with despair, it is true, but others regard it fondly as something as typical of the Islands as flower leis and pineapples. This attitude has grown with the realization that the dialect no longer brands a youngster—he can learn a standard or near-standard form of English for use in the classroom and during working hours, yet can revert to the Type III form of communication during casual hours at the beach, on the playing field, in the bus, during coffee breaks, and at home.

This "local language" is a mode of speech developed in the Islands as an outgrowth of Types I and II—a language filled with Hawaiianisms, imported phrases, teen-age talk, and slang. It has vigor and robustness, and, when used by men and boys, a certain roughness that may have come from the norms of "men's language" in Japan. In the speech of girls and women the roughness is not so apparent, but the Hawaiianisms, the pidginized forms, and the sharply falling intonation at the ends of yes-no questions are all present. Syllable-timed rhythm (see p. 50) can be heard sporadically from some speakers and consistently from others.

Explosive stop consonants and dental /t/ sounds often give a staccato effect. The locally developed auxiliaries used by some speakers are as much a mark of this type of speech as is the constantly repeated expression *da kine*. These "local" auxiliaries are: *stay* to indicate the present progressive, *been* or *wen* to indicate past or present perfect, and *go* to indicate the future tense or intention. (Examples: "I stay study—no mess wid me." "Las' night I been study ha:d." "Tomorrow I go study da library all morning.") Noun pluralizing inflections are used, but not always with complete success, appearing in such forms as *baggages, junks, stuffs, slangs, furnitures,* and *sceneries.*

In this form of expression, use is made of intensifiers such as *real,* key expressions such as *'ass why ha:d!* and terms like the popular *sharp* ("Das sha:p, boy!"). An attempt is made to use the contractions that occur constantly in the English of Type V—*didn't, couldn't, he's,* and so forth. These have become crystallized in the dialect of this level as *didint* (or sometimes *dint*), *couldint,* and *his,* partly because of difficulty with the pronunciation of consonant clusters. Words ending with two consonants often appear with only one: *las', firs', en'* for 'end', *stan'* for 'stand'. The stop consonants /t/ and /d/ are not developed after /s/ and /n/, respectively. The cluster /sts/ is reduced to /s/ (for example *nes'* for *nests*). The use of the present participle ending *-ing* in the (in) form is very general: *goin, doin, durin.* The Hawaiianisms listed in the Glossary (chapter 9) are freely used.

As representatives of Type III, two boys with high school educations are presented as they converse with each other in the casual talk of leisure hours. This is the rough style of the speech of men. The boys, who live in a middle-class neighborhood of Honolulu and are both second-generation Japanese, can change to the speech of Type IV when the need arises. As further examples of Type III, two high school girls are presented, speaking to each other in the popular jargon of their age-group—the "Hawaii-kine-talk." During school hours these girls can control a style of speech equal to that of Type IV. Speaker A is of Philippine extraction and Speaker B is cosmopolitan, a mixture of Hawaiian, Chinese, Caucasian, and other racial strains.

(See chapter 1 for an explanation of the symbols used in the transcriptions.)

CONVERSATION BETWEEN TWO STUDENTS

Speakers of Type III: Boys A and B.

B A: Ey, Marcus, wanna go show tonight?
     ²èɪ ³má:kìs²→ ³wànà gòu šòu túnàɪt¹↘

B B: Show? Where?
 ³šóʊ²→ ³wɛ́ə¹↘

B A: How's Waikiki?
 ³hàʊs ²wàɪkìkí²→

B B: Waikiki! Shee! All blads, eh?
 ³wàɪ²kì³kí¹↘ ²ší:²→ ²ɔ̀l blæ̀ds ³ɛ́:³↗

B A: Where you like go then?
 ²wɛ̀ə yù làɪk ³góʊ dèn¹↘

B B: Me, I no care— any place— up to you. What show
 ³mí àɪ nòʊ kæ̀²→ ³ɛ́ni ²plèɪs→ ³ʌp tù yù¹↘ ²wàt šòʊ
 you like go?
 yù ³láɪk gòʊ¹↘

B A: Ah— hope to go Waikiki though.
 ²à:²→ ²hòʊp tù gòʊ wàɪkì³kí dòʊ¹↘

B B: What get?
 ³wát gèt¹↘

B A: Chee, I think Peyton Place was playin, or something
 ²čí²→ ²àɪ ɵɪ̀ŋk pèɪtìn ³pléɪs ²was plèyɪn²→ oʊ ³sám²ɵɪ̀ŋ
 like 'at.
 làɪk æ̀t¹↘

B B: Peyton Place! Ey, ey, good movie eh dat.
 ³pɛ̂ɪtìn ⁴pléɪs²→ ²eɪ²→ ²eɪ²→ ²gud ³múvì ɛ̀ dæt¹↘

B A: Yeah—
 ²yɛ́:²→

B B: Us go then.
 ²ʌs ³góʊ dèn¹↘

B A: Yeah, may as well go cause, ah, nothing to do tonight.
 ²yæ̀²→ ²mèɪ æs wèl góʊ kɔ̀s²→ ²ɔ̀²→ ²nʌtìn tù dù tù³náɪt¹↘

B B: Okay. You come pick me up?
 ²óʊkèɪ²→ ³yù kʌm pìk mí ʌp¹↘

B A: Okay. About what time?
 ²óʊkèɪ²→ ²əbàʊ wá tàɪm¹↘

B B: Up to you!
 ²àp tù ³yú²→

B A: Ah, about seven o'clock.
²á:²→ ²əbàʊ ³sέn əklɑ̀k¹↘

B B: Okay.
²óʊ³kὲɪ¹↘

B A: Okay.
²óʊkὲɪ¹↘

B B: Easy!
²ì³sí³↗

CONVERSATION BETWEEN TWO STUDENTS

Speakers of Type III: Girls A and B.

G A: We goin' have one party— I like you come, eh?
²wì gòɪn hæ̀ wʌn pá:tì²→ ²àɪ làɪk yù kʌm ³æ̀³↗

G B: For what?
²fóʊ wɑ̀t¹↘

G A: Must goin' be one jam session.
²mʌ̀s gòɪn bì wʌn j̀æm ³sέšə̀n¹↘

G B: Where the kind goin' be, though?
²wὲə dɑ̀ kàɪn gòɪn ³bí dòʊ¹↘

G A: Puamana Day Care Center.
²pùɑmɑ̀nɑ̀ déɪ kὲə ³séntɑ̀¹↘

G B: What kind food you folks goin' get?
²wɑ̀ kàɪn fúd yù fòʊks gòɪn ³gét³↗

G A: Ah— like *laulaus*, some drinks, and cookies, ice
²á:→ ²làɪk ³láʊlàʊs²→ ²sʌm ³j̀ríŋks³↗ ²æn ³kúkìs³↗ ²àɪš
cream, and ah, all the kind can think of.
³krím³↗ ²ǽn ɑ̀:²→ ²ɔ̀l dɑ̀ kàɪn kæ̀n ³θfŋk ɑ̀f¹↘

G B: The kind records— what kind you folks goin' get?
²də̀ kàɪn ³rékə̀ds²→ ²wɑ̀t kàɪn yù fòʊks gòɪn ³gét³↗

G A: All rock and roll.
²ɔ̀l rɑ̀k æ̀n ³róʊl¹↘

G B: An' the guests— what kind?
²æ̀n dɑ̀ gés²→ ²wɑ́t kàɪn¹↘

G A: Ah, let's see. Hardly any *haoles*, an' some school
²á:→ ²lès ³sí¹↘ ³hà:dlɪ énì háʊlìs²→ ²æ̀n sʌm ³skúl
friend— Makaha Vultures, the AC Club, an' some friends
frèn²→ ²màkàhà vʌlčə̀s²→ ²ðə èɪsí klʌb→ ²æ̀n sʌm frèns
you don't know.
³yú ²dòʊn nòʊ¹↘

G B: The kind Makaha Vultures— where they live?
²ðə kàɪn màkàhà vʌlčə̀s²→ ³wè ³déɪ lìv¹↘

G A: Makaha— of course! All over the island—
³màkàhá²→ ²àf kɔ́s²→ ³ɔ́l ²òʊvɑ də àɪlìn²→

G B: Well—
²wǽl²→

G A: Not all over the island— some Waianae and some
³nát ²ɔ̀l òʊvɑ dà àɪlìn²→ ³sʌm ²wáɪənàɪ²→ ²æ̀n sʌm
Makaha.
màkà³há¹↘

G B: What time the party goin' be?
²wà tâɪm dà pà:tì gòʊɪn ³bí³↗

G A: Around— let's see, I don' know. I tell you bumbye.
²əràʊn→ ²lès ³sí²→ ³áɪ dòʊn nôʊ²→ ²àɪ tèl yù bʌmbáɪ¹↘

G B: Bumbye!
²bʌm³báɪ¹↘

G A: I got tell my mother.
²àɪ gàt tèl màɪ ³mádà¹↘

G B: What I goin' tell *my* mother? My mother tell, "What
²wàt àɪ gòʊɪn tèl ³máɪ màdà¹↘ ²màɪ ³mádɑ tèl²→ ²wàt
kind party this goin' be? What time? No more time?"
kàɪn pà:tì ³dís gòɪn bî¹↘ ³wát tàɪm¹↘ ²nôʊ mòʊ ³táɪm³↗

PHONOLOGY

Although Type III speech differs from standard spoken English in many
ways, its phonological differences are perhaps the most immediately
apparent to the ear. These can be only guessed from the printed words
of the informants and are therefore more or less lost to those who do not
read phonetic symbols and the special symbols used for intonation. The

summary following may serve to convey the extent of these changes, even though it is much less than a complete phonemic analysis.

CONSONANTS

B A's consonants, as shown in this limited material, are [p b t d k g m n ŋ s š č h ɵ l w y]. The only initial cluster is [pl-]. Two final clusters are [-kl] and [-ŋk]. Lacking are [f v z ž ǰ ɵ ð r].

B B's consonants are [p b t d k g m n v s š h l w y]. Initial cluster [pl-] and final cluster [-dz] are present. Lacking are [ŋ f ž č ǰ ɵ ð r].

G A's consonants are [p b t d k g m n ŋ f v s š č ǰ h ɵ r l w y]. Consonant clusters are more developed than are those of other speakers. Initial clusters are [dr- kr- fr- kl- sk-]; medial clusters are [-mb- -dl-]; final clusters are [-ts -ns]. The consonant cluster [-nd] is not successfully completed. Missing consonants are [z ž ð], although the speaker produced one successful [ð] in the initial position.

G B's consonants are [p b t d k g m n f s č h r l w y]. Clusters completed are the final [-ks -dz], although the latter was unvoiced. Clusters not completed successfully are [-sts -nd]. Missing consonants in this conversation are [ŋ z ž ǰ ɵ ð]. GA pronounced one initial [ð] successfully.

VOWELS

B A's simple vowels are [i ɪ ɛ æ ʌ ə u ɔ ɑ]. His diphthongs are [eɪ aɪ aʊ oʊ]. Missing are [ʊ ɔɪ].

B B's simple vowels are [i ɪ ɛ æ ʌ ə u ɔ ɑ]. Diphthongs are [eɪ aɪ oʊ]. Missing are [ʊ aʊ ɔɪ].

G A's simple vowels are [i ɪ ɛ æ ʌ ə u ɔ ɑ]. Diphthongs are [eɪ aɪ aʊ oʊ]. Missing are [ʊ ɔɪ].

G B's simple vowels are [i ɪ ɛ æ ʌ ə u ɑ]. Diphthongs are [eɪ aɪ oʊ]. Missing are [ʊ ɔ ɔɪ aʊ].

An inventory of consonants and vowels is relatively unimportant in the description of Type III, since the material is limited and the study was not meant to be a seine to catch all possible segmental phonemes. It was devised, rather, to capture intonation and to record the handling of inflectional forms and the use of Island idiom—features which are more or less lost in a rigid test involving the reading of prepared printed material containing all the sounds. Several comments can be made, however, about the consonants and vowels.

The tapes show that five consonants are relatively undeveloped [ɵ ð z ž ǰ], the same ones that are lacking in the utterances of Type II. The three consonants [z ž ǰ] are rare, partly because of unvoicing in final positions. An observable gain is seen in the ability to produce final consonant clusters, especially [-ŋk -dz -ts -ns]. Among the vowels, [ʊ] is relatively undeveloped and [ɔɪ] is missing.

Instances of phonetic assimilation make an interesting study in the speech of Types I through IV. GA, in her fourth statement in the dialogue, says, "some drinks," and the transcription shows her pronunciation to be [sʌm ǰríŋks], an instance of the change of /d/ to /ǰ/ before /r/ in words such as *dry, dray, dream,* and *drive,* resulting in [ǰraɪ ǰreɪ ǰrim ǰraɪv]. Directly parallel to this change is the similar change of /t/ to /č/ before /r/ in such words as *try, tray, tree,* and *tribe,* resulting in [čraɪ čreɪ či čraɪb]. In both cases, the phonetic change is by regressive assimilation, caused by the palatalization of the stops /d/ and /t/ by the /r/ immediately following them. These two changes often go unnoticed by people who have grown up in Hawaii. The more complicated change of /str/ to /ščr/ in many words including *street, strange, strong,* and *history,* is perceived by a larger percentage of people, because the dual change results in the rather noticeable forms [ščrit], [ščreɪnǰ], [ščrɔŋ], and [híš čri]. It is an example of double regressive assimilation whereby the /r/ influences the preceding /t/, which in turn influences the /s/ in front of it.

INTONATION

There are striking differences between the intonation patterns of Types II and III. Mrs. Akana, Type II speaker of chapter 3, is a person of Hawaiian-Chinese background, who has always lived in an isolated area and whose speech has not been influenced by the newer syllable-timed rhythm which crept into Island English after the arrival of the Japanese and the Filipinos. Three of the four speakers representing Type III, on the other hand, are either Japanese or Filipino and the fourth grew up with the group.

The features of syllable-timed rhythm are described by Samuel E. Martin in these words, "Instead of putting a heavy stress on some syllables and various weaker stresses on the others (as in English), the Japanese allows about the same amount of time for each of his syllables, regardless of the apparent prominence of the syllable" (Martin 1954: 4–5). This metronomic stress pattern has made itself felt in areas of Hawaii that have been influenced by the languages of Japan and the Philippines. It has spread to the speech of many other people who are of neither Japanese nor Filipino ancestry. Island English and speech teachers have long referred to this feature as choppy, or staccato, rhythm.

The contrast between syllable-timed and stress-timed rhythm is made clear by a comparison of the first question in the dialogue between BA and BB with the same question expanded to complete form and given in the normal 2–3–3 rising pattern of standard English (see chapter 1).

BA: ³Wànnà gò shòw tónìght?¹↘

Expanded to the standard form: ²Do you <u>wànt</u> to <u>gò</u> to the ³<u>shów</u> <u>tonìght</u>?³↗

The six syllables that receive weak stress in standard spoken English are those not underscored. All except one of these weak syllables have been omitted or changed in the pidginized question of BA. The syllables omitted include the following function words: the auxiliary *do*, the pronoun *you*, the *to* of an infinitive (which is actually retained, changed, and stressed in the second syllable of *wanna*), the preposition *to*, and the article *the*. The expanded sentence points up the *alternation* of strong and weak syllables, which is an important factor in the characteristic rhythm of spoken English. Strongly stressed syllables may be separated from each other by one, two, or even more weakly stressed ones. When the weak syllables are dropped out in the pidginized form, the remaining stressed syllables become a string of abrupt, distinct, and emphatic utterances, well suited to the application of syllable-timed rhythm.

Differences between the nonstandard and standard configurations are shown again in the first statement uttered by GA compared with the same statement expanded to the pattern of standard spoken English. Five weakly stressed syllables in the expanded sentence are left without underlining.

GA: ²Wè gòin hàve òne ³pártỳ.¹

Expanded to the standard form: ²We're gòing to <u>hàve</u> a ³<u>párty</u>.¹

Syllable-timed rhythm, then, as it occurs in nonstandard English, is caused in part by the omission of syllables (or monosyllabic words) that in standard English would be unstressed, and in part by the application of one of the degrees of strong stress to each of the remaining syllables of the sentence.

The speakers of Type III were chosen not only to illustrate this syllable-timed rhythm, but also to give examples of question patterns that are different from the conventional interrogative forms of American English. In the following list, the interrogative sentences of the boys are given, followed in each case by a reconstruction of the question in the intonation pattern of a person speaking the Central Midland type of American English.*

---

* Pronunciation of the Central Midland variety of American English, as described by Charles K. Thomas (1958:236–238), is native to the author of this book.

(1) BA: ^{3}Wan^{3}na ^{3}go ^{3}show ^{3}tonight?^{1}↘ ^{2}Do you want to go to the ^{3}show tonight?^{3}↗

(2) BB: ^{3}Show?^{2}→ ^{2}Where?^{1}↘ ^{2}The ^{3}show?^{3}↗ ^{3}Where?^{1}↘

(3) BA: ^{2}How's ^{2}Waikiki?^{2}→ ^{2}How about the Waiki^{3}ki?^{1}↘

(4) BB: ^{2}All blads, ^{3}eh?^{3}↗ ^{2}They're all stuck-up ^{3}haol^{2}es ^{2}down there,→ ^{2}aren't ^{3}they?^{3}↗

(5) BA: ^{2}Where you like ^{3}go then?^{1}↘ ^{2}Where do you want to ^{3}go then?^{1}↘

(6) BB: ^{2}What show you ^{3}like go?^{1}↘ ^{2}What show would you like to ^{3}go to?^{1}↘

(7) BA: ^{3}What get?^{1}↘ ^{2}What's ^{3}on there?^{1}↘

(8) BB: ^{3}You ^{3}come ^{3}pick ^{3}me up?^{1}↘ ^{2}Will you ^{2}come to ^{2}pick me ^{3}up?^{3}↗

(9) BA: ^{2}About what time?^{1}↘ ^{2}About what ^{3}time?^{1}↘

Among the nine questions asked by the boys in their dialogue, questions (1) and (8) show the most definite contrast to the pattern usually followed in standard American speech. These are questions that can be answered by yes or no, and that, in full form, begin with a verb or an auxiliary. The expected final intonation is rising. The Island pattern—a high tone (level 3) at the beginning which is sustained until the last syllable and then dropped abruptly to level 1—is a prominent feature of the so-called pidgin intonation. This pattern and others have been studied descriptively by Vanderslice and Pierson (1967:156–166). The exact points of difference from standard American English are: the high initial pitch, the sustaining of this high pitch throughout until the last syllable of the question, and the sharp drop from level 3 to level 1 on the last syllable. American speech ordinarily gives this question the 2–3–3 rising intonation pattern shown in the reconstruction of BA's question (1). BB's question (8) is another example of this difference in pattern. Question (4) shows still another kind of interrogative form—the statement followed by a tag question. The standard form most often heard is 2–3–2 followed by 2–3–3 rising (for the tag question). BB's question, although drastically reduced in structure, follows the same intonation pattern.

All of the other examples are of the basic pattern used in the United States for questions beginning with *what, where, why, how,* and similar interrogative words. In American English these normally take the 2–3–1 falling intonation pattern. The boys' questions in this category follow the same pattern.

It is the so-called yes-no question, then, that has developed its own characteristic pattern in Hawaii, and there has been much speculation concerning its origin. One plausible explanation is that it may have developed from a British pattern, since in earlier times British English was heard frequently in Hawaii. Examples of the intonation pattern of simple interrogative sentences in "received standard" British English are given in a text for teaching English to foreign students, published in London, in which Peter Strevens, a well-known instructor, provides a set of model sentences marked for intonation (Strevens 1968:2, 32, 84). Below are several yes-no questions from the Strevens text, with the intonation as indicated there. For the purpose of close comparison, the same questions are marked to indicate the intonation of American English and that of Hawaii's dialect, Type III.

TYPE OF ENGLISH	INTONATION	INTONATION PATTERN
British (Strevens, page 2)	³A̲r̲e̲ ̲y̲o̲u̲ ²Bill Jones?¹	3–2–1 rising
American (Central Midland type)	²Are you ³Bill Jones?³	2–3–3 rising
Hawaii's dialect (Type III)	³Ey, you Bill ¹Jones?¹	3–1–1 falling
British (Strevens, page 84)	³Have you ²got a book?¹ ↗	3–2–1 rising
American (Central Midland type)	²Have you got a ³book?³ ↗	2–3–3 rising
Hawaii's dialect (Type III)	³You get one ¹book?¹ ↘	3–1–1 falling

The British and American patterns are alike in their final upward turn of the voice, while in Hawaii's dialect a yes-no question takes a downward turn. British and Hawaiian patterns are alike in that such questions begin on the high, level 3, pitch but in the local dialect the high pitch is maintained for a longer time than in the British pattern, dropping sharply to level 1 without intermediate level 2 syllables, and ending with a downward turn of the voice.

As to possible influences from the British pattern upon the dialectal Hawaiian pattern, the point is only a conjecture and needs further investigation. Other observers suggest a possible influence from the Portuguese language, but this suggestion remains to be traced by students familiar with the Portuguese language as it is spoken in Madeira and the Azores, the origin of Hawaii's Portuguese population. Portuguese intonations, introduced before the turn of the century, may have had an effect upon the developing patterns of English in the Islands.

An intonation pattern for a request occurs in the dialogue between the boys when BB says, [2]"Us [3]go then,"[1]↘ a phrase equivalent to the standard [2]"Let us [3]go then,"[1]↘ or commonly [2]"Let's [3]go then."[1]↘ Here the Island and the standard intonation patterns coincide. The use of *us* instead of *we* in "Us go then" seems to result from the omission of *let* rather than from the substitution of the accusative form of the pronoun for the nominative. One of the girls uses the request pattern "Let's see," and the final utterance in the boys' dialogue is actually a request, the curious word of parting used in Hawaii—"Easy!"—which may have come from the "Take it easy!" of American usage, a bit of advice in the form of a request. It is discussed in the Glossary (chapter 9).

GRAMMAR

Progress in the ability to use inflectional endings of nouns is noticeable in Type III as compared with the speech of the Type II sample studied. Of eleven plural nouns used, nine have complete inflections (with some unvoicing) while two are incomplete. The use of pronouns parallels standard usage except for the "me-I" of one of the male speakers.

In the speech samples of Types I, II, and III, the indefinite article does not occur. The word *one* serves as a substitute for *a* (or *an*) in Type III speech, for example, when GA says, "We goin' have one party," and "Must goin' be one jam session." This use of *one* is a feature discussed in the Glossary. The definite article is present in the Type III speech of this chapter but is far from stable. In fifteen instances during the two dialogues, the article *the* is required in standard usage, yet in six of these instances it is omitted entirely, in seven it is produced in the form [dɑ] or [də], and in only two cases does it occur in its full form. *They, then,* and *that* appear, but without the fully developed consonant [ð].

Verbal forms in Type III speech show fewer differences from standard English than do the verbs of Type II. Topics talked about are more easily handled, calling for the use of present and future tenses, and not exclusively for the past tense, as in the reminiscences of Mrs. Akana, Type II. Only one past tense is called for in the dialogues; it is produced when speaker BA says that a certain moving picture "was playing" earlier. Although verbs are used in the present tense, these speakers do not resort to the "local auxiliary" *stay* described in the Glossary. They frequently omit the copula, in a way characteristic of children's speech and pidginized languages (Ferguson 1968). The dialogue between the two girls contains eleven instances of statements in the future tense, all constructed in the same way by the use of *going* plus an infinitive without the introductory *to*. Examples of this construction are: *goin' have, goin' be, goin' get, goin' tell*, and, as a variation, *got tell*. On one occasion, this future construction is strengthened by *bumbye* 'by-and-by', a term inherited from pidgin-English expressions of very early times. The actual gain in the verb at this level, then, is only in the addition of the inflectional ending *-ing* in the form [-ɪn], at least insofar as these speakers may represent the group. The curious adverbial *no more* is used in the sense of an emphatic *no, no more time* meaning 'no time at all'.

Prepositions used appropriately are *about, to, around, for, of*, and *over*. Those omitted are *to, at*, and *of*. As in the case of Type II speakers, the preposition *to* and the *to* of the infinitive are frequently omitted.

VOCABULARY

Several loanwords from the Hawaiian language appear in the dialogue of the girls. *Puamana* is the name of a plant of the daisy family that is used medicinally. *Makaha* and *Waianae* are place names for localities on the leeward side of Oahu. *Haole* and *laulau* are listed in chapter 7.

The adverbial *bumbye* 'by-and-by' is found in the glossaries of pidgin and creole speech in other parts of the world, both East and West. With the meaning 'any future time', it served, in Cantonese-pidgin days, as a tense-marker long before the inflectional endings of English verbs were even attempted by Asian peoples learning English by the pidgin route. In another part of the world, *bumbye* is heard in Jamaican creole where it probably stems, as Cassidy and Le Page suggest (1967:23), from the dialectal form *bamby* used in Devonshire and Cornwall.)

GB uses the word *tell* in two different senses: "What [am] I going [to] tell my mother?" (conventional sense); and "My mother [is] going [to] tell, 'What kind [of] party [is] this going [to] be?'" (local sense). Bracketed terms are function words omitted by GB, in the way characteristic of Type III speech. A similar use of *tell* for *say* is reported in Jamaican creole by Cassidy and Le Page, and it is also found in Bahamian folk speech, along with the use of *talk* for *tell* (Crowley 1966:v).

Space is given in the Glossary to the locally developed expressions *blads, da kine*, and *easy* (as a leave-taking).

The most striking features of the speech of Type III are likely to be lost in a close scrutiny of its segments. It is Hawaii's own local language, remarkable for its tremendous gusto and vitality and its stability over the decades. This "neo-pidgin" is a living, constantly changing language and the chosen speech of thousands of citizens who use it during moments of relaxation, even though they may have mastered a more nearly standard brand of English for formal and semiformal occasions. For countless teen-agers, it serves as a fun-language. Other types of speech in this book, with the exception of Type I and Type V, can be thought of as relic forms, soon to disappear, but Type III is active, alive, and productive of new forms. It has high peer-group value within a certain social environment, and it is likely to persist, probably side by side with standard English as one dialect of a bidialectal group.

Chapter 5

Hawaiian Near-standard English: Type IV

The variety of English which we may call "Hawaiian near-standard" is the daily speech of thousands of men, women, boys, and girls who are the very backbone of the State. The line between the form called "standard" and the form judged to be not quite standard is a tenuous one—not hard to identify by ear but difficult to explain because of its complexity, and usually quite unclear to the near-standard speakers themselves. To those who try to take the major step from one form to the other, this line of demarkation is a critical thing—puzzling, elusive, and often totally frustrating.

The boundary between the near-standard and the standard is not a single line but a large number of imaginary lines separating differences in phonology, grammar, and other features. There are always more features that are alike, however, than features that are different, because the two forms, in a linguistic sense, are close together. The differences assume particular importance for some speakers because the standard is not only the socially acceptable form but is often required for professional advancement.

An example of these fine lines of demarkation is that between the two pronunciations of the clause *he said:* the standard [hi séd] versus the near-standard [hi séɪd]. The exact point of difference is between the two vowels [ɛ] and [eɪ], or, expressed in the briefest way, [ɛ/eɪ]. The same contrast may be shown between the two pronunciations of the clause *he says:* [hi séz] and [hi séɪz], again [ɛ/eɪ]. This does not mean that there is difficulty with all words in which these two vowels are in contrast, but rather with a few particular words, some of which are given "relic pronunciations" in Hawaii. All regional dialects contain archaic pronunciations that have been superseded by other pronunciations in the normal evolution of the language (Wise 1957:193).

A complete set of such distinctions, contrasting the forms used by a nonstandard speaker with those used by a standard speaker pronouncing the same material, would constitute a contrastive analysis. Such an analysis might be useful to an Island nonstandard speaker who wished to become proficient in standard English. In this book, contrasts have been made between characteristics of various types (for example, between Types I and II) in an effort to show progressive gains in the mastery of English forms. Although this chapter is not a complete contrastive analysis between Types IV and V, an attempt is made to show many of the lines of demarkation, especially in the area of phonology.

During the nineteenth century, the English heard in the Islands was predominantly the northeastern American variety—the model set by the early missionaries from New England and the many teachers whom they trained. British speech was also heard, and the two types had similarities in their "non-r" features and in their treatment of some of the vowels.* During the twentieth century, however, the northern, midwestern, and western varieties of American pronunciation have been more widely followed, possibly because of the influence of the radio and because of the influx of teachers from those areas called (inexactly) the general American speech areas. A great many non-r speakers still remain in the Islands.

As a representative of the speech of Type IV, a woman has been chosen who retains some of the phonological characteristics of the New England pattern, along with traits of Hawaiian near-standard speech. Any of the ethnic groups that have lived in Hawaii for a long time could have furnished examples of Type IV speech, but a Portuguese representative was chosen because her speech shows non-r features as well as near-standard ones and because her reminiscences are interesting from a historical point of view. Mrs. G, second generation in Hawaii, gives a word sketch of the life of her immigrant mother who came from Madeira to Hawaii in one of the principal Portuguese migrations between 1878 and 1887. At the time of the interview Mrs. G was about sixty years old. Although her formal education was limited to elementary school, her

---

* When speakers omit the final [r] in words such as *actor* and *river* (ending the words with [ə], and omit the medial [r] following vowels in such words as *farm* and *party*, at the same time lengthening the vowel, the type of pronunciation is popularly called "non-r" speech. It is heard in eastern New England and in the southern states.

speech may have been influenced to some degree by her term of service in the home of a *kama'āina* family in Honolulu. Only certain sections of this interview have been transcribed, but the entire tape is available for study.

(An explanation of the notation used for sounds, stress, and intonation is given at the end of chapter 1.)

WORD SKETCH OF ONE OF THE FIRST IMMIGRANTS FROM MADEIRA

Speaker of Type IV: Mrs. G, second generation in Hawaii. Questions and comments of the interviewer are in parentheses.

(Were your parents born in the Islands?)
No, my mother was three years old when she came from
²nóu³↗ ²maɪ mʌðə wəs ³ərí yɪəs òuld²→ ²wɛn ši kèɪm frəm
Portugal.
³pɔ́:čəgəl¹↘

(Oh, what place in Portugal?)
Well, I don't know, we just say Madeira—
²wél³↗ ²aɪ dount ³nóu²→ ²wi jʌs seɪ mə³dérə²→

(Oh, yes.)
Madeira. That would be— there's two sections, of course,
²mə³dérə¹↘ ²ðǽt wud bì²→ ²ðɛəs tù ³sékšənz²→ ²əf kɔ̀rs²→
the St. Michael, and the Madeira, and my mother was from
²ðə sə ³máɪkəl²→ ³ǽn ðə mədèrə²→ ²æn maɪ mʌðə wəs frəm
Madeira. And she was three years old when she came from
mə³dérə¹↘ ²æntə ši wəs ³ərì yìəs òuld wɛn ši ³kéɪm ²frəm
Madeira and then, my grandparents, when they came from
mədêrə æn ðèn²→ ²maɪ ³grǽnpæ̀rənts²→ ²wɛn ðèɪ ³kéɪm ²frəm
Madeira, they lived in Kauai, they worked in the plantation.
mədêrə²→ ²ðeɪ ³lívd ɪn kɑwàɪ²→ ²ðeɪ ³wɔ́:kt ²ɪn ðə plæntèɪšən¹↘

(Is your mother still living?)
My mother's still livin', she's eighty-five years old.
²maɪ mʌðəz ³stɪ̀l lívɪn²→ ²šis ³êɪtɪfáɪv yìəs òuld¹↘

(Goodness, she must remember a lot about the plantation!)
Yes, she does, she know 'cause she was raised there. She was

²yés³↗ ³ší dʌs²→ ³ší noʊ² ²kɔs ši wəs ³réɪst ðêə¹↘ ²ši wəs

seventeen years old when she got married [on Kauai], and after

³sévəntìn yɪəs òʊld²→ ²wɛn ši gʌt ³mǽrɪd³↗ ²æn æftə

I was born, then I was one year old when she sent me here

³áɪ wəs bɔ̀:n²→ ²ðɛn aɪ wəs wʌn yɪr òʊld²→ ²wɛn ši sɛnt mi ³hfə¹↘

[to Honolulu]. Then she had two other children, a boy and a girl. . . .

²ðɛn ši hæd ³tú ʌðə čìldən²→ ²ə bɔ̀ɪ ³ǽn ə gɔ̀:l¹↘

(I know a Portuguese lady who used to make sweet bread, and just before
Lent she would make malassadas.)

Well, my mother did that for few years, she made— Oh!—

²wél²→ ²maɪ mʌðə ³díd ðæt²→ ²fə ³fyú yìəs²→ ²ši méɪd²→ ²óʊ²→

she made malassadas, as you say, and-a for the whole neighborhood,

²ši mèɪd mùlə³ádəs²→ ²æs ³yú seɪ²→ ²æntə fɔ ðə hòʊl ³néɪbəhʊd²→

she used to give them but now she's eighty-five and she's too

²ši yus tə ³gív ðèm²→ ²bət nàʊ šis ³éɪtɪfàɪv²→ ²æn šis ³tù

old and can hardly get around—still, last year she was doin'

òʊld²→ ²æn kən ³hά:dli get əràʊnd²→ ²stɪl ³lǽst yìə²→ ²ši wəs dùɪn

a lot of sewin'— makin' dish towels— you know— she put a border

ə ³lát ə sòʊɪn²→ ²meɪkɪn ³díš tàʊls²→ ²yə nóʊ²→ ²ši put ə bɔ̀:də

of colors and things like that, and makin' bootees, like crochet,

əv ³kʌ́ləz ²æn θɪŋs laɪk ðǽt²→ ²æntə mèɪkɪn ³bútɪz²→ ²làɪk kròʊšéɪ²→

but of course with wool. . . . She's very active for her age, very

²bət əv kɔ̀rs wɪd ³wúl¹↘ ²šis ³véri ǽktəv ²fə hə ³èɪj²→ ²vèri

active. She loves to sing yet, she sings. Yes, if there's a party,

³ǽktɪv¹↘ ²ši ³lʌ́vs tə sɪŋ yèt²→ ²ši ³síŋz²→ ²yès ɪf ³ðès ə pá:tɪ²→

she like to sing. . . . Well, you don't see much Portuguese people

²ši ³láɪk tə sìŋ¹↘ ²wèl yu doʊnt ³sí ²mʌč pɔ̀:čəgis pìpəl

gettin' together like before. It seems that the old-timers are all

getɪn təgêðə laɪk bɪfɔ̀ə¹↘ ²ɪt ³sìms ²ðət ðə òʊld ³táɪməs ²ə ³ɔ̀l

gone. Around here, I hardly see anybody now.

gɔ̀n¹↘ ²əràʊnd ³hfə²→ ²aɪ hὰ:dlɪ ³sí ɛnɪbɑdɪ nâʊ¹↘

PHONOLOGY

In this interview Mrs. G demonstrates her ability to use all the consonants of English with the exception of [ʒ]. Her final voiced stops and
fricatives are frequently unvoiced. She has a good command of the diffi-

cult fricatives [θ] and [ð] in nearly all words containing them that she uses, and in various positions in the words. However, she retains the relic pronunciation of a few words, as do other speakers in her peer group. These include *with* pronounced as [wɪd] or [wɪt], and *throw* pronounced as [trou]. The word *both* is such a word, usually pronounced [bout] by Type IV speakers, but it is not included in Mrs. G's comments and remarks.

The speaker uses eleven words containing [r] in the final position and, if repetitions of the same word are included, the total becomes twenty-two. She consistently pronounces these in the non-r manner, for example, the term *mother* as [mʌðə]. In the phrase *one year old*, however, the [r] before the following vowel is retained, in accordance with the habits of non-r speakers.

Her treatment of the post-vocalic [r] in the words *hardly, border, party, born*, and *Portuguese* is almost as consistent. The [r] is omitted and the preceding vowel is lengthened, for example, *hardly* which is [háːdlɪ]. Only in the expression *of course* does she seem to have a fully pronounced post-vocalic [r].

The speaker uses [w] rather than [hw] in words spelled with *wh* (such as *when, where, whale*), a usage that seems to be all but universal with the speakers of Types I through IV. A great number of Type V speakers likewise use [w] in these words, for example, *when* [wɛn].

As to the nonstandard use of /n/ for /ŋ/ in present participles (for example, *doin'* for *doing*), Mrs. G is indeed a good subject for study, showing six instances within the tape transcribed. The variation, in no sense a Hawaiianism, can be heard in the speech of Types I through III, but it persists and is especially noticeable in Type IV, where most of the nonstandard Island features are lacking.

In comparison with the speakers studied in previous chapters, Mrs. G demonstrates a substantial advance in the mastery of final consonant clusters. She uses twelve clusters in the interview—in general, the kinds of clusters that help her in producing inflectional forms. Clusters that end in [s] and [z] are, of course, essential in producing many of the English plural and possessive nouns, verbs in the present tense, third person, and some contractions such as *he's* and *Sam's*. In this category, Mrs. G uses [-ts], [-lz], [-mz], [-nz], [-ŋz], and [-vz] (with some unvoicing), in the words *grandparents, dishtowels, seems, sections, things*, and *loves*. In cases where the final [z] is unvoiced, it has been transcribed with its voiceless counterpart [s]. Clusters ending with [t] and [d] in English are equally important in the pronunciation of the preterit and past participial forms of many regular verbs. Mrs. G uses [-kt], [-nt], [-st], [-ld], [-nd], [-vd], and with these she is able to utter the past tense of the verbs she uses, for example, *worked*, *sent*, and *lived*, in addition to the words *last*, *old*, and *around*, and the negative contraction *don't*. In the transcriptions, final unvoiced [d] has been transcribed with its voiceless counterpart [t].

The informant has all of the English vowels and diphthongs in her speech and few are unstable. In the utterances of most of the types studied earlier, the two high-front and the two high-back vowels were somewhat unstable. Of these pairs of vowels, the lax ones, [ɪ] and [ʊ], are particularly difficult for speakers in Hawaii. The inventories of vowels for the speakers from Types I through III showed that these persons lacked the lax [ʊ] and tended to use the tense [u] for it, or a sound intermediate between the two. Those speakers also had more or less difficulty with the lax front [ɪ]. Mrs. G utters [ʊ] with ease and precision in the words *would*, *put*, and *wool*. She produces the vowel [ɪ] with the standard acoustic effect in the words *in*, *still*, *did*, *give*, *things*, *with*, and *sing*, but she shifts the sound toward the high-front tense vowel [i] in the words *lived* and *living*.

Many Portuguese speakers of the older age group have difficulty in distinguishing between [ɛ] and [æ], but Mrs. G keeps these two vowels well apart. Similarly, she has no difficulty with the distinction between [ʌ] and [ɑ]. It is worth noting that she does not use the vowel [ɒ], intermediate between [ɔ] and [ɑ], in her pronunciation of such words as *not*, *hot*, *on*, and *doll;* that vowel is firmly fixed in the pronunciation of many other speakers of near-standard and standard speech in Hawaii. As far as can be determined from this interview, she chooses the vowel [ɑ] regularly for this set of words. In the word *aunt*, where there is a choice in standard speech between [ɑ] and [æ] in all areas of the United States, Mrs. G uses [ɑ], as do many persons in Hawaii of all types described. The weak vowel [ə] is fully unstressed, not only within words such as *Madeira* [mədérə], but also in function words appearing in sentences such as "She w[ə]s doing [ə] lot [ə]f sewing." The mastery of this unstressed vowel has a significant effect upon Mrs. G's ability to use English rhythm. Representatives of all types of speech before Type IV have tended to overstress it.

As to intonation, Mrs. G's speech exhibits stress-timed rhythm, in contrast to the syllable timing of the speakers of Type III (see chapter 4). The degrees of stress are well defined and there is a marked difference between the weak and strong syllables throughout her sentences, with the strong stresses distributed according to the meaning she has in mind. Spaces between the pitch levels are wide enough to give her voice a certain amount of vocal variety. She makes frequent use of level 3, and she does not always return to level 1 at the ends of statements, but lets her voice trail along on level 2 until the next sentence comes to her mind.

GRAMMAR

Mrs. G's skill in handling inflectional endings has been discussed under the heading of phonology. In the interview, she completes all the plural forms that she undertakes but is not quite so successful with inflected verb forms, since she utters two incomplete present-tense inflections, *she like* and *she know*, among fourteen spoken. In other portions of the tape, a few additional failures in agreement may be noted. With preterit inflectional endings of regular verbs, she is uniformly successful.

The speaker's use of *much people* rather than *many people* is a variation commonly heard in Hawaii. Similarly, the use of *few* for *a few* in Hawaii's English is a habit of considerable interest, involving a subtle semantic difference that has often gone unnoticed. Example: "My mother did that for few years." This usage is listed in the Glossary (chapter 9).

Mrs. G, along with other speakers of Type IV, uses *hardly* in sentences where *hardly ever* would be expected, for example, in her last sentence: "I hardly see anybody now." She does not use the curious and interesting Hawaiianism *used to to*, meaning 'accustomed to', which most Type IV speakers retain, as in the sentence "I finally got used to to [yústətù] my noisy neighbors."

The interview failed to elicit interrogative sentences or request patterns. The speaker's declarative sentences are much more complex than those of the speakers of Type III, as would be expected, yet her ability to frame complex sentences is rather limited.

VOCABULARY

At the present time, Portuguese people in Hawaii use only a few words from their ancestral language. These few are mentioned in chapter 7. Mrs. G here uses only the term *malassadas*, the name of Portuguese doughnuts. Her English vocabulary is simple, but adequate to express her memories and comment upon household matters, such as handwork. During the course of her recollections, she uses Hawaiian place names connected with the islands of Kauai and Maui. Her observed English vocabulary contains words of not more than three syllables.

In the speech of this representative of Type IV we have a kind of linguistic Hawaiiana, including much that is parallel with standard American spoken English, but also a number of archaisms and locally developed relic pronunciations. Youthful Type IV speakers, although they may have attained a near-standard level of speech for formal use, delight in reverting to Type III speech as a language for leisure hours. Listening to the words of Mrs. G, however, one is certain that she would never intentionally drop below the standard she has exhibited in this interview. She conveys an impression of sincerity and dignity, and these qualities would keep her at her best level of speech at all times.

SUMMARY: NONSTANDARD TYPES

Each individual speaker, at any level of achievement, uses his own idiolect, a total individual pattern which is similar to the speech of his peer group but not identical with that of any other member of the group. For this reason, the persons chosen to represent the various types of speech discussed in this book could not possibly exhibit all of the special features of the dialects of Hawaii. Speakers studied in chapters 2 through 5 have demonstrated some of the characteristics of Hawaii's English, but not all of them. A more comprehensive survey would show that many speakers find it difficult to discriminate between the following pairs of vowel sounds: [i] and [ɪ], [eɪ] and [ɛ], [æ] and [ɛ], [u] and [ʊ], [ɑ] and [ʌ]. In each pair, the second sound is the more difficult. The first often takes the place of the second, or a sound is produced that is intermediate between the two. No single person could be found whose speech would illustrate all of these discrimination problems.

As for the consonants, some speakers find it difficult to distinguish between the following pairs: [t] and [θ], [d] and [ð], [n] and [ŋ], [j] and [ž]. The first consonant of each pair is the more easily produced and frequently takes the place of the second, or a sound is produced at some point between the two. The use of [d] for [ð] has become a relic pronunciation, occurring most conspicuously in the very simplest function words, for example in the word *the* [də]—the most frequently used word in the English language. The consonant [ž] is almost never uttered in the final position by Island nonstandard speakers, for example, in *garage*, which becomes [gəráj], although it is heard consistently and correctly in the medial position, as in *casual* and *usual*.

Unvoicing of final voiced consonants occurs so regularly that it must be thought of as a major factor in giving Island nonstandard speech the acoustic effect of a "foreign accent." Of all the voiceless and voiced pairs of stops, fricatives, and affricates, such as [p] and [b], [t] and [d], and so forth, the two most difficult (yet most interesting) are the [s] and [z]. In all standard and near-standard spoken English everywhere, these consonants are in constant use, playing their role as inflectional affixes to indicate plural forms, possessives, some contractions, and the third person singular form of the verb. Yet the difference between [s] and [z] in these affixes is rarely indicated in the English spelling—*roses* and *Bob's* are spelled with the final *s*, although both end phonetically with [z]. Therefore, in a large community where the foreign-language background has been of major significance, as in Hawaii, it is inevitable that the innumerable final [z] sounds in inflections, unvoiced, as they are, to [s], should cause dialectal speech to have an abnormally "hissing" sound, at least to the ears of nonresidents.

The difficulty with [n] and [ŋ] is not necessarily due to failure to distinguish the sounds. Speakers do not say [rɪn] for *ring*, or [sɪn] for *sing*, but substitute [n] for [ŋ] almost exclusively in the endings of present participles. The persistence of [-ɪn] in these endings is a very old English trait, an archaism, in fact, which is still accepted as standard pronunciation in some parts of England (Cassidy 1961:39).

Examples of phonetic assimilation were given in chapter 4 of this book, but many additional studies could be made. Phonetic loss and the simplification of final consonant clusters occur widely. The final stops [-t] and [-d] are especially unstable when they follow other consonants and clusters, for example, after [k], [s], [ks], [n], and [v]. *Cracked* becomes [kræk] (as in "crack-seed"), *shaved* becomes [šeɪv] (as in "shave-ice"), *next* is [nɛks], *last* is [læs], and *end* is [ɛn]. The three-consonant final cluster [-sts] is simplified to [-s] by the phonetic loss of [t] and the falling together of the two [s] sounds, resulting in forms like [nɛs] for *nests* and [brɛs] for *breasts*. Similar occurrences of phonetic loss involving stops are common in other areas of the world where English is spoken in nonstandard forms. Laura L. Shun has made a study of these phenomena in Hawaii (1961: 226–227).

It is frequently said in the public schools that the agreement of noun and verb is the leading grammatical problem in the Islands. The author has been deeply impressed with the extent to which phonology affects grammar, and the very apparent fact that the lack in nonstandard English of final consonants and consonant clusters can make English agreement impossible. The treatment given to other aspects of grammar in this study has been minimal. Problems in this area await the work of descriptive linguists and transformational grammarians.

A great many speakers of Types I through IV show the typical stress-timed rhythm of English, although often in rudimentary stages of development. Others speak consistently with the staccato-like syllable timing, and still others drop occasionally into syllable-timed rhythm. The form of interrogation called in this book the "local question pattern" is very widespread indeed. It is probably more quickly imitated by standard speakers than any other Island trait—even by children who have recently arrived in Hawaii from the mainland of the United States.

More than one hundred words and phrases used in Hawaii in special forms or with special meanings are studied in the Glossary (chapter 9). Some of these local idioms can be found in the vocabularies of speakers of all types—including Type V, the standard form.

Chapter 6 **Hawaiian Standard English: Type V**

The amount and nature of social stratification varies greatly from one society to another. . . . We often find that the speech of the privileged classes is more uniform from one locality to another than is that of the less fortunate: educated British English is much the same in London, in Manchester and in Southampton, but the local dialects in and near those three cities show great divergence. . . . Standards of correctness derive largely from the natural habits of speech of the privileged classes and are promulgated mainly for the guidance thereof. Adherence to the rules becomes one symbol of class membership. In a stratified society with little vertical mobility—that is, one in which the son of a farmer is predestined to become a farmer himself, and knows it—the special connotation of correctness does not arise: the privileged class has its usages and the lower classes have theirs, and that is that. But when there is the belief that humble origin is no necessary barrier to social advancement, the doctrine of correctness comes into the picture, with its whole panoply of rationalizations and justifications. The acquisition of "correct" habits of speech and writing becomes one of the rungs in the ladder of social success. The doctrine may then survive long after the social structure which gave rise to it has been altered. This seems to be largely what has happened in the United States. [Hockett 1958:471–472]

Charles Hockett's comments have a special meaning for Hawaii, a community where society is not stratified and where the son or daughter of immigrant parents may earn a master's or a doctor's degree in English. Hockett's explanation of the word *standard* provides a reason for its use as a term meaning the end of the speech-spectrum, which speakers at other points seem to be moving toward in a conscious or unconscious drift.

66

The tendencies that Hockett noted in other parts of the United States are clearly apparent in Hawaii, where the climate has been unusually favorable for the rise from the status of immigrant to that of community leader. Even though the term *standard* is disliked by some linguists, it is used in this book for convenience in comparing the most developed varieties of speech in Hawaii with those less fully developed. It is used also in referring to parallel varieties of "standard" speech on the mainland of the United States. Although the dated term "General American speech" is also a convenience, its use has been avoided. Extensive field research by Charles K. Thomas, Hans Kurath, John S. Kenyon, Miles L. Hanley, and others has shown that the former so-called General American area of speech comprises in reality a number of different areas. The new map published by C. K. Thomas subdivided the vast region into seven smaller dialect areas: New York City, Middle Atlantic, Western Pennsylvania, Central Midland, North Central, Northwest, and Southwest (Thomas 1958:232). General American speech as a term, therefore, is no longer useful and may be actually misleading.

The style of pronunciation in Hawaii in the nineteenth century was patterned after eastern American models, as noted in chapter 5, but it has shifted during the twentieth century until now, for the majority of speakers, it resembles more closely the patterns of pronunciation found in the western and northern sections of the country. When comparing the speech of individuals of Type V with the speech of the Mainland, we may say that it is like that of the Central Midland, the Northwest, or the Southwest, for example, as identified by Charles K. Thomas; or we may employ the terms used by W. Nelson Francis: the Midland, the Middle West, or the Far West—in short, the "r-producing dialects of American English" (Francis 1958:128, 147).

Among standard speakers of the English-speaking world, the differences in pronunciation between individuals or groups are usually narrowed to the area of vowels, diphthongs, stress, and intonation. Consonants and consonant clusters are relatively stable. Stress changes often become more noticeable than changes in pitch. The speakers of Type V, Hawaiian standard English, will illustrate these characteristics.

As representatives of Type V, it was important to choose speakers who are descendants of the early immigrants to Hawaii—those who might be thought of as having completed the journey to the end of the language spectrum. It would be less than reasonable to choose Caucasians, most of whom have regularly spoken, or at least heard, standard English, or Hawaiians, whose forefathers have had twice as much time as the Asians, the Portuguese, and others to perfect their English in the Islands. More than one-half of Hawaii's present population of approximately

748,000* is composed of the "sugar immigrants," their children, their grandchildren, and their great-grandchildren (Lind 1967:9). Thousands of these people, from all of the diverse backgrounds in Hawaii today, use a form of English which falls within the limits of Type V, and representatives from any of these ethnic groups might have been chosen. In the end, however, the choice was made on the basis of expediency and not because one ethnic group has surpassed the others in mastering standard English.

The speakers presented here are two Japanese-Americans, a woman and a man. Their forefathers spoke a language sharply different from English. The syllable-timed rhythm of Japanese is so unlike the stress-timed rhythm of English that the *nisei* and *sansei* have had a difficult hurdle to cross in attaining the intonations of standard American English. In speech sounds and grammatical features also, the Japanese group has had to span the wide gulf between the structure of Japanese and the very different forms of English. Adding to the problem is the constant possibility of language interference in early childhood, since Japanese is still spoken in many homes and shops in Hawaii. The quality and effectiveness of the standard English of the speakers presented here is therefore particularly impressive.

Both representatives of Type V speech were born on outer islands of the Hawaiian chain. They are products of the public elementary and high schools of their respective islands, and both, after earning degrees at the University of Hawaii, attended universities on the Mainland for advanced academic study. Patsy T. Mink, Congresswoman from Hawaii, studied science and law before she entered politics. Shunzo Sakamaki is a professor of history at the University of Hawaii and dean of the Summer Session. Extensive experience in public speaking has been a vital part of their respective careers. Mrs. Mink is in her early forties; Dr. Sakamaki is about sixty years old.

(The phonetic notation used in the following transcriptions was explained in chapter 1.)

FROM SCIENCE TO NATIONAL POLITICS

Speaker of Type V: Patsy Takemoto Mink, Congresswoman (third generation in Hawaii). Questions and comments of the interviewer are in parentheses.

* The preliminary United States census report for 1970 gives 748,182 as the population of Hawaii, according to the *State of Hawaii Data Book 1970*, published by the Department of Planning and Economic Development, Honolulu, Hawaii. The figure includes 41,000 members of the Armed Forces, 62,000 Armed Forces dependents, and 11,000 residents temporarily out of the State.

(After your graduation from Maui High School in 1944, did you decide at once to attend the University of Hawaii or did you think of other schools too?)

Oh, no! In my time it was almost an impossible thought to

⁴ðu ³nóu²→ ²ɪn màɪ ³táɪm²→ ²ɪt wəz ɔ́lmoust ən ɪm³pá:səbļ ə̀t²→ ²tə

even entertain the idea of going to a college other than the

ìvən ɛntə˞³téɪ:n ðə àɪdîə ²əv gòuɪŋ tu ə kàlɪj ³ʌðə˞ ðæn²→ ²ðə

University of Hawaii! It was just beyond the reach of anyone.

yùnəvə́˞·sətɪ əv hə³wáɪ¹\ ²ɪt wəz jə̀st biyʌ̀nd ðə rìč əv ³ɛ́nɪwən¹\

(I know that your major subjects at the University of Hawaii were chemistry and zoology. When did you decide to study law? What made you change your mind?)

During my senior year at the University of Hawaii, really for the

²durɪŋ maɪ ³sínyə˞ ²yɪr ət ðə yùnəvə́˞·sətɪ əv hawàɪ²→ ²rilɪ fə˞ ðə

first time, I left the scientific field in terms of course

fə́˞st ³táɪm²→ ²aɪ ³léft ²ðə sàɪəntîfɪk fìld²→ ²ɪn tə˞mz əv kɔ̀rs

selections. I took some courses in philosophy and logic, and

sə³lékšənz¹\ ²aɪ tuk səm kɔ̀rsɪz ɪn fəlàsəfi ən ³lájɪk²→ ²ən

various other things. In the course of self-analysis, I guess,

vèrɪəs ³ʌðə˞ θîŋz¹\ ²ɪn ðə kɔ̀rs əv sèlfə³nǽləsɪs²→ ²aɪ gɛs²→

and again consulting with Dr. Saunders, I decided that I would

²ənd əgèn kənsʌ́ltɪŋ wɪə dàktə˞ ³sɔ́ndə˞z²→ ²aɪ dɪsàɪdɪd ðæt aɪ wʊd

try, at least, to see if I could get into law school, and to see if

³tráɪ²→ ²ət list²→ ²tə sì ɪf aɪ kʊd gɛ̀t ɪntə ³lɔ́: skûl²→ ²ən tə sì ɪf

I liked it.

aɪ ³láɪkt ɪt¹\

I wrote to the University of Chicago and to Columbia, and

²aɪ ³ròut ²tə ðɪ yùnəvə́˞·sətɪ əv šə³kágou²→ ən tə kə³lʌ́mbɪə²→ ²æn

to my amazement, I was accepted at Chicago, and two weeks

tə màɪ ə³méɪzmənt²→ ²aɪ wəz æk³séptɪd ²ət šəkàgou²→ ²ən tù wìks

later, boarded the plane and left. It was an entirely new kind

³léɪtə˞²→ ²bɔ̀rdɪd ðə plèɪn ən ³léft¹\ ²ɪt wəz ən ɪntâɪrlɪ nù kàɪnd

of discipline, but it was very exciting— very interesting— and

əv ³dísəplɪn²→ ²bət ɪt wəz ³vérɪ ɪksàɪtɪŋ²→ ²vèrɪ ³íntrɛstɪŋ²→ ²ænd

I think I was fortunate in selecting the University of Chicago

aɪ θìŋk aɪ wəz ³fɔ́rčənət²→ ²ɪn səlèktɪŋ ðə yùnəvə́˞·sətɪ əv sə³kágou²→

because their approach in teaching was unique and it was impossible
²bɪkɔz ðɛr əpròʊč ɪn tìčɪŋ wəz yu³nîk²→ ²ənd ɪt wəz ɪm³pá:səbl̩
to be bored.
²tə bi bôrd¹↘

(In your political career, we have heard a great deal about your work for
education.)
It's to me the only real promise of an open and free
²ɪts tə ³mî²→ ²ðə oʊnlɪ ³rîəl ²prʌmɪs²→ ²ʌv ən òʊpən ænd frì
opportunity that we can offer our citizens— the ability to
ûpɚ³túnəti²→ ²ðæt wì kən ³ófɚ ²aʊr sìtəzənz²→ ²→ðɪ əbìlətɪ tə
say to them that you can rise to the heights of your own initiative
³séɪ tə ðèm²→ ²ðət yu kən ràɪz tə ðə ³háɪts²→ ²əv yʊr oʊn ɪnìšətɪv
and talents and abilities. . . . If that has any meaning, then we've
ən tǽlənts ən ə³bîlətɪz²→ ²ɪf ³ðǽt ²hǽz ɛnɪ mìnɪŋ²→ ²ðɛn wiv
got to provide students with the opportunity to fulfill it. I think
gʌt tə prə³váɪd stùdənts²→ ²wɪθ ðə ûpɚtûnətɪ tə fəl³fîl ɪt¹↘ ²aɪ θɪŋk
that this is the most important function of government, and really,
ðət ðìs ɪz ðə ³móʊst ²ɪmpòrtənt fʌŋkšən əv gʌ̀vɚnmənt²→ ²ænd ³rîlɪ²→
I guess, why I became interested in politics.
²aɪ gɛs²→ ²hwaɪ àɪ bɪkeɪm ìntrɪstɪd ɪn ³púlətɪks¹↘

(You must have had many other interests in your political career, but
education is your principal one, then?)
That's right. You have to diversify your interests, but my first
³ðǽts ràɪt²→ ²yu ³hǽf ²tə dəvɚ̀səfàɪ yur ìntrɪsts²→ ²bət maɪ fɝ̀st
love is education.
lʌ̀v ³îz ²êǰukêɪšən¹↘

PHONOLOGY

A useful contrastive study may be made between the stress pattern of
this speaker and that of the speakers of Type III English in chapter 4.
The teen-age representatives of Type III had metronomic, syllable-timed
stress, with an almost equal amount of force applied at the onset of each
syllable—a pattern characteristic of Japanese, Korean, Ilocano, Visayan,
Tagalog, and Spanish, as well as of some other languages. Mrs. Mink's
utterances provide a direct contrast to this rhythm, being extraordinarily
clear examples of the stress-timed rhythm which is characteristic of

standard English. The strong primary stress, with simultaneous lengthening of the stressed vowel or diphthong, forms the key difference. Such
forceful application of primary or secondary stress allows the diphthongs
to be heard clearly as two-part sounds. The first sentence of the interview, from the words "Oh no!" through "the University of Hawaii,"
illustrates three fully diphthongized sounds, [ou], [aɪ], and [eɪ], with the
glides to [ʊ] and [ɪ] clearly perceptible.

This vigorous stress on key syllables of content words brings with it a
corresponding weakening of emphasis on unstressed syllable peaks and
makes for a wide range of difference between the strong and weak vowels
—a feature that is basic to the rhythm of standard English. This is a
wider range of stress than many Island speakers are accustomed to per-
ceiving or to using. Although not all speakers of standard American
English use the same amount of emphatic stress, the pattern illustrated
here is one commonly heard in conversational speech throughout the
mainland United States.

Later in the interview, a clause introduced by an infinitive occurs
which contains four clearly perceptible degrees of stress: primary [ʹ],
secondary [ˆ], tertiary [ˋ], and weak (unmarked):

to sèe if I could gèt into láwschôol

In the syllable-timed rhythm of Type III, these words might have been
spoken as follows:

tò sèe ìf Ì còuld gèt ìntò láwschòol (or) làwschóol*

With level stress of this second kind, the various content words, *see*, *get*,
and *lawschool*, do not emerge as the significant ones for meaning. As a
pointer to meaning, stress is extremely important in English, but not in
Japanese, where pitch plays a primary role.

A somewhat foreign, or non-English effect in the pronunciation of
speakers of Types I through IV can be traced, in part, to the unvoicing
of final voiced consonants. The regular voicing of these final sounds by
both representatives of Type V is a significant part of the total effect
achieved in native English speech. Some instances of phonetic loss become a part of the standard spoken language, especially in function
words. Thus the normal pronunciation of the unstressed conjunction
and, when it is followed by a word with an initial consonant, is [ən]. This

---

* Compound words in English usually have primary stress on the first of the two
words compounded, for example, *stámp collêction* and *pineâpple*. In Hawaii's nonstandard dialects, the stress pattern is frequently reversed, so that the two words
might become *stâmp colléction* and *pineápple*. For this reason, the compound *láw
schôol* might be pronounced by Type III speakers with the primary stress on *school*.

unstressed form can be observed in the pronunciation used by the first representative of Type V, who is speaking informally.

Mrs. Mink uses the stressed [ɝ] and the unstressed [ɚ] with consistency. In this respect her speech is similar to the standard patterns of the northern, central, and western parts of the United States—the so-called r-producing areas. Examples of words which show the full acoustic effect of the [ɝ] are: *university, first, terms,* and *diversify.* Examples of words showing the unstressed final [ɚ] are *other* and *doctor.*

She uses the [u] rather than the [yu] or [ɪu] in words such as *new* and *opportunity.* This trait also suggests the northern, central, and western areas of the nation. The use of [ɑ] rather than the lip-rounded back vowel [ɒ] is consistent, in words such as *logic, got, of* (when unstressed), *Chicago,* and *philosophy.* This pronunciation is characteristic of those parts of the United States called by Thomas the Central Midland, Northwest, and Southwest areas, although it can be found in other sections as well.

OTHER FEATURES

Mrs. Mink employs a variety of patterns in constructing sentences, and these become more apparent in a study of the entire recording, only a part of which is transcribed here. Because of the format of the interview, she had no opportunity to employ interrogative and imperative sentence patterns.

The speaker has an impressive vocabulary encompassing her two major specializations, science and law. In her everyday speech in the Islands, she undoubtedly employs numerous loanwords and loanblends from other languages, such as those listed in chapters 7 and 8. She would be sure to know the connotations of most of the Hawaiianisms and other local idioms listed in the Glossary (chapter 9), but she would use those expressions only to establish rapport with persons in Hawaii who have at their command only the speech of Types I, II, or III.

The second representative of Type V also demonstrates a speech rhythm that is entirely different from the syllable-timed rhythm of his Japanese forebears. Dr. Sakamaki's speech offers an interesting addition to the interview with Mrs. Mink for two reasons. First, he was reading an address of his own composition when the recording was made, while Mrs. Mink and the other speakers of the various types were speaking extemporaneously in interviews or dialogues. Second, Dr. Sakamaki's voice is, of course, in a lower register than Mrs. Mink's, and for emphasis he tends to depend less on widely differentiated degrees of stress than on pauses and changes in pitch. In his style of speaking, the pause becomes a means of getting and holding attention, and an instrument for projecting fine shades of meaning.

THE UNIVERSITY OF HAWAII'S FIRST DEBATE

Speaker of Type V: Shunzo Sakamaki, university administrator (second generation in Hawaii).

We might say that debating history at the University of Hawaii
²wi ³máɪt sèɪ²→ ²ðæt dibêɪtɪŋ hìstrɪ ³ǽt ²ðə yùnəvɝ·sɑti əv həwàɪ²→
began that evening, the twelfth of February, 1925,
²bɪ³gǽn ðæt ìvnɪŋ²→ ²ðə ³twɛ̀lfə əv fêbyuwèrɪ nâɪntìntwèntɪ²fáɪv²↗
with a debate held between a team representing the University
²wɪð ə dɪ³béɪt hɛ̀ld²→ ²bɪtwìn ə tìm rɛprɪzɛ̀ntɪŋ ðə ³yùnəvɝ·sətɪ
of Hawaii and a team representing none other than Oxford
əv hə²wáɪ²↗ ²ənd ə ³tím ²rɛprɪzɛ̀ntɪŋ nʌn ʌ̀ðə²→ ²ðən ɑ̀ksfəd
University. In 1925 the University of Hawaii was
yùnə³vɝ·sətɪ¹↘ ²ɪn ³náɪntìntwêntɪfàɪv²→ ²ðə yùnəvɝ̀sətɪ əv həwàɪ wəz
the youngest university in the English-speaking world; Oxford
ðə ³yʌ̀ŋgɪst ²yùnəvɝ·sətɪ²→ ²ɪn ðɪ ìŋglɪšspìkɪŋ ³wɝ́ld¹↘ ³ɑ́ksfəd²→
was the oldest. And certainly, while the University of Hawaii is
²wəz ðɪ ³óuldɪst¹↘ ²ənd sɜ̀tənlɪ hwàɪl ðə yùnəvɝ·sətɪ əv həwàɪ ɪz
not now the youngest, Oxford will forever be the oldest.
nɑt ³nàu ðɪ ²yʌ̀ŋgɪst²↗ ²ɑ̀ksfəd wɪl fə³évə bî²→ ²ðɪ ³óuldɪst¹↘

    Debating was an ancient and honored art at Oxford, while
²dɪ³béɪtɪŋ²→ ²wəz æn ³eìnšənt ənd ɑ̀nəd ɑ̂ːt ət ²ɑ́ksfəd²↗ ²hwaɪl
Hawaii, in 1925, had never yet had one public
həwàɪ ɪn ³nâɪntìntwèntɪ²fáɪv²↗ ²həd nèvə yêt hæd wʌ̀n pʌ̀blɪk
debate. The three Oxford debaters were J. Douglas Woodruff,
dɪ³béɪt¹↘ ²ðə ³orí ɑ̀ksfəd dɪbêɪtəz wɝ̀³→ ³jèɪ dʌ̀gləs ²wúdrəf²↗
M. Christopher Hollis, and Malcolm J. McDonald. Malcolm,
³ɛ̀m krìstəfɚ· ²hʌlɪs²↗ ²ən mælkəm jèɪ mək³dánəld¹↘ ³mǽlkəm
incidentally, was the son of Ramsey McDonald, Britain's first
ìnsədêntlɪ²→ ²wəz ðə sʌ̀n ɑv ³ræmzɪ mæk²dánəld²↗ ²brìtnz ³fɝ́·st
labor prime minister. These three men, Woodruff, Hollis, and
lèɪbə²→ ²pràɪm ³mínəstə¹↘ ³ðíz ərí mèn²→ ²wúdrəf²↗ ²hʌlɪs²↗ ²ənd
McDonald, were the top debaters of the famed Oxford Union

³mæk²dánəld²↗ ²wə ðə ³táp dɪbèɪtəz²→ ²əv ðə fèɪmd ɑ̀ksfəd ³yúnyən²→
Debating Society. Before coming to Hawaii they had met and
²dɪ³béɪtɪŋ ²səsàɪətɪ¹↘ ²bɪfəə ³kʌmɪŋ tù hə²wáɪ²↗ ²ðeɪ həd mɛ̀t ən
defeated teams from thirty American and Canadian universities
dɪfîtɪd ³tîmz frəm ˌəɟ̇ˈtɪ²→ ²əmérəkən ənd kənèɪdiən yùnəvɜ̂sətɪz
and colleges. And from here they went on to more debates in
ən ³kɑ́lɪǰɪz¹↘ ²ænd frəm ³hɪ́r²→ ²ðeɪ wɛ̀nt ɑ̀n tə ³móur dɪbèɪts²→ ²ɪn
Australia and New Zealand.
ɔ̀strêɪlyə ənd nyû ³zíĺənd¹↘

       They sent us a— that is, they sent the University of Hawaii
   ²ðeɪ ³sɛ́nt əs èɪ²→ ²ðæ̀t îz ðeɪ sɛ̀nt ðə yùnə³vɜ̇ˈsətɪ əv hə²wáɪ²↗
a challenge by letter. The challenge or invitation to a public
²eɪ čɑ̀lɪnǰ baɪ ³létɚ¹↘ ²ðə čɑ̀lɪnǰ ər ɪnvə³téɪšən tu ə pʌ́blɪk
debate was accepted by a faculty committee despite the fact
dɪbèɪt²→ ²wəz əksèptɪd baɪ ə ³fǽkəltɪ kəmìtɪ²→ ²dəs³páɪt ðə fæ̀kt²→
that we had no debating team and no tradition or record of
²ðət wi ³hǽd ²nou dɪbèɪtɪŋ tìm²→ ²ænd nòu trədîšən ɚ rèkɚˈd ³áv
debating at this university. Students were invited to compete
dɪbèɪtɪŋ²→ ²ət ðîs yùnə³vɜ̇ˈsətɪ¹↘ ²stùdənts wɚ ɪnvàɪtɪd tə kəmpìt
for selection to the debating team representing Hawaii, and after
fɔr sə³lékšən²→ ²tù ðə dɪ³béɪtɪŋ tîm rèprɪzêntɪŋ ²həwàɪ²↗ ²ənd æftɚ
a series of elimination contests, a team of three men was finally
ə sìrɪz əv ɪlìmənêɪšən ³kɑ́ntɛ̀sts²→ ²eɪ tìm əv ³θrí mɛ̀n²→ ²wəz ³fáɪnlɪ
selected by a faculty committee. The team selected consisted of
sɪlèktɪd²→ ²bàɪ ə fæ̀kəltɪ kə³mîtɪ¹↘ ²ðə ³tîm sɪlèktɪd kənsìstɪd əv
three boys, all in the College of Arts and Sciences— Kensuke
θrí ²bɔ̀ɪz²↗ ²ɔ̀l ɪn ðə ³kɑ̀lɪǰ əv ɑ̀ːts ən ²sáɪənsɪz²↗ ³kɛ̀nsùke
Kawachi, a senior, Walter Short, a junior, and myself,
kɑ̀wɑ̂či ə ²sínyə²↗ ³wɔ̀ltə šɔ̂ːt eɪ ²júnyə²↗ ²ənd màɪ³sêlf²→
Shunzo Sakamaki, a sophomore.
²šûnzòu sɑ̀kɑ̀³mɑ́kɪ²→ ²eɪ ³sɑ́fəmɔ̀ː¹↘

PHONOLOGY AND ORAL STYLE

This recording of Dr. Sakamaki's speech shows a further development in
the control of spoken English and is an appropriate one with which to
end this graded series of examples of speech types. In this reading of a

prepared talk, the skillful use of pauses as a means of achieving clarity and emphasis is readily apparent. In early stages of language development, as in Types I and II, a speaker uses pauses because he is groping for words—because he is not yet in command of the language. Speakers of standard English learn to use pauses for an entirely different purpose: as a means of regulating the speed of their words to insure understanding by their listeners and to gain response from them. However, pauses alone would not be effective without the sustained tone which this speaker is able to command.

Pausing and the control of pitch patterns are illustrated in the speaker's handling of a series of items. Four phrases beginning with "The Oxford debaters . . ." are spoken with the following pitch patterns: 2–3–3 sustained, 3–2–2 rising, 3–2–2 rising, 2–3–1 falling. If these phrases are placed on a staff representing the pitch levels, similar to that used in musical notation, they appear as follows:

4	_____	4	_____
3	three Oxford Debaters were→	3	J. Douglas
			ruff↗
2	The	2	Wood
1	_____	1	_____

4	_____	4	_____
3	M. Christopher	3	Don
	lis↗		
2	Hol	2	and Malcolm J. Mc
1	_____	1	ald.↘

Because the public speaker must project his voice to a larger audience than the informal speaker, he tends to make use of pitch level 3 for a larger number of syllables than he might in conversation. In handling the members of a series of items (before the final item), he may drop his voice from level 3 to level 2, followed by a rise, in the intonation pattern 3–2–2 rising, as shown in the diagram above. In conversation, however, he might give the same material in the intonation pattern 2–3–3 rising, as explained in chapter 1. The effort to attain projection also leads him to give strong stress to some of the function words; for example, Dr. Sakamaki pronounces the indefinite article *a* as [eɪ] rather than [ə] on several occasions. A skillfully sustained vocal tone carries his voice in smooth transitions from one phrase to another.

This speaker's pronunciation does not fit completely into either the r-producing or the non-r-producing types of American speech. In most instances he pronounced the word *university* as it is heard in the western states; that is, he used [ɝ] for the vowel with primary stress. But in two other occurrences of the same word he used the eastern and southern variations [ɜ] or [ʌ]. Similarly, in the pronunciation of the so-called unstressed vowel-r (transcribed as [ɚ] and written variously as *-er, -or, -ar,* or with other spellings), he is inconsistent. In pronouncing the words *letter, after,* and *Christopher,* he used the [ɚ]. Yet in the words *other, forever, never, debater, labor, minister, junior,* and *Walter* he used the [ə], following the habits of the non-r areas. Such inconsistency in the use of r-producing and non-r patterns is not at all unusual in the speech of persons who have grown up in the Islands, and it serves to illustrate the fact that speech patterns have been changing from those set by the early New England missionaries to the styles of the present day, which reflect those generally heard in northern and western sections of the United States.

In the use of [ɑ] rather than the lip-rounded back vowel [ɒ], this speaker is completely consistent. Examples are: *college, not, top, on, honored, McDonald,* and *of* (when stressed). In this respect he follows the usage of the Central Midland, Northwest, and Southwest areas of the United States, as he does also in using [hw] rather than [w] in such words as *where* and *while.* As for the use of [ɑ] rather than [æ] in the word *challenge,* this is probably a case of over-correction (Wise 1957:166), illustrating the feeling many persons have that [ɑ] is a "better" vowel than [æ].

Regarding the choice between the use of [u] and [yu] in such words as *news,* and *tune,* the speaker is not completely consistent, using [u] in *students* and [yu] in *new.*

Dr. Sakamaki has a wide vocabulary centering in the areas of history and language. Always interested in language, he is alert to the changes that words undergo in Hawaii, in their forms and semantic content.

This graded series of speech samples from five selected segments of the spectrum of Hawaii's English illustrates the diverse varieties of spoken English in the Islands. In writing a simple description of these five types, comparisons have been made between the sample under discussion and the type just preceding it—the type less developed—as a means of showing changes and advances toward fully developed structural forms. In the discussion of Type V (the standard speech of Hawaii), however, such a treatment was not enough. Comparisons had to be made also with standard American speech on the Mainland. This procedure presented difficulties because (1) descriptions of the regional standards of Mainland speech have not been a part of this book and references to them are necessarily brief; (2) descriptions of regional types of standard American spoken English have been published by Thomas, Francis, McDavid, and others, as to the segmental phonemes, but not as to intonation; (3) descriptions of the intonation patterns of a single (ideal) standard for all American English have been published by Hockett, Gleason, and others, but regional variations have not been worked out. The intonation patterns among standard speakers in different parts of the country vary considerably, however, and a comparison of Hawaii's standard patterns with regional Mainland patterns must await further careful research.

The evidence presented in this book substantiates the hypothesis that the fully developed spoken English in the Islands, Type V, includes the stress and intonation patterns of standard Mainland speech as described by Hockett and Gleason for the whole country. Features of the pronunciation of consonants, vowels, and diphthongs, as described in the regional studies of Thomas, Francis, and McDavid, have their counterparts in Hawaii. The speech of the older *kama‘āina** and Hawaiian families may resemble the pronunciation of eastern New England, reflecting even today the influence of the early missionaries. Among younger speakers and among families that have moved to Hawaii in recent decades, characteristics of pronunciation will be noted which resemble the central, northern, and western sections of the United States. The speech of some individuals, for example, the one presented last in the series of representatives, may cut across several geographical areas and show features associated with several different parts of the country, reflecting no doubt the influence of public school teachers who have come to Hawaii from the Mainland, as well as periods of study the individual has had in various parts of the United States.†

---

* *Kama‘āina* is a word from the Hawaiian language meaning 'native born'. In one of its modern meanings, however, it refers to old-time Caucasian families in the Islands who frequently are descendants of the New England missionaries.

† Unlike the situation in England, where only one type of speech is considered standard—the so-called received pronunciation—a number of different regional standards of speech are recognized in the United States.

Part II **Vocabulary in a Multilingual Community**

Chapter 7 Loanwords

Although many languages are not receptive to foreign words, English has borrowed words freely since the late Middle Ages, particularly from Latin and French (see, for example, Bloomfield and Newmark 1965:361). In America, English-speaking pioneers borrowed terms from the American Indians, and in later times residents of the southwestern states adopted countless Spanish words from the culture across the border. Early American missionaries to the Hawaiian Islands learned Hawaiian place names and proper names and used them regularly in their speech (Stewart 1970:121–123), just as they were beginning to teach English words to their Island pupils. During the last decades of the nineteenth century and the first part of the twentieth, as plantation laborers arrived in the Islands, foreign words and loan translations by the hundreds entered the makeshift English of the fields and streets. Many of these terms became permanent acquisitions to the English speech of the Islands. As the twentieth century has progressed, foreign words (especially from Asia) have continued to be absorbed, although the kinds of words borrowed have changed somewhat. The earliest Asian loanwords were simple terms, such as the names of tools used in sugarcane cultivation, but the more recently acquired words have been terms suited to middle- or upper-class living and to educated speakers.

A study of Hawaiian and Portuguese loanwords has been carried on for a number of years by two or three energetic scholars. Borrowed words from other languages have received much less attention. The hybrid compound called the *loanblend*, made up of an English word and a word of non-English origin (for example, *poi dog*), has not had the study it deserves; and the *loan translation*, or *calque*, and the *loanshift* have been for the most part ignored, even though they account for the form or the meaning of numerous Hawaiianisms. This chapter is devoted to a survey of the loanwords currently in use among speakers of all levels, while chapter 8 gives attention to the curious and colorful loanblends and to other forms of change that result from language contact. Such lists cannot possibly be exhaustive. Examples missed will be included in possible future editions of this book.

HAWAIIAN LOANWORDS

The Hawaiian language is first in importance as a donor of loanwords to the English speech of Hawaii at all its levels of dialectal variation, including the standard. During the nineteenth century, Hawaiian was still the mother tongue of a great many Island people. Other ethnic groups coming in contact with Hawaiian people learned useful words connected with the Hawaiian scene and with the occupations of Islanders. In the early days, agricultural workers and plantation *luna*s were often Hawaiians and some of their Hawaiian words were incorporated into the pidgin English as it developed on the plantations. Today, many of those early loanwords are still used in agricultural districts.

New and very different forces now foster the word-borrowing process. The tourist industry promotes the use of Hawaiian words as a means of capturing and spreading the local color and warmth that are so appealing to visitors. Local song writers and entertainers, who come in contact with many thousands of tourists, play a major role in this effort. City planners keep the language always in view by giving Hawaiian names to new streets and subdivisions. On the academic side, courses in the Hawaiian language are given every year to increasing numbers of students at the University of Hawaii and at several high schools. From these formal courses, many appealing words find their way into daily use as a part of Hawaii's English.

Hawaiian loanwords were carefully listed during the 1930s by several observers. The earliest of these collections is the one compiled by U. K. Das in 1930 for the agricultural department of the experiment station of the Hawaiian Sugar Planters' Association. A revised form of this list, dated 1945, is available in the Sinclair Library of the University of Hawaii. The Das list includes Japanese, Ilocano, and Visayan words, although three-fourths of the total number of items are Hawaiian. Between 1932 and 1935, John E. Reinecke compiled a list of loanwords from the Hawaiian with the assistance of his high school students and friends at Honokaa on the island of Hawaii. In 1937 Miss A. Keakealani Lee submitted to the University of Hawaii a master's thesis entitled "A Study of the Hawaiian Vocabulary of Certain Groups of Preschool Children in Hawaii." Reinecke added some of the words and definitions from the Das and Lee lists to his own collection before completing it in 1938 and submitting it to the University library under the title "A List of Loanwords from the Hawaiian Language in Use in the English Speech of the Hawaiian Islands." This collection has been revised and published (Reinecke and Tsuzaki 1967).

In its original form, the Reinecke list, by far the longest and most fully annotated, contained approximately 250 terms. If proper names are excluded, these may be divided into four classes: (1) names of plants, fishes, and birds, with a few insects and other animals; (2) terms so rooted in Hawaiian culture that exact translations are difficult or impossible; (3) technical terms used among juveniles, such as Hawaiian terms used in the game of marbles; and (4) words with more or less adequate English equivalents, which may be used side by side with the borrowed term. Reinecke subdivided the fourth and largest class as follows: (4-a) technical terms used on plantations, ranches, and in other fields of labor; (4-b) words used mainly for and to little children; (4-c) words of indelicate meaning which a non-Hawaiian may use more easily than the equivalent term in English; (4-d) words used chiefly in pidgin by persons who consider them equivalent to English words; (4-e) words used facetiously, often as conscious slang; and (4-f) words in general use for which adequate English equivalents are available, but which have special local flavor and connotations.

For their lists, Reinecke and Lee used definitions from *A Dictionary of the Hawaiian Language* by Lorrin Andrews, revised by Henry H. Parker in 1922. Reinecke supplemented the information in this dictionary with definitions and comments collected from a large number of persons who had an acquaintance with the languages used in the Islands.

In 1950, five hundred students attending the University of Hawaii—a mixed group from all classes, from freshman to graduate student, and of many national origins—were asked to list the Hawaiian words they knew and used, exclusive of proper names.* The total number of words listed was seventy-one. The word *pau* 'finished', apparently the most widely known, was included by 449 of the students in the group; *'ae*† 'yes', by

* The questionnaire was administered by the Department of Speech, University of Hawaii, circa 1950.

† A reversed apostrophe is used to indicate the glottal stop in Hawaiian words containing this sound.

only one. The number of words listed indicates that in college student circles, which included many Mainland transfer students, the number of Hawaiian words used at the time was relatively small, at least in comparison with the Reinecke list.

The revised list put out by Das in 1945 showed a total of 191 Hawaiian words in use on the plantations, along with 46 Japanese words and 23 words from languages of the Philippines. The speech of most plantation laborers would be classified as Type I or Type II (see chapters 2 and 3). Although the majority of the laborers on the plantations at mid-century were Japanese and Filipino by birth (most Hawaiians had left the plantation labor force for other kinds of work), three-fourths of the loanwords in the English dialect of the fields were from the Hawaiian language.

More recently, A. Grove Day (1951) has provided a pleasant, nontechnical introduction to many Hawaiian loanwords. He assembled many commonly known words, grouping them according to subject.

It is not possible or necessary to repeat here Day's list or any of those mentioned earlier in this chapter. However, in all of them appear a number of words that are of such widespread currency as to need no definition: *aloha, hula, lei, lū'au, pau, poi, 'ukulele.*

S. I. Hayakawa, an interested observer of the English language in the Islands, noted in 1962 that the number of words of Hawaiian origin included in *Webster's Third New International Dictionary* showed an impressive increase over the number in the Second Edition (Hayakawa 1962). In an actual count made at the University of Hawaii in connection with the present book, the increase was found to be 78 percent, Webster's Second Edition having included 102 Hawaiian words and the Third, 182. Some of the terms selected for the Second had been dropped from the Third, however, and additional words listed. Hawaii had become a state between the publication of these editions, and tourism had boomed. Thus it could be expected that many Hawaiian words would be included among the one hundred thousand new entries added to the Third. Some residents of the State were dissatisfied with the selection of terms, believing that a number of constantly used words had been omitted and a few rarely used ones had been included.

Judging from the definitions of the word *hula* in the two editions, the gain in understanding is encouraging, however. In the Second Edition, the term was defined thus: "A native Hawaiian woman's dance. It is of mimetic and often lascivious character and is usually accompanied with rhythmic drumming and chanting." This grossly incorrect definition of *hula* exasperated some residents of Hawaii, where parents from all ethnic groups encourage their daughters to learn the hula in the hope that they may acquire the grace of motion of the dance and an understanding of the poetic interpretation of scenes and events of the Islands described in the accompanying songs.

In the Third Edition, the definition of *hula* has been changed in several dimensions. It is now: "**hula** . . . 1: a sinuous mimetic Polynesian dance of conventional form and topical adaptation performed by men and women singly or together and usu. accompanied by chants and rhythmic drumming. . . . 2: the music to which a *hula* is performed. . . ."

Samuel H. Elbert, who served as consultant to the Merriam-Webster staff for the Third Edition, is given credit for much of the improvement in accuracy of definitions. Elbert believes, however, that there is more to be done in eliminating terms no longer used by non-Hawaiians, in adding other words now known and used, and in improving further the accuracy of the definitions.

Words from the Hawaiian language tend to become anglicized in pronunciation, especially when they are carried to the mainland of the United States. An example is the name of the State, which is incorrectly pronounced [həwáyə] by many Americans who have never visited the Islands. Within the State, the approved pronunciations are [hɑwáiʔi], [hɑváiʔi], or [hɑwái]. Tourists often return to the Mainland with an improved pronunciation of the word. Another example of the tendency to anglicize is the change from the approved Hawaiian pronunciation [ho no lu lu], with nearly even stress, to the pattern closer to American English [hɑ̀nəlúlə]. Critics are so vigilant that those guilty of mispronunciations are periodically scolded or teased in the newspapers or on the radio or television. The feeling in the State for the original language is strong enough to counterbalance, to some extent, the influence of those speakers who treat Hawaiian words exactly as they treat English words.

Place names in the Islands are taken largely from the Hawaiian language; many places, indeed, still bear the names given them by the ancient Hawaiians. The individual islands, most towns and villages, and almost all mountain and land districts on all the islands have Hawaiian names. In Honolulu, the names of streets, areas, and subdivisions are usually Hawaiian or English. Street names from Portuguese number about thirty in all. Mary Kawena Pukui and Samuel H. Elbert (1966) have published a volume of place names of Hawaii, but the ones included are only those in common use, which make up only a small proportion of the names actually current, since the Hawaiian people named every patch of earth, every bay and stream and ocean channel.

The very names of people who live in Hawaii have become a part of the Island language. An interested observer has only to look in the Oahu telephone directory, particularly under the letter *K*, to find evidence of the various ethnic groups living in Hawaii. Many Hawaiian names begin with *K* because the definite article, *ka* or *ke*, is the first element in a large number of them, for example, *Kapali*, *Kapana*, and *Kealoha*. A Chinese listing in the same division is *Kau*; a Japanese name, *Kawamoto*; a Korean name, *Kim*; and a Caucasian name, *Knight*. Hawaiian family names may be very short or extremely long. The shortest is the name spelled with a single letter: *I*, pronounced [i:]. Then there is the name of former Honolulu City Councilman *Kekoalauliionapalihauliuliokekoolau David Ka'apuawaokamehameha*, known informally as Kekoa D. Kaapu.

Persons who become intrigued with the constantly recurring loan-words from the Hawaiian language used in almost all phases of life in the Islands will find the best aid of all to be the *Hawaiian-English Dictionary* (1957) and the complementary *English-Hawaiian Dictionary* (1964) compiled by Pukui and Elbert and cited frequently in this study.

Interest in Hawaiian words, then, is lively, and from all indications, it is increasing. Booklets containing popular wordlists are to be found in libraries, bookstalls, and hotel lobbies on all the Islands. Each writer has his own favorite list. The one hundred eight popular words given below, with their meanings, were collected by the author of this book and others associated with the study. For notes on the pronunciation of these and other Hawaiian terms, Tsuzaki's "Common Hawaiian Words and Phrases Used in English" (1968) is interesting and helpful.

ONE HUNDRED EIGHT HAWAIIAN WORDS COMMONLY HEARD IN HAWAII'S ENGLISH

'a'ā. A rough kind of lava

'ae. Yes; agreement

ahahana or *ahana*. Shame on you!

akamai. Smart, clever

aku. Bonito, skipjack (an important food item)

ali'i. Chief or noble person

aloha. Love, affection, hello, goodbye; as used by Hawaiians, sometimes also an expression of pity

'a'ole. No, not

auwē. Oh! Alas!*

'ele'ele. Black, dark

'Ewa. The direction opposite from Waikiki and toward 'Ewa Plantation

hale. House, building

hana. Work, activity

hāpai. To carry, lift; pregnant

haole. White person, Caucasian

haupia. Coconut cream pudding formerly thickened with arrowroot and now with cornstarch

heiau. A pre-Christian place of worship

* Intonations and gestures used by the Hawaiians as they uttered this word during the wailing that formerly accompanied a royal wake and funeral are described by Stewart (1970:225).

hikie'e. Large Hawaiian couch

hilahila. Bashful, shy, ashamed

holokū. Hawaiian gown with a train

ho'omalimali. To flatter, flattery

huhū. Angry, offended

huli. To turn; to change, as an opinion or manner of living

hui. Club, association, corporation

hukilau. A seine; to fish with the seine

hula. Hawaiian dance

humuhumu-nukunuku-a-pua'a. The name for two species of triggerfish

imu. Earth oven

ipo. Sweetheart, lover

kāhili. Feather standard of royalty

kahuna. Priest, expert in any profession

kālua. To bake in the ground oven

kama'āina. A person born in Hawaii; literally, 'child of the land'

kanaka. Human being, man, individual; as a loanword used by non-Hawaiians, the meaning is sometimes 'native' or 'fellow'

kāne. Male, husband

kapa. Tapa, a cloth made from bark

kapakahi. One-sided, crooked

kapu. Taboo, forbidden

kea. White, clear, fair

kiawe. Algaroba or mesquite tree

koa. Brave; warrior; largest of the native forest trees

kōkua. Help

Kona. Leeward sides of the Hawaiian Islands; name of a leeward wind

kukui. Candlenut tree

kuleana. Private property; responsibility, jurisdiction

lānai. Porch, veranda

lani. Sky, heaven; spiritual; very high chief, royal

lau hala. Pandanus leaf, especially as used in plaiting

laulau. Packages of ti or banana leaves containing pork, beef, salted fish, or taro tops, baked in the ground oven, steamed or broiled

lei. Flower wreath, necklace

limu. General name for all kinds of plants living under water, fresh or salt; most commonly, seaweed

lōlō. Stupid

lomilomi. Massage

lū'au. Hawaiian feast; young taro tops

luna. Foreman

mahalo. Thank you, thanks

mahimahi. Dolphin, a game fish popular for food

maika'i. Good, well; good-looking, goodness

makahiki. Year, annual, yearly; ancient Hawaiian festival

makai. Toward the sea, seaward

make. To die, dead; to faint

malihini. Visitor, tourist, newcomer

malo. Loincloth

mālolo. The Hawaiian flying fish

manapua (a telescoped word from *mea* 'thing' + *ono* 'delicious'

+ *pua'a* 'pig'). Originally, any of several Chinese delicacies, but now usually referring to only one—a large steamed bun enclosing a small amount of meat or vegetable stuffing

manu. Bird

mauka. Toward the mountains, inland

mauna. Mountain

mele. Song or chant; to sing

Menehune. Legendary race of small people who worked at night and were noted for good deeds

moana. Ocean

moemoe (reduplication of *moe*). Sleep.

moku. Island; to cut, sever

mu'umu'u. Loose Hawaiian gown without a train

nani. Pretty, beautiful

nēnē. The Hawaiian goose, adopted as the official state bird of Hawaii

niu. Coconut

nui. Large, great

'ōkolehao. Liquor made from ti root

oli. A chant

'ono. Delicious

'opihi. Limpet, a small shellfish

'ōpū. Stomach, belly

pāhoehoe. Smooth lava, contrasting with *'a'ā*

pali. Cliff

pau. Finished

pā'ū. Sarong

pīkake. Arabian jasmine

pilau. Rotten

pilikia. Trouble

pio. To close, extinguish

pohō. Out of luck

poi. The staple food of the Hawaiians, made from cooked taro corms, pounded and mixed with water

pōpoki. Cat

pua. Flower

pua'a. Pig

pueo. The Hawaiian owl

puka. Hole, perforation

pūne'e. Couch

pupule. Crazy

taro (*kalo*). A tropical plant which was the staple food of Hawaiians; *poi* was made from its starchy corm, and the leaves (*lu'au*) were also eaten

'ukulele. A musical instrument; literally 'leaping flea'

ukupau. A work concept under which laborers are allowed to go home when their assigned work for the day is finished, regardless of the time it takes

'ulu. Breadfruit

ulua. Jackfish, pompano

wahine. Woman, female

Waikīkī. As a direction, toward Waikiki, opposite from 'Ewa

wikiwiki. Hurry, hurry up

JAPANESE LOANWORDS

Many material objects from Japan have proved popular and useful in Hawaii's particular setting. As they have been adopted, the words to name them have been added to Hawaii's English. At the same time, the

Japanese language has influenced the spoken English of Hawaii both phonologically and semantically. These influences are discussed in other chapters.

Japanese family names are widely known in the Islands. Three that are known throughout the nation are those of Hawaii's United States Senator Daniel K. *Inouye* and United States Congressmen Spark M. *Matsunaga* and Patsy *Takemoto* Mink.

Strangely enough, although the Japanese arrrived many years ago, Japanese place names are almost nonexistent in the cities. This lack is explained in two ways: the early immigrants came as single men who, for several decades, did not set up homes and create neighborhoods where streets might be named for them; later, when they had established themselves and had become citizens of influence, a policy of naming new streets from the Hawaiian language had already been adopted.

Among Japanese terms borrowed with cultural items is *shōji*. The object itself is a lightweight sliding door covered with durable paper, an importation well suited to the climate of Hawaii. The term is often heard (outside the circles of Japanese-speaking residents) as *shōji door*, a loanblend listed in chapter 8 and a redundant compound with the second word a kind of partial translation of the first. Many loanblends are introduced to the public in this way, as self-explaining compounds. *Tatami matting* is another example, the English word again being redundant since *tatami* means 'grass matting'.

Many terms, however, are completely accepted and used, without the crutch of compounding with English. One is *zabuton*, the large floor-cushions to be found in homes of people of all ethnic groups. Some non-Japanese homes have a built-in *tokonoma*, a niche for displaying an object of art or a flower arrangement. This innovation was connected originally with the Japanese tea ceremony. In Hawaii, the *tokonoma* has shown Americans what the Japanese have long known, that an object of art is more impressive if displayed alone for a short time and later replaced by another treasure. The formal *tokonoma* may display a *kakemono* 'something hung', which may be either a painting or a piece of artistic calligraphy.

It comes as a surprise to Japanese people in Tokyo to learn that non-Japanese residents of Hawaii are often well acquainted with *Nō* (or *Noh*), the classical Japanese dance drama, and with its unique masks. Island audiences are also familiar with *Kabuki*, the traditional popular drama, since several of these plays are presented each year in Honolulu, either in English translation or in the original Japanese.* The *Bunraku* puppet

---

* Earle Ernst, professor and chairman of the Department of Drama and Theatre at the University of Hawaii, has been the leading interpreter of Kabuki at the University of Hawaii. See the Bibliography.

theater has been brought to Honolulu, too, on several occasions. The *hanamichi*, an extension of the stage for some of the entrances and exits of actors, is a necessary part of the staging of many Japanese plays. Invented by Japanese dramatists in medieval times and peculiar to Japan, the *hanamichi* has nevertheless made an easy transition to the Hawaiian scene, where many people have forgotten that it is an importation. The *shamisen* and *koto*, musical instruments of Japanese origin, have been heard on the stage so often that the terms and their meanings are well known.

In the world of clothing, some words popular in Hawaii today actually predate (as loanwords in the English language elsewhere) the discovery of Hawaii by Captain Cook. *Kimono* first appeared in English in the seventeenth century (Serjeantson 1961). Other words, such as *tabi* and *zōri*, although known everywhere in Hawaii, were not included in *Webster's Third New International Dictionary*. *Tabi*, socklike foot coverings with a division between the large toe and the other toes, are worn by thousands of non-Japanese women, and *zōri*, the low Japanese thong slippers often called "go-aheads" and "grass slippers," are worn by men and women of all ethnic groups and for many more occasions than in Japan, even appearing on the streets of Honolulu, to the mild dismay of visitors from Japan. *Obi* and *obi* cloth are widely known and valued for their beauty. A useful word in the realm of applied art (for example, in the designing of clothing), the adjective *shibui* carries with it a connotation of elegance without undue ornamentation.

Ikebana, the Japanese art of flower arrangement, involving symbolism as well as a great deal of grace and beauty, has been established for many years in Hawaii with subdivisions into several schools of study. *Origami*, on the other hand, has not stopped in Hawaii but has become known throughout the Mainland, as evidenced by its entry in Webster's Third with the definition "the art or process of paper-folding." *Origami* is the more practical of the two, with great appeal for children, while *ikebana* (not yet entered in Webster) is actually a fine art, requiring years of study and practice.

The forty-seven Japanese restaurants in Honolulu at the end of 1969 were evidence of the local demand for Japanese cuisine. They are still outnumbered, of course, by Honolulu's seventy-odd Chinese restaurants. The Japanese dish known to the greatest number of people is *sukiyaki*, a combination of meat and vegetables cooked with soy sauce, sugar, and *sake* 'rice wine'. *Teriyaki* is a runner-up in popularity and is currently in vogue with American tourists. This special way of cooking beef or chicken is used by Chinese and Koreans, as well as by Japanese, although the Japanese word for it has become its common name in Hawaii. Each ethnic group seems to have its own variation of *teriyaki*. The Korean-style *teriyaki* calls for the use of sesame seeds and oil, which neither the Japanese nor the Chinese variations use, and is called *bul-kogi*, while the Chinese equivalent is called *ch'au niu yiou*. In Japan *teriyaki* fish is also a favorite, but the idea of using *teriyaki* sauce on fish has not become popular with the Oriental population in Hawaii.

Tempura, as a word and as a food item, is widely known. It is seafood or bits of vegetables covered with a special batter and fried in deep fat. *Sashimi* 'raw fish', served with sauces or condiments, and *sushi* are prime favorites with Asians and Westerners. Several varieties of *sushi* are made in Hawaii, all of them using *gohan* 'cooked rice' mixed with vinegar and sugar. A favorite kind has a delicacy at the center (such as a bit of shrimp, raw fish, caviar, or cucumber) rolled up in prepared rice with a thin outer wrapping of *nori* 'seaweed'. Indispensable items on the Japanese menu are *shōyu* 'soy bean sauce'; *miso*, a paste made from soy beans and rice and used mainly for flavoring soup; *tofu* 'soy bean curd'; *daikon*, an edible root similar to a radish or turnip; *sembei* 'crisped rice tidbits', used as appetizers; *ajinomoto* 'monosodium glutamate', which seems to improve the flavor of all edibles; and *sake*, which points up the Japanese meal. *Kamaboko* 'boiled fish paste' is well known in Hawaii as 'fishcake', and *udon* 'noodles' are staple items.

The word *saimin*, meaning 'noodle soup', is often identified with the Japanese in Hawaii. Its pedigree, however, is a puzzle. One observer has offered his theory of the origin of *saimin* and has placed the source squarely in a Japanese mind. Steinberg writes of the imagined "inventor" of *saimin:* "One contributor to this gastronomic integration [foods in Hawaii] was the unknown culinary genius who hit upon the idea of adding pork to *ramen*, a Japanese rendition of a Chinese noodle dish. His brainstorm became *saimin*, a richly flavored, uniquely Hawaiian noodle concoction that is today the most popular quick-lunch snack in the islands" (1970:12). Other possibilities are discussed on p. 99 and in the Glossary.

The term *hibachi*, used in Hawaii to mean a portable stove for cooking, provides an example of a loanshift (Hockett 1958:408–412). In Japan, the *hibachi* is a charcoal brazier for warming hands, whereas the *hichirin* is used for cooking. In Hawaii, where hand-warmers are not needed, the term *hibachi* has been transferred to the brazier for cooking.

Japanese sports and games are of intense interest to some persons in all ethnic groups. Most boys and many girls in Hawaii have had a year or more of *judō*, *karate*, or *aikido*. Although it is not commonly practiced in Hawaii, *sumō*, a form of wrestling, is becoming better known each year as an occasional Hawaii participant goes to Japan to compete there.

Go, the Japanese game of skill sometimes likened to chess, is played by some and is known to many.

A Japanese word much heard on radio and TV in the early 1970s is *shibai*, usually in the combination *political shibai*. From an original Japanese meaning of 'play, drama, theater', the term *shibai* has come to mean, in the political circles of Hawaii, 'making a dramatic production to obscure a point.'

A scientific term of wide use is *tsunami*, meaning an ocean wave commonly but inaccurately called "tidal wave." Because the Japanese chain of islands and the Hawaiian chain alike had suffered the devastations caused by the *tsunami*, and because the Japanese name seemed to be an unequivocal label, contrasting with the vagueness and ambiguity of "tidal wave," the word *tsunami* was adopted by scientists and has become a part of the English language. A project office at the University of Hawaii is called the Tsunami Research Center. Phonologically, this loan is one of the few words in English that begin with the consonant cluster [ts].

Words used in Hawaii's sugarcane and pineapple fields include Japanese terms for agricultural items, activities, and work relationships. A list of such foreign terms compiled by the Hawaiian Sugar Planters' Association (1945) contains forty-six Japanese words, representing nearly 18 percent of the total number on the list. Hawaiian words make up 73 percent, and words from the languages of the Philippines, 9 percent. Although more than two decades have passed since the list was circulated, many of the simple and basic expressions are still in use, particularly the following: *arigatō* 'thank you'; *atsui* 'hot'; *bangō* 'number', hence 'identification tag'; *kibikaji* 'cane fire'; *kusa* 'weeds'; *kuwa* 'hoe'; *mate* 'wait' or 'stop a while'; *mizu* 'water'; *nagai* 'long'; *satōkibi* 'sugarcane'; *shigoto* 'work'; *suki* 'plow'; *tsuchi* 'soil'; *wakaru* 'to understand'; *wakaran* 'not understand'; *Ohayō* 'Good morning'; and *Konnichi wa* 'Good day'. (No macrons were used to indicate long vowels in this list as it was originally published.)

Further examples of Japanese words of wide currency in Hawaii appear in the pages of the novel *Hey, Pineapple!* by Bob Nobuyuki Hongo (1948). Three of these are: *sayōnara* 'goodbye'; *ichiban* 'number one'; and *banzai*, a cheer meaning 'ten thousand years of life'.

Terms used in referring to Japanese-Americans are of more than minor interest. *Naichi jin* refers to people from Japan proper (*naichi* meaning 'inner land'); *Uchinanchu* and *Okinawa-ken jin* indicate the people whose pioneers came from the Ryukyu Islands. Informal shortened forms used by non-Japanese persons in Hawaii are *naichi* and *Okinawa group*. *Issei* denotes 'first generation', and is applied to immigrants born in any part of the Japanese Empire. *Nisei* is literally 'second generation' away from Japan, but it has acquired the meaning 'first generation born in Hawaii', while *sansei* means 'third generation' away from Japan but 'second generation born in the Islands'.

The term *kibei* is more difficult to explain. The morpheme *ki* means 'to return' or 'the act of returning', and the morpheme *bei* is the abbreviation of *beikoku* 'the United States of America'. When the two are combined, the resulting word *kibei* means the act of returning to the United States. In Hawaii, semantic widening has caused this noun to denote a person who has come back to the United States, especially to Hawaii, after a term of residence in Japan. The actual *kibei* may have a curious linguistic history. Born in Hawaii, he usually learns as a child a dialectal form of English. Then, taken to Japan to spend a number of years with relatives, he attends school there and learns to speak the language of his forebears. Upon his return to Hawaii, the dialectal phonemes in his English speech may still be present, complicated by the effects of Japanese phonemes and grammar upon his much-traveled English.

Two humorous terms used during World War II were *Buddahead* (technically a loanblend), a name for Japanese-Americans born in Hawaii, and *Kotonk*, for those born on the mainland of the United States. (The thesis of Patricia Morimoto [1966] discusses the origin of these terms.)

Examples of loanwords so far given have been from standard Japanese. Edgar Knowlton (1961) has gathered a few expressions that originated in the Ryukyu Islands and are familiar to some persons outside the Okinawa group. They include *tsura kagi* 'pretty girl', *yana kagi* 'ugly girl', and the mild exclamation *Akasimi yo* 'Gracious me!' Two other Okinawan expressions are *Dika* 'Let's go' and *Cha ga* 'How are you?'

Hawaiian and Japanese words are similar in phonological structure. In both languages, words end with vowel sounds (with the exception of the final *n* of some Japanese words). Neither language has consonant clusters. Both possess large numbers of polysyllabic words with regular alternation of consonant and vowel. English-speaking people in Hawaii, accustomed to the use of Hawaiian words, easily adopted loanwords from Japanese as they became necessary and attractive. Chinese words, on the other hand, with their varied tones and monosyllables, have proved far harder to distinguish and remember. The popularity in Hawaii of features of Japanese culture, such as its architecture, has added force to the word-borrowing inclination of English speakers here. This exchange of words has its reciprocal aspects. In Japan itself, since the close of World War II, the language has been absorbing English words in large numbers, subtly altering the pronunciation until they are almost indistinguishable in sound from Japanese words.

Of the sixty Japanese words discussed in this chapter, which are heard in the everyday speech of Hawaii in various forms of activity, thirty-one are not yet listed in Webster's Third: *ajinomoto, arigatō, atsui, bangō, gohan, hanamichi, hichirin, ichiban, ikebana, kibikaji, Konnichi wa, kusa, kuwa, mate, mizu, nagai, naichi, Ohayō, satōkibi, sembei, shibui, shigoto, sushi, suki, tabi, teriyaki, tsuchi, wakaran* (or the standard *wakaranai*), *wakaru, zabuton,* and *zōri.* The most surprising omissions are *ajinomoto, ikebana, shibui, tabi, teriyaki, zabuton,* and *zōri.* At least the most popular of these should be suggested to the editorial board of the next edition of the unabridged dictionary, with precise definitions and supporting evidence as to their actual use in America.

All in all, the Japanese language has had a far-reaching influence on Hawaii's English speech. In chapter 4 it is shown that the syllable-timed rhythm of Japanese, transplanted long ago to the Islands, can be heard to this day in the English phrases of some dialectal speakers, particularly those of Types I and III. Word borrowing from the Japanese language, on the other hand, is evident in all levels of speech from the relatively unschooled to the most educated and accomplished. The more dialectal speakers tend to use the simpler terms of early importation, such as those connected with agriculture, while persons of near-standard or standard speech supplement their vocabularies with the newer borrowings appropriate to middle-class or upper-class living. Educated and widely traveled residents have access to a variety of imported objects and ideas, and hence to the names that accompany them. Because loanwords widen the choice of synonyms available to a speaker, they provide an enrichment of expression that is notable in artistic and professional circles in the Islands.

PORTUGUESE LOANWORDS

Twice in the course of its development Hawaii's English speech has been influenced by the Portuguese language. The original contact was made in Asia, as a side effect of the development of commerce between East and West. In the sixteenth century, the Portuguese were granted the territory of Macao in China "as a factory for trade with Canton" (Livermore 1966). In the interchange between the Portuguese and Chinese merchants, certain Portuguese words became part of the pidgin English developing around Canton. Some of these terms later filtered into the Hawaiian Islands along with other bits of pidgin as explorers and traders came and went. The first Portuguese word to be recorded in Hawaii was heard in the speech of Hawaiians by the Spaniard, Manuel Quimper in 1791. He entered in his Hawaiian journal the word *piquinini*, translated as 'small thing', and according to Quimper, pronounced by the Hawaiians *pikanele* (Quimper 1822). The original Portuguese word is *pequenino*, meaning 'small child'.

In 1820, Lucia Holman, wife of the physician with the first company of Christian missionaries to arrive in Hawaii, heard this word and recorded it in her diary after her first verbal encounter with Hawaiian women (Holman 1931). The huge Hawaiians, after scanning the slender figures of the missionaries' wives, laughingly called them *piccaninny*. This was Mrs. Holman's spelling of the word which was translated for her as 'too little'.

Before 1878, Portuguese-speaking people settled in Hawaii. Knowlton summarizes:

By the middle 1870's there were over four hundred Portuguese living in Hawaii, many of them former sailors from whaling ships. . . . One of the most distinguished was Jason Perry . . . from Fayal, the Azores, proprietor of a dry goods store in Honolulu. Perry was an early consular agent and was instrumental in the decision to recruit contract laborers (at first from Madeira) to come to Hawaii for contract work. [1960:212]

The most intensive period of contact between the Portuguese language and Hawaii's English began in 1878, when more than seventeen thousand Portuguese laborers, with their families, arrived in the Hawaiian Islands from Maderia and the Azores. Effects upon the developing dialect were soon felt, as Portuguese children mixed in play and at school with Hawaiian children. They learned English quickly, and passed on characteristics of their native language to the stream of English speech, just as the Hawaiian children were themselves injecting lauguage habits from their Polynesian tongue into that same dialectal English. Knowlton has made a clear summary of this period of language contact:

It should be remembered that if the subtle influence of Portuguese is far-reaching, it is not surprising. In the late nineteenth century, in the schools of Hawaii when English was being taught as *the* language of the schools, the two groups comprising the bulk of the school population were the Hawaiians and the Portuguese. They outnumbered the British and Americans. The Chinese and Japanese, though forming a large percentage of the population in earlier days, migrated almost entirely as unaccompanied adult males, so that children of Chinese or of Japanese ancestry were comparatively few. This period may have been most important in shaping Hawaii's English dialect. [1967:236]

In Portuguese neighborhoods that grew up, such as the early one on the slopes of Punchbowl, a few streets and lanes were named in honor of

cities and districts in the home country and for distinguished citizens of
Portuguese ancestry. Knowlton again furnishes an excellent summary:

> Material for the study of Honolulu's street names is at hand in seventy-six
> articles in the *Honolulu Star-Bulletin*. These articles were prepared by George
> Miranda and were published between January 17 and April 13, 1956. About
> thirty street names in Honolulu reflect the Portuguese in Hawaii. Among them
> are names of distinguished Hawaiians of Portuguese descent—Alencastre,
> Correa, Machado, Osorio, Pacheco; some reflect geography: Azores, Funchal,
> Madeira; history is recalled in the name of Magellan; Concordia, Lusitana, and
> San Antonio preserve the memory of Portuguese benevolent societies; Monte
> derives from the name of the Catholic church of Nossa Senhora do Monte. A few
> buildings have Portuguese names: Araujo, Farias, Mendonça. [1960:213]

Oahu's 1970 telephone directory shows many columns of Portuguese
names. For the family name spelled *Pereira* in Portugal, three different
spellings occur in Hawaii. There are sixty-five listings for *Perreira*, four
for *Perriera*, and nineteen for *Pereira*. For the name *Perry* (a shortened
form of *Perreira* adopted by some members of this family), there are 145
entries. Other family names taken at random from the directory are
Cabral, Caldeira, Cunha, Gonsalves, and *Pacheco*. Portuguese names have
long been connected with some of the substantial industries of the
Islands, notably with Hawaii's bakeries.

Hawaii's Portuguese heritage, gastronomically speaking, comes to
mind in connection with the popular *pão doce*, the sweet-bread known to
all, and the *malassada*, a kind of doughnut raised with yeast. In recent
years, enlarged supermarkets and increased radio and television adver-
tising have made Portuguese products well known outside the circles of
the Portuguese-Americans. Certain meats are associated with this ethnic
group, particularly Portuguese sausage. Jacintho M. De Gouvea is said
to have introduced link sausage into Hawaii commercially in 1880 from
his native island, São Miguel, in the Azores. *Choriso* (or *chorizo*) is another Portuguese sausage, usually sold in tins. (*Chouriço* is the dictionary
form of this word.)

As in the case of the Japanese immigrants, the Portuguese in Hawaii
have acquired nicknames. Because of the frequent appearance of codfish
on their tables, the Portuguese long ago were dubbed *baccaliaos*. The
Pukui-Elbert Hawaiian-English dictionary lists this word as *pakaliao*
from the Portuguese *bacalhau* 'codfish', treating it as a loanword in the
Hawaiian language from the Portuguese. A more dignified Hawaiian
name for the group is *Pukikī* ('Portuguese'), a transliteration from
English.

Knowlton's list of sixteen points at which this language may have influenced the syntax of local speech is readily available (1967:234–235).

The "Portuguese lilt" from Maderia and the Azores (where dialectal forms of Portuguese are used) has frequently been named as the source of some of Hawaii's intonation patterns, yet this statement has never been completely documented. For the student of language, the less evident influences (in phonology and in loan translations) are likely subjects for continued interest and study. The influence of Portuguese upon the English language in Hawaii is considerable even though the actual number of loanwords heard today is small.

That early Portuguese settlements have influenced the pidginization of English in another part of the world has been shown by Le Page and De Camp:

> On the Gold Coast the Portuguese did everything they could to maintain their monopoly of the gold exports which gave the coast its name. By the time they were expelled by the Dutch in 1642 they had had settlements on the coast for 160 years, the chief being Elmina. They had introduced from their possessions a great many useful plants—oranges, lemons, limes, rice and sugar-cane from the Far East, and maize, tobacco, pineapple, cassava and guava from America. In addition their presence had given rise to a widespread knowledge of Portuguese and to the development of a trade language from which many words of Portuguese origin survived both in the Gold Coast languages and in the pidgin English which evolved as a trade language later. Some of these words in due course found their way to the West Indies and became naturalized there. [1960:30]

CHINESE LOANWORDS

Loanwords come into being because of contact between ethnic groups, and there are records of contact between the Hawaiians and the Chinese nearly two centuries ago. In Kuykendall's words, "The lure of foreign travel strongly attracted many of the Hawaiians. . . . The most distinguished of these early Hawaiian tourists was the high chief Kaiana, who went with Meares in 1787 and returned the following year after having visited China and the Northwest Coast" (1938:22).

There is also a record of one or more Chinese persons visiting Hawaii and being included in the group at the court of the king. Kuykendall again reports: "From about 1790, there grew up, very slowly at first, a foreign population in Hawaii. . . . In the early part of 1794, there were eleven foreigners with Kamehameha at Kealakekua; they were of several nationalities, including Chinese" (1938:26–27).

Archibald Campbell, author of *A Voyage Round the World from 1806 to 1812*, remained for more than a year on the island of Oahu in 1809–1810 and recorded seeing nearly sixty white people at one time during his stay there, about one third of them Americans and the rest almost all Englishmen (Campbell 1967:118).

Chinese words could have entered Hawaii from direct contacts between Hawaiians and Chinese or they could have been brought in by
Americans and Englishmen, since at least two Chinese words had been
taken into the English language in the seventeenth century. The word
tea, brought to Europe by the Dutch, had reached England by 1650, and
chopsticks (an early Chinese-English loanblend) was recorded in written
English in 1699 (Serjeantson 1961:239).

Manuel Quimper, making his glossary of Hawaiian words in 1791, set
down a word which he spelled *caucao*, assuming it to be a native term.
It was the Hawaiianized form of the Chinese pidgin *chowchow* 'food' or
'to eat'—the present-day popular term *kaukau*—which had already
found its way to the Islands. In the year 1820, this word was recorded
in the diary of Lucia Holman (1931:19), when the gigantic Hawaiian
women who had called Mrs. Holman *pickaninny* advised her to *kaukau*
and grow *nunui* 'eat' and grow 'big'. It seems likely that these borrowed
words were part of a special vocabulary used by the Hawaiians when
talking to foreigners.

Considering these contacts, the early arrival of the Chinese immigrants
for plantation labor, and the very substantial Chinese contribution to
Island life, we might expect to find a great many expressions from their
language in Island English. This is not the case; there are relatively few
Chinese loanwords in general use other than family names and terms
connected with foods. As suggested before, the short and tonal Chinese
words have proved to be elusive and, unlike Japanese and Hawaiian
words, they have remained difficult for English-speaking persons to learn
and remember. There are several notable exceptions.

Chinese family names, for example, are everywhere in evidence in
Hawaii. There were thirteen and a half columns of entries for the family
name *Wong* in the 1970 telephone directory for Oahu and eight and a half
columns of *Ching*s, compared with eight columns of Smiths. (The average
number of names in each column of this directory is seventy-five.) Two
widely known names are Hiram *Fong*, United States Senator from Hawaii
and *Chinn Ho*, a leading businessman. In the years after the Chinese
laborers came to Hawaii as single men, many of them married into Hawaiian families. Later some of these Chinese-Hawaiian families changed
their names slightly to give them a more "Hawaiian" sound, usually by
attaching an initial *A* to the family name. Thus we have *Afong*, *Akau*,
Achong, *Achin*, and *Achiu*. This practice is said to have derived from the
Cantonese expression *A Sam*, used in speaking to a third son in a family:
it carries a meaning something like the Caucasian "Oh, John!"

Most of the Chinese laborers who came to Hawaii between 1876 and
1897 were from the vicinity of Canton in South China. They were given

a nickname by people of other ethnic groups in Hawaii—the term *Pākē*, possibly fashioned after a colloquial reading of the Cantonese *pai-yā* 'father' (Pukui-Elbert Dictionary, 1957). The language that came with these immigrants and the style of cooking they later popularized were Cantonese.

Among the myriad contributions of the Chinese to Island living, perhaps the most highly prized category has been food—from the characteristic tangy snacks to the nine-course formal dinner. Children from all ethnic groups consider *crack seed* and *see mui*, usually pronounced [sí mòi], to be better than candy. The terms have become generic ones for a variety of preparations of dried plums or other fruits, salty, sour, or sweet, and sometimes with the seed actually cracked to give additional flavor. The most popular variety has a label that reads *mui* 'plum' and *see* 'sour' or 'salty'. It brings puckering to the lips and tension to the jaws, but it is a delight to Island youngsters. Packages labeled *tim mui* contain sweet, whole dried plums, while the very salty *li hing mui* is of uncertain pedigree. These words and the contents of the little bags are a part of growing up in Hawaii. Island parents frequently mail packages of assorted *mui* to youngsters away at college on the Mainland; the pleasure of the recipients equals the bewilderment of non-Island roommates.

The Cantonese word *min* 'noodles' introduces another complex of delicacies. The best known is *saimin*, a noodle soup which is disclaimed by both the Chinese and Japanese (see p. 146). The vast number of *saimin stands* throughout the Islands (interestingly enough operated by Japanese), prove that this is a favorite local dish. The best judgment as to a Chinese origin of the word is that *sai* is a Cantonese rendering of the word 'water' and that *saimin*, therefore means 'water noodles' or 'noodle soup'.* Today, packages of dried or frozen *saimin*, some from Japan and some prepared locally, are available in Island supermarkets. They are not to be confused with the Japanese *somen*, a packaged vermicelli.

One of the first Chinese terms learned by newcomers to Hawaii is *wun tun*, a name for meat dumplings. Fried in deep fat (*crisp wun tun*), they appear on the menus of all Chinese restaurants and are served as appetizers at many cocktail parties. *Wun tun* are also served in soups (*wun tun min*). Several other items are such favorites that their Chinese names have become a part of the local language, for example, *egg fu yung*, *chow fun*, and *chow mein* (which may appear in Cantonese romanization as

---

* Lily C. Winters, professor of Chinese and chairman of the division of East Asian literature, Department of Asian and Pacific Languages, University of Hawaii, was particularly helpful with this word and with other terms in this section.

chau min). In the markets one can see *char steak* and *char siu*, explained to customers as 'fork steaks', that is, meat cooked on a spit or fork over an open fire—in other words, barbecued. On vegetable counters will appear *wun bok* or Chinese cabbage.

The cover word for Chinese food throughout the United States including Hawaii is *chop suey*. Translated from the Cantonese *daap sui*, the name means 'miscellaneous bits', 'various items', or 'odd assortment', but the famous dish is not actually on Chinese tables at all. To the Chinese people, *chop suey* is known only as an agreeable foreign dish. Although there are various stories as to its origin, one is that the chefs of Diplomat General Lee Hoong Jeung served a quickly prepared dish to unexpected foreign guests, consisting of pork sauteed with onions, celery, mushrooms, and bean sprouts. It pleased the guests so much that they asked its name and the general replied "daap sui," meaning an odd assortment of things. This general would be astonished, if he were alive today, to learn that he had invented the typical American Chinese dish (Ching 1967:7). Almost all of the more than seventy Chinese restaurants on Oahu are listed in the yellow pages of the telephone directory as "chop suey houses" even though each provides its customers with a savory array of dishes with precise names of their own.

Two well-known words may reflect the gregarious nature of the Chinese. *Tong*, the Cantonese word for 'hall' or 'large room', seems to have a less ominous meaning in Hawaii than on the mainland of the United States. Non-Chinese Island people think of this word as meaning 'a fraternal organization'. It has been recorded in the English language since 1918 and is defined in Webster's Third as "a secret society or fraternal organization especially among the Chinese in the United States, formerly notorious for gang warfare and popularly associated with racketeering, gambling, and traffic in narcotics." It is possible that this definition needs to to be updated.

The other word connected with group activity is *hui*, said to be from the Mandarin, meaning 'a club'. By a strange coincidence, this word is the same as the Hawaiian and Maori *hui*, which means a group formed for a purpose, sometimes a syndicate. Thus, doubly reinforced, the word is useful and popular in the Islands. During World War II, driving *hui*s were formed because of gasoline rationing. Since that time, all kinds of temporary *hui*s have been formed for the mutual interests of the participants.

There are almost no streets named for the Chinese in Honolulu or on the rest of the island of Oahu. We find *Chun Hoon Lane, Wong Lane, Sing Loy Lane, Wong Ho Lane, Achiu Lane*, and *Heen Way*, but that is about all. No survey has been made of the outer islands. Although the Chinese arrived early in the Islands, as with the Japanese it was many years before they established families and produced distinguished citizens. By the time they had developed a substantial cultural unit, a policy had already been formed of giving new streets and subdivisions names from the Hawaiian language. Of all the immigrant groups, only the Portuguese have given their names to more than a few Island streets and districts.

The Chinese have often provided colorful English translations for their native terms, coined in patterns of elegance and glamour. Several restaurant names in Honolulu are cases in point: *Four Seas, House of Dragon, Four Seasons, Golden City, Ming Palace, Imperial Jade,* and *Lotus Inn.* On their own New Year's holiday, however, celebrated with festive food and noisy fireworks, the Chinese-Americans do not translate their Cantonese greeting, now familiar to all—*Kun Hee Fat Choy.*

LOANWORDS FROM LANGUAGES OF THE PHILIPPINES

Except for the Filipino's enthusiastic shout of joy and approval—*mabuhay*—the average resident of Hawaii has known very few words from the Philippine Islands until rather recently. This was to be expected, since the Filipinos were the last of the ethnic groups to immigrate to Hawaii in large numbers. Of their arrival, Kuykendall and Day wrote:

After the Japanese immigration was stopped in 1907, the sugar planters began the importation of Filipino laborers in great numbers. Many others came voluntarily ... In all, about 125,000 Filipinos came to Hawaii. Enough of these have remained to give the territory a substantial Filipino population group, amounting in 1957 to more than 73,000. [1961:212]

Bruno Lasker has provided pertinent details concerning the origins of the immigrants who arrived in Hawaii between 1916 and 1928 (1969: 167). In 1916, the island of Cebu, where Visayan is spoken, took the lead in sending 669 laborers, and Visayans arrived from other provinces as well. In the same year, various Ilocano-speaking provinces sent more than 460 workers, while immigrating Tagalog speakers numbered about 150. By 1919, the Ilocano-speaking immigrants outnumbered all others and during 1928, the Ilocanos from Ilocos Norte, Ilocos Sur, and La Union contributed 62 percent of the total number of Filipino immigrants to Hawaii. Thus the Ilocano language was most often heard during the years when Filipinos were restricted to plantation labor, and, as Lasker explains, this was because of the greater ability of the Ilocano group to adjust to the arduous work of the sugarcane fields. The Visayan language was a close second, but in more recent years, the Philippine national language, Tagalog, has been heard in Hawaii increasingly because younger Filipinos coming to Hawaii have studied Tagalog as a required subject in Philippine schools. During plantation days, the syllable-timed rhythm of the newcomers' speech reinforced that of the Japanese, their rapid staccato enunciation was noticed, and the term "Filipino pidgin" was coined to describe their own characteristic variations on American English.

During the nineteenth century in the Philippines, a majority of the people took Spanish names, often voluntarily but sometimes with pressure from Spanish authorities. Thus the names of many Filipino families in Hawaii are indistinguishable from the names of Spanish and Puerto Rican, and, in some cases, of Portuguese, citizens. Yet there are numerous examples of names from the language stock of the Philippines, often interesting for the frequency of their consonantal endings /g/, /ŋ/, /n/, or /t/. Examples of Tagalog names, with the number of entries in the Oahu telephone directory for 1970 are: *Galang* (five), *Ilagan* (four), *Lapitan* (four), *Tapat* (two) and *Liwanag* (one). A few of the names in this directory from other Philippine languages are: *Paglinawan* (eight entries), *Maglangit* (three), *Mamauag* (two), *Pabalan* (one), and *Samabat* (one).*

Certain Filipino proper names are of such importance in the history of the Pacific area that they are known by long-time residents of Hawaii in all ethnic groups: *Rizal*, the revered martyr-poet and patriot, *Quezon* and *Magsaysay*, two great Philippine presidents, and *Romulo*, the distinguished author and diplomat. On Oahu today, two second-generation Filipinos whose names are known because of ability and achievement are Judge Alfred *Laureta* and Domingo *Los Baños*, a district superintendent of schools (the word *los baños* is an interesting Spanish borrowing meaning 'the baths'.)

As in the case of proper names, other loanwords from this language group are of two kinds: Spanish words that had been absorbed by the Filipino people in their homeland before their immigration to Hawaii, and words from the language stock of the Philippines, a branch of the Malayo-Polynesian family. In the list of 260 foreign terms used on Hawaii's plantations, revised by C. K. Das for the Hawaiian Sugar Planters' Association (1945), twenty-three words (or 9 percent) of the total were labeled "Filipino words." Of these, fourteen are actually from

* Ethel Alikpala Ward, formerly an East-West Center grantee, native speaker of Tagalog, and teacher of English as a second language, Farrington High School, furnished some of the material in this section, including the identification of family names.

Philippine languages while nine are Spanish words. The latter will be listed in another section of this chapter.

Some words on the list are Ilocano terms exclusively, but because Ilocano, Visayan, and Tagalog are closely related, some other words are shared by two of these languages and some by all of them. They may be found in dictionaries of the Philippine languages (see the Bibliography), often with the newer spellings now being established in the Philippines, and usually with accent marks provided. The words listed below appear as given by Das. *I*, *V*, and *T* stand for Ilocano, Visayan, and Tagalog.*

babai 'girl' or 'woman' (I,V,T)
balay 'house' (I,V)
bata 'child' (boy or girl) (V,T)
bayao or *bayaw* 'brother-in-law' (I,T) 'brother-in-law' or 'sister-in-law' (V)
dakayo 'you' (plural) (I)
danom 'water' (I)
ditoy 'here' or 'over this way' (I) .
ikau or *ikaw* 'you' (singular) (V,T)
lalaki 'boy' or 'man' (I,V,T)
sabidong 'poison' (I)
tao 'person', 'people', 'mankind' (I,V,T)
tubig 'water' (V,T)
tubo 'sugarcane' (V,T)
unas 'sugarcane' (I)

The word *bayaw* from the list above has long been taken as a humorous nickname for the Filipinos in Hawaii. The term *bayaw style*, as used in Honolulu, refers to their supposed habit of segregating at gatherings, with the men on one side of the room and the women on the other. It is applied in jest to any situation where people tend to divide in this way.

Nearly three decades have passed since the word list by Das was last revised, and the people from the Philippines have made themselves known far beyond the rural areas by means of the many attractive features of their culture, particularly their clothing and their food. Their national costume is sometimes worn for special occasions by Hawaii's non-Filipino residents. For men it is the *barong Tagalog*, a cool open-necked shirt made of pineapple fiber and embroidered in designs quite in keeping with recent trends in men's clothing. For women, it is the *terno*, a long dress with high, winglike shoulders and airy sleeves—an addition

* Ernesto Constantino, professor of linguistics and chairman of the Pilipino Department at the University of the Philippines, provided information about the Philippine words on the Das list.

to Hawaii's complex of floor-length dresses for formal and semiformal wear.

Philippine foods, with their distinctive flavors and striking names, tend to emphasize the sour and salty rather than the sweet and bland, and to furnish surprises by their unexpected combinations of ingredients. Katherine Bazore, in her book *Hawaiian and Pacific Foods* (1940:85, 87), furnishes interesting examples. *Tinola*, a name from the Tagalog language, is a chicken soup often made with the addition of garlic, ginger, and green papaya cubes. Tamarind, the tart brown fruit from the tamarind tree, sometimes provides the characteristic sour taste in dishes such as *sinigang* (or *sigang*), a soup of meat or fish and tomatoes, cooked in water with tamarind, guavas, or green mangoes added for the tart flavor. *Bagoong*, a hot sauce or paste, is as powerful as its name suggests. To prepare it, shrimp or small fish are mixed with salt and allowed to ferment for several days, after which they are pressed and the liquid is drained off. *Patis*, this clear liquid, is used for salads and seasoning. The rest of the mixture is pounded, salted again, and allowed to stand for one or two days longer. It may be used to flavor pork or vegetables or may be eaten alone. At least five varieties of *bagoong* are sold in the Filipino shops in Hawaii; one is known as *monamon*.

Early risers on Sunday mornings on Oahu may hear via radio the Filipino music hour with its tinkling instrumental music, its romantic songs, and the extraordinarily fast, syllable-timed rhythm of its announcer, Prose Martinez, as she trips along in Ilocano syllables and breaks intermittently into English loanwords. A popular television program, "Mr. Respicio's Filipino Fiesta," is also in Ilocano with English and Tagalog added.

By means of their distinctive clothing and food and the other lively and sparkling features of their culture—which complement the quieter traits of many other ethnic groups—the Filipinos are steadily gaining recognition, and it seems certain that Hawaii's English will be the richer as new loanwords are adopted from their languages.

SPANISH LOANWORDS

Spanish words were acquired by both the English and the Hawaiian languages during the colorful decade between 1830 and 1840 in the country around Waimea, Hawaii. Here, in 1793, Captain George Vancouver had left a bull, several cows, and some calves which were allowed to run free for more than ten years under a strict tabu enforced by Kamehameha I. By 1830, the wild descendants of these cattle had become so numerous that they presented a serious problem. Cowboys were recruited from California in that year for their skill in handling both horses and cattle;* during their residence and activity at Waimea, they passed along not only words but cultural items to the Hawaiians and the American missionaries. Bernice Judd gave an account of this period of activity, including the following comment about a loanword: "These men were of Spanish, Mexican, and Indian origin. The Hawaiians called them *paniolo* from the word *espagnol*. Indeed, today, the Hawaiian word for cowboy is *paniolo*" (1931:14–25).

Curtis J. Lyons, son of the missionary Lorenzo Lyons who was stationed at Waimea during this time, has listed a number of objects brought in during the activity of the *paniolos*, including Mexican decorated saddles, spurs, twisted-hair rope, hand-wrought bits, and—most useful of all to the missionary families—the ox cart (Lyons 1892:25–27). Of the word *poncho*, he wrote: "Did not the serape—'poncho' we always called it and the name must have come from South America—commend itself to our common sense as a defence against rain? We adopted it, and the red silk sash in the bargain" (p. 26).

Much more important than the word *poncho* as a contribution to Hawaii was the word *adobe*, and the new method of building houses and schools introduced with it by the Spaniards at Waimea. Lyons gave his impression of the making of *adobe* in the Islands as a process of using "the clayey soil of the yard [house site] itself with *pili* grass mixed in." (Pili was a common grass used for thatching.) Lyons was fully aware of the significance of this innovation: "People in these days [1892] can hardly realize how important an element that was in the early building up of Honolulu" (p. 25). The fact that the early Mission School, as well as several other Honolulu landmarks, was built with this local form of *adobe* adds to the interest of Mr. Lyons' statement.

The Spaniards at Waimea were employed by Kamehameha III, and the hides and tallow produced from the cattle taken there were to go toward the payment of a debt owed by the king. Their contract was therefore a terminal one; they had not come to Hawaii as immigrants intending to remain. In 1840 a five-year kapu was laid upon the killing of wild bullocks (Kuykendall 1938:318), and the decade of the original *paniolos* came to an end. But the word remained.

Sixty years went by before the arrival of the next large groups of

---

* Kuykendall (1938:318) reported that "Spanish or Mexican cowboys" had been brought to the Islands "not later than 1830"; Lyons (1963:27) included in his recollections: "At Waimea, Hawaii, on the high plateau . . . there the Mexican Hispano-Indian found his home and occupation. . . . He had with him, sometimes, full-blooded Indians of Mexican origin, whom I saw in my boyhood."

Spanish-speaking immigrants. Lind has written of these newly recruited sugarcane field workers:

Nearly 6,000 Puerto Ricans arrived chiefly in 1901 . . . while an equal number of Spaniards were recruited in the years 1907 to 1913. So great was the emigration of the Spaniards to California that there were never more than 2,430 recorded by the census (in 1920), and since 1930 they have ceased to figure at all as a separate group in the census. The Puerto Ricans, on the other hand, have remained and reproduced within the Islands. [1967:31]

The Hawaiian people called Puerto Ricans *Pokoliko* or *Poto Riko* (Pukui and Elbert 1964:121) and the general public occasionally gave them the humorous title *Borinki* (Judd 1961:134). Because they remained as permanent residents, it is probable that their dialect of Spanish has been heard more frequently than any other form of that language in the Islands. A study of the English speech of selected Honolulu Puerto Ricans was made in 1960 by Maita M. Kindig, and it may lead to other investigations of loanwords taken into Hawaii's English from that source. A loanblend introduced by local Puerto Ricans, according to the Kindig study, is *gandude rice*, a special dish flavored with the plant *Cajunus indicus*, commonly called *gandures* in Puerto Rico. Mrs. Kindig notes that the consonants *l*, *r*, and *d*, are interchangeable in certain positions of some words, varying with the dialect, but that *d* always occurs in *gandudes* in Hawaii (1960:151, 184).

The coming of large numbers of Filipinos to Hawaii between 1907 and 1931 (and a later group in 1946) has been discussed in another section of this chapter. During the time of Spain's rule in the Philippine Islands, many Spanish loanwords entered the Philippine languages; over the years, some of these were assimilated and changed. Nine Spanish loanwords which appear in the list of terms used on Hawaii's plantations provide an intriguing puzzle as to their separate routes of entry into Hawaii. Some may have arrived with the Filipinos as loanwords in their speech. Others, perhaps, came into use on the plantations from the speech of Puerto Rican or Spanish laborers. Again, some may date from the days of the *paniolos*. The solution of this Hawaiian word puzzle offers interesting possibilities for students familiar with several dialects of Spanish and with some of the Philippine languages.

Although the task of tracing the words to their original donors is far beyond the scope of this book, the nine Spanish loanwords from the Das list are presented in table 3, together with the Spanish dictionary spelling and the forms of these words as they occur in Ilocano, Visayan, and Tagalog, and the meanings. In the new spelling developed for Philippine languages in recent years, the *c* of Spanish becomes *k*—for example,

TABLE 3   Spanish Loanwords

DAS LIST	SPANISH	ILOCANO	VISAYAN	TAGALOG	MEANING
arraro	arado	arádo	dáro	araro	'plow'
asado	azada azadón	–	saról	asarol	'hoe'
corta-pluma	corta-plumas	corta-pluma	kórta	korta-pluma	'penknife' 'pocket-knife'
caro	carro	carro	káro	karo	Spain and Hawaii: 'cart' Philippines: 'car', 'hearse', 'religious float'
kaballo	caballo	cabáyo cabállo	kabáyò	kabayo	'horse'
oficina	oficina	oficína	opisina	opisina upisina	'office'
sako	saco	sáco	sako	sako	'sack'
sigui-sigui	sigue (imperative of seguir, 'follow')	–	sígi sigi-sígi 'continual', 're-peatedly'	sige sigi-sigi 'continuously'	Hawaii: 'quick' 'hurry up'
trabajo	trabajo	trabajo	trabáho	trabaho	'work'

Ilocano becomes *Ilokano* or *Iloko*—and other changes have been made. The sources for Philippine spellings of Spanish words may be found in the Bibliography (*Ilocano:* H. P. Williams, revised by A. B. Guerrero; *Visayan:* T. V. Hermosisima; and *Tagalog:* J. V. Panganiban.)*

Two Spanish loanwords in the three major Philippine languages refer to dishes prepared by Filipino (or Filipina) cooks in Hawaii. *Adobo* (from the Spanish *adobar* 'to pickle', 'to cook') is a dish of infinite variation, but basically it is chicken and pork cooked in a brown sauce that gives the rich, sour taste so prized by the Filipinos (Steinberg et al. 1970:131). *Lechon* 'roasted pig' is another Spanish word shared by the Ilocano, Visayan, and Tagalog. The original Spanish *lechón* means 'suckling pig'.

Ratoon and *ratooning,* from the Spanish *retoño* 'fresh shoot or sprout',

* Edgar G. Knowlton, Jr., professor, and chairman of the division of Spanish, Department of European Languages, University of Hawaii, gave valuable assistance in tracing the Spanish loanwords.

have a more restricted use and more limited definitions in Hawaii than elsewhere. In Hawaii the words are used only in reference to the second (ratoon) crop of pineapples that comes from shoots of the mother plant, either at the soil level or above. Elsewhere, as in Jamaica, *ratoon* applies to other cultivated plants such as yams, ginger, cotton, and indigo, as well as pineapples; there it means the second harvest that comes from roots left in the ground after plants are cut down.* The earliest reference in the Oxford English Dictionary to the word *ratoon* is 1779. Known in the Caribbean for many years, it may well have come to Hawaii with the first shipment of Smooth Cayenne pineapples brought to the Islands from Jamaica by Captain James Kidwell in 1886.

A transferred meaning is contained in the hybrid compound *ratoon crop*, used in Hawaii to refer to a child or children born late in the lives of their parents, after the rest of children in the family have grown up. This meaning may be a Hawaiianism. Another jocular meaning has been recorded by De Camp in the parish of Clarendon, Jamaica, where a *ratoon* may mean an unborn child fathered by a man who has left town and cannot be found (Cassidy and Le Page 1967:375).

Spanish loanwords in Hawaii have come from diverse sources over a period of almost a century and a half. They are interesting enough to warrant further study by specialists in standard forms of Spanish, Mexican and Puerto Rican Spanish, Tagalog, Ilocano, and Visayan.

KOREAN LOANWORDS

The immigrants in the Korean group learned English rapidly after their arrival in 1904 and 1905 (Reinecke 1969:132). Their number (eight thousand) was small in comparison with the Chinese and the Japanese workers; they did not live in segregated areas; and their language seemed to leave few traces in the fabric of Island English. Gradually, however, a number of Korean words have appeared in English, as the culture of this group has made itself felt. Some linguistic influences are difficult to detect. The similarities of Korean and Japanese, in syllable-timed rhythm and in the semantic range of many words, served to reinforce those characteristics being incorporated from Japanese into some types of English. Examples of this reinforcement are given in the Glossary (chapter 9).

Among loanwords of wide circulation are two terms of respectful ad-

* Beatrice H. Krauss, a botanist associated for many years with the Pineapple Research Institute in Honolulu, has contributed generously to this section of the book from her knowledge of the early days of pineapple production in the Islands.

dress: *abuji* 'father' and *ajusi* 'uncle'. *Yobo* 'Korean', a term used humorously by non-Koreans, corresponds to *Pākē* employed for the Chinese and *Bayaw* for the Filipinos. The term is objectionable to the Koreans themselves because in Korea it is used only when addressing a younger person or someone lower in social status. In an attempt to make the term acceptable to Korean ears, *Yoboji* was coined locally by adding the syllable *-ji*, which non-Korean speakers misconstrued to be an honorific ending because it is found at the end of *abuji* 'father'.

Korean family names are reasonably well known in Honolulu, Kim and Park leading the list. In 1970, families bearing the name Kim had more than 450 entries in the telephone directory. This name is spelled in other ways: *Khim* (two entries in the directory), *Kiehm* (six), and *Kimm* (two). The name *Park*, almost as well known as *Kim*, is also a Caucasian family name, whereas *Kim* seems to be exclusively Korean. The name *Lee* is shared by Koreans, Chinese, and Caucasians, for a total of fourteen columns in the Oahu directory, while as *Li*, a variant Chinese spelling, it has twenty-one additional entries.

Sung by the Korean contingent whenever international students gather in Hawaii, *Arirang* is a haunting folk song describing the sadness of two lovers at parting. The song's title, actually the proper name of a hill path near Seoul, has been adopted as the name of a Korean restaurant in Honolulu. Two new Korean restaurants bear the name *Doraji* 'bell flower', taken from the folk song next in popularity to *Arirang* in Korea.

The taste for Korean food has grown in Honolulu since the time of the Korean Conflict. One popular dish, *kun koki* 'broiled meat', is beef broiled with toasted sesame seeds, sesame oil, garlic, green onions, and hot pepper. Its potency is suggested by its other name, *pul koki* 'fire meat'. *Chun* is meat or fish cut into small pieces and rolled in flour before being fried. *Mandu* is similar to meat pie except that the pies are made very small and are steamed rather than baked. The filling is made of meat, bean curd, bean sprouts, vegetables, and *kimchee*, all chopped together. *Kimchee*, by far the most widely known of Korean foods, comes in several varieties involving bases of cucumbers, Chinese cabbage, watercress, radishes, seaweed, or mixed vegetables. In the minds of non-Koreans, the essential ingredients of this unique dish are chopped Chinese cabbage, quantities of red peppers, and a great deal of garlic. Korean families have traditional, unwritten recipes for *kimchee*, passed down from mother to daughter to granddaughter.

All in all, aside from family names, no more than a dozen Korean words are in general circulation in Hawaii today. If the Korean restaurants continue to increase in number, however, they will surely introduce additional loanwords along with their popular menus.

LOANWORDS FROM OTHER LANGUAGES

In addition to the immigrations already discussed, thirteen hundred Germans and Galicians, two thousand Russians, and twenty-five hundred Pacific Islanders from widely separated areas have been brought to Hawaii to satisfy the continuing demand for plantation labor (Lind 1967:8). The effects of their languages on Hawaii's speech have been negligible. It has always been the large immigrant groups, coming to remain and be naturalized in Hawaii, who have contributed words to the speech of the Islands.

Hundreds of Samoans, who have immigrated in recent years with the intent to remain permanently in the Hawaiian Islands, have settled, for the most part, in two areas on Oahu. Elements of their culture that contrast with the culture of the Hawaiians are becoming apparent, for example, the Samoan fire dances and variations on the well-known *lu'au* cooking of the Hawaiians. Undoubtedly Samoan words will soon become common in the speech of the Islands. One already known is *lavalava*, which was recorded in Webster's Second and again in the Third. The ambiguous definition recorded in the Second was "A printed calico waist cloth or kilt worn around the loins."

That definition was expanded and clarified in the Third to read: "A rectangular cloth worn like a kilt or skirt by men, women, and children in Polynesia and esp. in Samoa that is now usu. of a bright cotton print often with white or yellow floral designs on a red or blue background." The improvement in definition is comparable to that already noted for the word *hula*.

Fale 'house' is the Samoan equivalent for Hawaiian *hale*, and *alofa* 'love, greetings', for the Hawaiian *aloha*. Both pairs of words show the interchange of /f/ and /h/—evidence of the close relationship of these two languages. These Samoan words are known in Hawaii but have not yet appeared in a dictionary of American English.

Micronesian languages of the Trust Territory and Guam will probably contribute loanwords to Hawaii's English in the future, because the University of Hawaii has become the principal institution for the higher education of young Micronesian leaders and because Honolulu is a gateway between the Micronesian Islands and the mainland of the United States.

The recording and study of loanwords in Hawaii's English is in itself a project large enough to fill a book. Until such a book is written, the author of this study will welcome additional terms and needed corrections for the words thus far recorded and defined.

Chapter 8 **Loanblends or Hybrid Compounds**

Poi dog is an example of a hybrid compound or loanblend (Hockett 1958:412–413). The first half of the term is from the Hawaiian language; the second half, from English. The small Polynesian dog, brought to the Islands by the early Hawaiians, is now sometimes referred to as the *poi dog*. He has a pedigree of his own making, because no other dog can equal him in hunting wild pigs in the mountain undergrowth. He has a past, too, since he was sometimes served up, along with *poi*, at the feasts of the ancient Hawaiians. The term is now commonly used in the Islands to mean any dog of mixed or uncertain breed.

The process of coining expressions such as this one goes on continually in Hawaii, where there are many imported and exotic objects to be named and many languages from which to borrow words. Sometimes, when a foreign object is introduced, an English word is affixed to the foreign name to explain and relate it to English. An example is *shoji door*, even though *shoji* itself contains the meaning of door. These lightweight, sliding doors, covered with durable paper, suited the climate of the Islands so well and harmonized with various types of architecture so easily that they were widely adopted (see chapter 7, Japanese loan-words). Another much-used loanblend is *aloha shirt*, the colorful, open-necked shirt for men which originated in the Islands but has traveled to the mainland of the United States and to several foreign countries.

Approximately eighty compound expressions are listed in the following pages. Nearly all of them have been coined in Hawaii—extemporane-

111

ously at first, to suit a given set of circumstances, then popularized by repetition. All but a very few function as nouns, but occasionally a compound term becomes an adjective, as in the case of *'ono-looking* 'good-looking', 'delicious-looking' and *manini-looking* 'skimpy-looking'. About three-fourths of these hybrid compounds have the foreign term in initial position, with an English word after it. Most of the others have an English word first, followed by a foreign term. A few have no English words at all, for example, *kagami ulua*, *Pākē muʻu*, and *Vita tōfu* (for definitions, see the following lists). One expression is an agent noun, *lei seller*, and several others are full predications in the request form: *Hele on!* 'Come on!' *No huhū* 'Don't be angry', and *Pio the light* 'Turn out the light'. Most of the hybrid compounds are of the class analyzed as "attributive-noun-plus-noun"—one of the most common patterns of word compounding in American speech on the Mainland today (Carr 1953:161–170).

The list of loanblends given here is not exhaustive. Hundreds of these expressions are currently used in the Islands, and they are well worth collecting for their expressiveness and exuberance.

SOME COMMON LOANBLENDS OF HAWAII

aku boat (Hawaiian + English). Seagoing vessel used in fishing for *aku* (bonito or skipjack).

Aku Head Pupule (Hawaiian + English + Hawaiian). 'Crazy fishhead', the professional name of a popular radio commentator in Honolulu.

'alae salt (Hawaiian + English). A coarse-grained, red salt used in Hawaiian food. The Hawaiian word *'alaea* is defined as "water-soluble colloidal ocherous earth, used for coloring salt, for medicine, and for dye" (Pukui and Elbert 1957:16).

aloha party (Hawaiian + English). A farewell party given for someone about to leave the Islands. The word *aloha* itself may be a greeting or a farewell, but an *aloha party* is almost always for leave-taking.

aloha shirt (Hawaiian + English). A bright-colored, short-sleeved shirt, open at the neck—the informal attire of men in Hawaii.

Aloha Shōyu (Hawaiian + Japanese). A trade name for a brand of soy sauce (see *soy sauce* in this chapter).

Aloha Week (Hawaiian + English). An annual celebration held in October featuring Hawaiian singing, dancing, and feasting. A king and queen are crowned and reign throughout the festive week.

bayaw style (Ilocano + English). 'Filipino style', with the men in one group and the women in another. Another spelling for this Ilocano word is *bayau*.

bōbora head (Portuguese via Japanese + English). A Japanese citizen as distinguished from a Japanese American. *Bōbora* is used by the local Japanese to mean 'pumpkin', although it is derived from the Portuguese *abóbora* meaning 'gourd'. The more dignified term for a Japanese person born in Japan is *naichi ken.*

bon dance (Japanese + English). A Japanese folk dance performed in mid-July in Hawaii as a part of the *O-bon* 'festival of the dead'.

Buddahead (Sanskrit via Japanese + English). A name given by non-Japanese or by AJAs (Americans of Japanese ancestry) from the Mainland, to Japanese Americans born in Hawaii.

business wahine (English + Hawaiian). 'Business woman', a prostitute.

buta kaukau (Japanese + pidgin English). 'Pig food', 'garbage'.

buta kaukau man (Japanese + pidgin English + English). A pig farmer who, in the old days, collected slop in the city.

calabash cousins (Spanish, possibly from Arabic, + English). Very close friends, but not blood relatives, who in most cases have grown up together and who 'eat from the same calabash'. The compound term was apparently coined in Hawaii.

chawan cut (Japanese + English). 'Rice-bowl cut', a haircut that looks as if a bowl had been placed on the head, and the hair trimmed around its edges. Asian youngsters often had this haircut, with bangs in front.

chicken lū'au (English + Hawaiian). Chicken cooked with young taro tops (*lū'au*), one of the dishes served at a Hawaiian feast (the feast is also called a *lū'au*).

coast haole (English + Hawaiian). Literally, a Caucasian from the west coast of the United States. By extension, this term is used to designate a person newly arrived in Hawaii from any part of the Mainland, a person who has not yet adjusted to the Hawaiian scene, a "greenhorn" by local standards.

driving hui (English + Hawaiian or Chinese). A group of automobile owners who take turns in driving the children of their families to school or in performing other group errands, in other words, a car pool. The plan, and with it the term, originated because of gasoline rationing during World War II.

hanahana man (pidgin Hawaiian + English). A laborer on a plantation. *Hanahana* is the reduplicated form of the Hawaiian noun *hana* 'labor' or 'activity'.

hānai child (Hawaiian + English). 'Foster child', often not legally adopted. The Hawaiian *hānai* means 'foster child'.

haole bait (Hawaiian + English). A local girl who prefers to date Caucasians rather than non-Caucasians.

hapa haole (assimilated English in Hawaii + Hawaiian). A part-white person or a person of part-Caucasian extraction. As an adjective, this loanblend produces interesting, and often humorous, combinations, for example *hapa haole hula,* a *hula* which is visibly influenced by Western dances. *Hapa* is the English word *half,* assimilated phonologically into the Hawaiian language, the /f/ replaced by /p/ and the final vowel added.

Hele on! (Hawaiian + English) 'Come on!' This expression is distinguished from most of the others by being a predication in the form of a request, rather than merely a phrase.

hoe hana (English + Hawaiian). 'Labor with the hoe', as chopping weeds on a plantation. This part of plantation labor is sometimes done by women, hence *hoe-hana wahine* 'a woman who chops weeds'.

Holoholo Slippers (Hawaiian + English). 'Slippers to go *holoholo* in', and, since *holoholo* means 'to go out for pleasure', these are 'slippers for a good time', 'party slippers'.

ho'ohuli bipi (Hawaiian + English assimilated into Hawaiian). 'Roundup of cattle'. The Hawaiian prefix *ho'o* 'to cause to', *huli* 'turn', and *bipi* 'cattle', taken together mean 'to turn the cattle', 'to bring them in' (Lyons 1892:27). Pukui and Elbert list this term as *ho'ohuli pipi* (1957:83). *Bipi,* or *pipi,* is the English word *beef* with the consonants changed to conform to Hawaiian phonemes and with a vowel added.

Hula Bowl (Hawaiian + English). A term analogous to Rose Bowl, Sugar Bowl, and Pineapple Bowl, referring to special football games held in Hawaii.

hulihuli chicken (Hawaiian + English). Chicken roasted on a spit or rotisserie and hence, turned. *Hulihuli* is the reduplicated form of *huli* 'to turn'. Organizations often earn money by making and selling *hulihuli chicken.*

huli stomach (Hawaiian + English). 'Turned stomach'. Some people, especially among the Hawaiians and Portuguese, formerly believed that a baby suffering from colic had had its stomach turned upside down by a jealous, evil-eyed person.

kagami ulua (Japanese + Hawaiian). 'Looking-glass fish', a name given to a kind of *ulua* 'jackfish', because of its gleaming body. *Kagami* is Japanese for 'mirror'.

kālua pig (Hawaiian + English). A pig that is roasted in an *imu* 'underground oven'; the principal dish at a *lū'au* 'Hawaiian feast'.

Kona weather (Hawaiian + English). The muggy weather that comes when the northeast trade winds are replaced by the *Kona wind* from the south or southwest. A *Kona storm* brings with it heavy rains from the south or leeward side of the islands.

kukui nut (Hawaiian + English). The fruit of the *kukui* 'candlenut tree'. These oily nuts were formerly used for lighting. Now they are polished and strung into much-prized *kukui nut leis*.

lei seller (Hawaiian + English). A person, usually a woman, who makes and sells flower leis. These well-loved Island personalities preside in *lei stands*, usually small frame shelters thatched with coconut leaves.

lomi salmon (Hawaiian + English). Salmon or other fish, usually raw and salted, worked with the fingers and mixed with green onions, tomatoes, and seasonings. The verb *lomi* means 'to rub, press, squeeze'. *Lomilomi salmon*, the reduplicated form, is very frequently used.

lū'au feet (Hawaiian + English). The large bare Hawaiian feet seen at a *lū'au* 'Hawaiian feast'. *Lū'au*, in the literal sense, means 'young taro tops', especially baked with coconut cream and chicken; it also has come to mean the Hawaiian feast, named for the taro tops that are always served there (Pukui and Elbert 1957:197).

lū'au torch (Hawaiian + English). A form of outdoor or garden lighting used in Hawaii. The original fuel was the *kukui* nut; now kerosene or gas is used.

make-die-dead (Hawaiian + English + English). An expression used by children at play to mean 'good and dead', as in "I shot that robber good and dead." *Make*, pronounced [máke] or often nowadays [mʌ́kɪ], is the Hawaiian word for 'dead'.

make-man flower (Hawaiian + English). 'Dead-man flower', a name formerly used for the plumeria blossom because it grew so abundantly in graveyards.

Mama Kahu (English + Hawaiian). The wife of the minister of a Hawaiian church. The minister himself is called *Kahu Hipa* 'shepherd'.

Mama-san (English + Japanese). 'Good mother' or 'worthy mother', a term often used in Hawaii by non-Japanese speakers in addressing or speaking of an older Japanese woman. It implies friendship and affection. *Papa-san* is similarly used. *San* is the well-known honorific term in Japanese.

manini-looking (Hawaiian + English). 'Skimpy looking' or 'inadequate'. The *manini* is a common reef fish. *Manini* also means 'stingy' (see Pukui and Elbert 1957:220).

manuahi man (Hawaiian + English). 'Extra man' or 'free man', that is, a lover or side-kick. *Manuahi* (or *manuwahi*) means 'gratis, free of charge', also 'adulterous'.

No huhū! (English + Hawaiian). 'Don't get angry!' "No Huhu" is the name of a popular song of some years ago. This phrase has also appeared on road-repair signs in Honolulu as an informal Hawaiian way of saying, "Pardon the inconvenience."

No pau yet! (English + Hawaiian + English). 'It's not finished!' 'I'm not finished yet!'

No pilikia! (English + Hawaiian). 'That's all right!' 'It's no trouble!' *Pilikia* means 'trouble'—of any kind, great or small.

number-one-luna (pidgin English + Hawaiian). The head boss in charge of a gang of laborers on a plantation. *Luna* means 'foreman', 'supervisor'.

number-one pilau luna (pidgin English + Hawaiian). 'The very worst overseer on the plantation'. *Pilau* is the Hawaiian word for 'spoiled', 'rotten', 'decomposed'.

Obake Battalion (Japanese + English). The name by which members of the Hilo National Guard became known because they had no arm patch or identification. *Obake* is Japanese for 'ghost'.

one-finger poi (English + Hawaiian). *Poi* that is thick enough to be scooped up with one finger from the calabash. *Poi*, the Hawaiian staff of life, is made from cooked taro corms, pounded and thinned with water. For *two-finger poi*, a thinner mixture, two fingers are needed to transport it from the calabash to the mouth.

'ono-looking (Hawaiian + English). 'Good-looking', 'beautiful', 'delicious-looking'. *'Ono* 'delicious', as an adjective, enters into many expressions such as an *'ono-looking strawberry* 'a delicious-looking strawberry'. A sign recently seen in a supermarket of Honolulu read: "Ruby-red Texas grapefruit—so *ono!*"

'opihi pants (Hawaiian + English). Blue jeans, cut off above the knees, worn for the job of picking *'opihi* 'limpets', much prized by the Hawaiians for food.

Pākē muʻu (pidgin Chinese + Hawaiian). A colorful, fitted *muʻumuʻu* modified to resemble the Chinese gown, with its high collar and side seams slashed to the knee. The *muʻumuʻu*, often shortened to *muu* and popularly pronounced [mu], is the Mother Hubbard style of dress for women, adopted by the Hawaiians under the influence of the New England missionaries, but subsequently adapted to the color and ease of Hawaiian informal living.

Pākē style (pidgin Chinese + English). 'Chinese style', 'done in the Chinese way'.

pau-hana time (Hawaiian + English). 'Quitting time'. *Pau* means 'finished' and *hana* is 'work'.

pilau bugger (Hawaiian + English). 'Depraved, contemptible person'. *Pilau* is defined as 'spoiled', 'rotten', 'decomposed'.

pili grass (Hawaiian + English). A grass known in many warm regions. formerly used for thatching houses in Hawaii, and, mixed into clay, for making adobe walls (see chapter 7, Spanish loanwords).

Pio the light (Hawaiian + English). 'Turn out the light'.

pipi stew (English via Hawaiian + English). 'Beef stew'. *Pipi* is the assimilated form of the English word *beef*.

pipi kaula (English via Hawaiian + Hawaiian). Beef which has been salted, dried in the sun, and broiled before eating. *Kaula* means 'rope' or 'string'.

Poi Belt (Hawaiian + English). A phrase noted in the *Honolulu Advertiser*, July 2, 1968, analogous to "Bible Belt."

poi dog (Hawaiian + English). The typically Hawaiian strain of dog, used in hunting wild pigs; the term is often used in the sense of 'mongrel'. These dogs were formerly fed on *poi*.

pork tōfu (English + Japanese). A popular dish in Hawaii, similar to sukiyaki, made of cooked pork, onions, and other vegetables, with cubes of *tōfu* 'bean curd' added.

puka head (Hawaiian + English). 'Head injury', such as a cut scalp. *Puka* means 'hole' or 'perforation'.

puka net (Hawaiian + English). A net full of holes, thus a fishing net—probably a recent humorous coinage of neo-pidgin.

pūpū pups (Hawaiian + English). Small cocktail sausages, or miniature "hot dogs." *Pūpū* is the Hawaiian equivalent of hors d'oeuvre or appetizer; it was formerly the fish, chicken, or banana served with *kava*.

pupule head (Hawaiian + English). 'Addled head', a crazy person. *Pupule* is the Hawaiian term for insane.

pupule house (Hawaiian + English). A hospital for the mentally ill.

ratoon crop (Spanish + English). A second crop of shoots that grow from the mother plant; metaphorically, a child or children born late in the lives of their parents, after other children in the family are grown. This is probably a local coinage.

shōji door (Japanese + English). Japanese-style sliding door, made of lightweight wood covered with paper. Because they are so well suited to the Hawaiian climate, these doors are often used in homes that are otherwise entirely Western in architecture.

shorty muʻu (English + abbreviated Hawaiian). A short, or dress-length, *muʻumuʻu*.

soy sauce (Japanese + English). The salty sauce made from soy beans that is indispensable in Japanese and Chinese cuisine. In Hawaii, it is used also in many Western dishes.

tamago head (Japanese + English). 'Egg head', a stupid person. Here 'egg head' does not include the Western connotation 'intellectual'.

teriburger (Japanese + English). Hamburger prepared with *teriyaki sauce* (made of soy sauce, ginger, sugar, and other seasonings).

teriyaki steak (Japanese + English). Steak marinated in *teriyaki sauce*, then broiled. This is popular in Hawaii with residents and tourists alike.

'uku bla (Hawaiian + pidgin English). 'Ugly boy'. Literally, 'flea brother' or 'louse brother'. *Bla* is said to be a reduced form of 'brother'.

Vita Tōfu (Latin + Japanese). A commercial name for Japanese-style bean curd which is supposed to give strength and vitality.

wikiwiki burger (Hawaiian + English). A hamburger put together in a hurry and sold at drive-in restaurants. *Wikiwiki* is the popular re-duplicated form of *wiki* 'to hurry', 'to hasten'.

Chapter 9 **Glossary
of Typical
Island
Expressions**

The words and phrases recorded in this chapter were collected by the author over a period of more than three decades in the Islands. A few entries date back to accounts, written by students, of the attack on Pearl Harbor. A few stem from a rare, and all too brief, experience of tape-recording conversations on the remote island of Niihau. The majority, however, have been recorded (by the notebook method) as they were heard on local buses, in grocery stores, on street corners, and on the playgrounds and campuses of schools and colleges. Nearly all are examples of the spoken language of the Islands; only a small number were taken from written material such as student themes. The exact words of the speakers have been given in most instances; in only a few cases has the author invented examples, and then only when the expressions were quite familiar. The format of the entries has been kept simple. The word or phrase is given, together with its standard counterpart; an example is quoted with a few words of explanation; and, finally, records of parallel forms found in other languages or dialects are presented.

An absorbing question to Island residents and to visitors alike is: Where did these unique expressions come from? Whether undertaken as research work or merely as a game, the search for sources or parallels in other languages is an activity of never-ending interest. Possible sources surveyed for this book were the language of the native inhabitants of the Islands—Hawaiian—and the languages of the principal immigrant groups: Chinese, Japanese, Portuguese, Spanish, Korean, and the several tongues of the Filipinos. Scholars with special knowledge of these languages have assisted with the research. In tracing the origins of words and expressions to pidgin and creole areas elsewhere, word lists and dictionaries of Cantonese pidgin, Melanesian neo-pidgin, and Jamaican creole have been used, since the Hawaiian Islands were in contact for years with the coast of China and with Melanesia during the days of active trade in furs, sandalwood, whale oil, and whalebone, and later had contact with Jamaica through common agricultural interests, for example, in sugarcane, pineapples, and avocados.

An aspect of language study never yet sufficiently explored in Hawaii is the part that loan translation from foreign languages into English has played in forming the nonstandard speech of the Islands. In the process of loan translation, immigrants frequently seize upon a rather obscure meaning of a word in the donor language (in this case, English) and use that meaning as if it were the principal denotation of the word. On the tongue of the immigrant himself, the usage may go unremarked, but, carried along in the speech of his children and grandchildren, the idiom becomes an oddity to visitors and a bit of the "local language" to residents. Loan translations are involved in many of the terms listed in this glossary.

A summary of the study of the collected terms is given in chapter 10; it is, however, only a beginning in a place like Hawaii, where the possibilities for such a study are limitless. Readers with a special knowledge of Cantonese, for example, may find other parallels not reported here. It goes without saying that the author will welcome additions to the glossary and corrections for the material it contains, and, most particularly, new theories as to the origins of these words and phrases.

Dictionaries and other books and articles referred to are listed in the Bibliography. The glossary entries have been studied by several persons, each in the light of his own special language proficiency; their names and the initials by which they are referred to, are as follows: Pualani [Alberta] Pung Anthony (PPA); O. A. Bushnell (OAB); Denzel Carr (DC); Samuel Elbert (SE), and Dong Jae Lee (DJL).

THE GLOSSARY

across vs. **across from**

"I sat across you at church las' Sunday." 'I sat across from you . . .'

"Meet me at the bus stop across the library." '. . . across from the library.'

Certain pairs of expressions, often seemingly simple, cause problems in Hawaii, and one of the most typical is the pair *across* and *across from*. The differences in meaning and use are elusive even for bright students with foreign-language backgrounds, and native speakers of English themselves have difficulty expressing exactly the difference between the two. Observation, listening, practice, and guidance are apparently the routes by which students eventually manage to avoid the pitfalls. No theory has been advanced as to the influence that might have caused this persistent use of *across* for 'across from'.

alphabet vs. letter

"My name begins with the alphabet *A*, so I have to go first in line."

As used very widely by speakers in all nonstandard types, *alphabet* covers the meaning 'a single letter' as well as 'a set or system of letters'. There are parallel usages in Japanese and Korean: the Japanese word *kana* means not only a single *kana* symbol but also the total syllabary (DC); in Korean, there is no distinction between the words meaning 'alphabet' and 'letter' (DJL).

already vs. yet

"I called you up but you weren't there already."

In standard English, such negative expressions require *yet* rather than *already*, but in Hawaii *already* is used widely in both affirmative and negative expressions. This may be because *already* has long been a very common word, used as a tense-marker in reduced English without regard to finer points. Reinecke and Tokimasa noted its use as a tense-marker in "You been eat lunch already?" "Yes, I been eat" (1934:123). There is no word in the Hawaiian language equivalent to *already*, and native speakers of Hawaiian must have had difficulty with this much-used English word (SE). Knowlton, suggesting an influence from the Portuguese, cited five examples from Mário de Costa Pires of the use of the Portuguese *já* in a sense close to that of *already* in Hawaii's dialect (Knowlton 1967:234).

anybody vs. everybody; any kind vs. every kind

"Anybody go church today!" (the Type II speaker's way of saying that the church was full of people).

"Man, get any kind candy in dat box!"

In both cases, *any* covers the semantic range of *every*. There is no distinction between *anybody* and *everybody* in the Hawaiian language (SE).

Since the Korean *nugudunji* and the Japanese *daredemo* serve for both 'anybody' and 'everybody', the failure of Hawaii's dialect to make this distinction has received reinforcement from the speech habits of many Asian immigrants (DJL). (Cf. Cassidy 1961:168, *somebody*.)

attend to vs. attend

"I attend to Farrington High School. What school are you attending to?"

Because *attend to* is often heard in another sense, 'to take care of', the Hawaiianism above may be a cross association. However, in the Korean and Japanese languages, *attend* and *go to* are translated in exactly the same way. Koreans and Japanese wonder why, in English, *go* (in this sense) is followed by *to* while *attend* is not (DJL).

omission of the verb to be

"Now— no full two hundred people down dere."

The Type II speaker of chapter 3 here illustrates the omission of the copula or linking verb. During her interview she expressed the linking verb six times out of twenty-one instances where it might have been expected. Of the Hawaiian language, Pukui and Elbert wrote: "There is no verb *to be* in Hawaiian. The copula may be entirely omitted, or represented by verb markers" (1964:12). The Chinese language, too, has no counterpart for the English copula. The effect of these influences on the English of Hawaii has never been fully assessed.

bed clothes vs. night clothes, pajamas

"No can go show in bed clothes!"

In American speech, *bed clothes* refers ordinarily to blankets and sheets, *night clothes* to pajamas and gowns. In Hawaii, *bed clothes* seems to cover both meanings. The Japanese *shin-i* means 'bed or sleeping clothes', that is, 'night clothes', while *shingu* means 'bed or sleeping gear', 'bed clothes', 'covers'. Some Japanese-English dictionaries translate both words as 'bed clothes' (DC).

been

"We nevah go in, but my uncle, my auntie been go." 'We haven't gone in, but my uncle and aunt have.'

The speaker, Type II, is using *never* to express the present perfect tense (negative) in the first clause and *been* as an auxiliary for the same tense in the second. When *been* is used as an auxiliary in the past perfect tense we hear, for example, "After I been graduate high school, I went down Honolulu." The speaker has acquired the standard preterit form, *went*, but continues to use the "local" auxiliary in the dependent clause. This auxiliary *been* is used in the speech of Types I, II, and III although it is gradually abandoned by Type III speakers in favor of traditional methods of forming the past tenses. Many of them can revert instantly to the "local" auxiliaries when talking to speakers of Types I and II or when using the dialect as an in-group "fun-language."

Reinecke and Tokimasa (1934): "*Been* is so similarly used in Bechela-mar [Melanesian pidgin] that it must have been derived therefrom." Hall, however, did not list the use of *been* in Melanesian pidgin English but cited other methods of indicating the preterit and perfective tenses, such as *finis* 'already' (1943:27). New Guinea (Sepik) pidgin and New Guinea highland pidgin, as taught at the Australian National University, do not use *been* or *wen*, but have such time expressions as *behain* 'later', *bipo* 'formerly', and *pinis* 'finished' to express tenses (for example, *Mi kaikai pinis,* 'I have eaten').

Mihalic cited the use of the auxiliary *bin*, particularly in the Rabaul and Morobe areas, and commented: "Some grammarians say it comes from Australian Pidgin, others say it has a Papuan origin" (1957, dictionary:19).

Cassidy and Le Page, in the *Dictionary of Jamaican English*, noted that *ben* probably stems from the English and American dialectal use of *been:* "The boss been askin' for you." Variant forms in Jamaican English are *ban, bin, en, hin, min, n,* and *wen*. Of these, Hawaii also has the form *wen*, which is listed in this glossary.

before, before-time vs. **earlier, formerly**

"Befoah, I make net one week—easy!"

"Befoah-time, Mrs. Tanaka live next door."

These speakers, and others of Types I and II, use the simple tense of the verb, beginning the utterance with *before* or *before-time* as a past-tense marker to indicate 'earlier' or 'some time ago'.

This usage is very common in the Hawaiian language, as *mua, mamua,* or *i mua* (SE). See *mua* in Pukui and Elbert (1957). Leland cited the usage in Chinese pidgin: *before-time* 'formerly', 'previously' (1904:120). Hall noted that Melanesian pidgin uses *bifor* to indicate 'previously', 'formerly' (1943:28). Mihalic listed the same meanings with an example:

ol man bilong bipo 'ancestors' (1957, dictionary:19). Chinese, Japanese, and Korean also have parallel forms (DC).

Before, used in some types of Hawaii's speech to indicate past action, is thus paralled by a tradition of pidgin usage elsewhere, and by similar usage in the Hawaiian, Chinese, Japanese, and Korean languages.

below of vs. below, under

"Below of dis fall, you can see da road."

This is a sentence from Mrs. Akana's recording, the speaker representing Type II. Instances are reported of *below of your head* (PPA).

Translated into Hawaiian, the phrase *below of the waterfall* would be "i lalo o ka wailele" with *o* representing 'of' in meaning (SE). Japanese treats *before, below, above, after,* as nouns, often with *no* preceding and *ni* following the distinctive word. *Watakushi no shita ni* means 'at my underside', 'below of me' (DC). Korean has similar forms (DJL).

bla, blala vs. brother

"Look at that *blala!*" uttered by a *haole* who is unsympathetic may be insulting. "Ey, bla!" uttered by a member of the peer group may be a warm and affectionate greeting. Reductions of the word *brother,* these are terms of address used by, and for, Island-born men and boys, whether relatives or friends. In the Hawaiian language, the term parallel to *brother* may include a male first, second, or third cousin (SE).

blad

"Shee! All blads, eh?"

In the dialogue between the two speakers in chapter 4, this word was used with an apparent derogatory connotation. The theater-goers in Waikiki, to him, were *blads*—possibly 'conceited tourists' or 'objectionable *haoles*'. *Blad* may be related to *bla* or possibly to the slang term *broad.*

blast vs. very good

Q: "How da party was?" A: "Was blast, boy!" 'It was tremendous!'

In teen-age high school talk, the meaning is 'wonderful', 'very good'.

borrow vs. use

"May I borrow your telephone?"

Borrow is the verb heard in Hawaii in many instances where *use* is expected on the mainland United States.

In the Hawaiian language, there is no specific word for *borrow*, and hence Hawaiians in earlier days were uncertain how to use the term (SE).

In Chinese, Japanese, and Malay a speaker always "borrows" a telephone when he asks to use one (DC). In Korean, the word corresponding to *borrow* is often used if one person asks to use another person's belongings, even when there is no intention of returning them (DJL).

broke vs. torn, tear

"I hungry, an my pants all broke!"

"Paper like dis might broke."

Broke as used here means 'torn' or 'worn out'. If it is a reduction of *broken*, it has widened in range to take in fabrics and paper as well as the usual breakables: wood, crockery, bones, and so forth. Although the Hawaiian language has no general term for *break* or *broken*, it has more than two dozen terms for specific kinds of breakage, all of which could be translated by the term *broke* in reduced English (SE).

Mihalic gives the Neo-Melanesian parallel as *bruk* 'to be torn, broken, cracked, or smashed', with the examples: *klos i-bruk* 'the dress is torn', and *kap i-bruk* 'the cup is broken' (1957, dictionary:23).

"*Break, tear, rip, split, rend,* and so forth, are expressed by different words in most standard languages, but pidgins tend to lump many of these concepts together. *Broke* is 'ghettoese' among eastern European immigrants, pidgin or semi-pidgin in Hawaii. It is not a Japanese, Chinese or Korean influence." (DC)

burn firecrackers, play firecrackers vs. shoot firecrackers, set off firecrackers

"Us—we go burn firecrackers tonight!"

"You wen play firecrackers befoah!"

Fireworks are used in all important celebrations in Hawaii, most spectacularly at weddings and on New Year's Eve. The Cantonese verb *shiu* means 'to burn', 'to roast', and the term *shiu in foh* means 'fireworks' (Meyer and Wempe 1947:581). *Sieu pau-jeung* (in another spelling of the Cantonese) means 'burn firecrackers'.

Play firecrackers may be a local coinage.

but (at end of utterance) vs. **though**

Q: "Wheah you went aftah school?" A: "I wen pick up my shoes. Nevah was ready but."

But is often shifted to the end of an utterance in Hawaii and used in the sense of 'though'. If we consider this word as a coordinating conjunction, its position at the end of a sentence is a nonstandard innovation in syntax. If we consider it as a conjunctive adverb, it shows a widening of meaning to include 'though', and the change is a lexical and semantic matter. No theories have been offered as to the influence which might have brought about this change.

bumbye, bymby vs. **after a while**

"Bumbye we go beach—catch tan."

Pronounced as a two-syllable word, this term is used by speakers of Types I, II, and III to mean 'later', 'some other time'. In Chinese pidgin, Leland cited it as referring to any future time or occasion (1904:120). It is firmly fixed in Melanesian pidgin, Hall citing *bajmbaj* 'soon' (1943:28), and Mihalic reporting *baimbai* as the future-tense marker of Neo-Melanesian speakers (1957, grammar:32). *Bymby* has been noted in Gullah speech (*Dialect Notes*, V [1925]:358), and in Jamaican creole as *bambai*. A possible origin was suggested as the *bamby* of the dialects of Devonshire and Cornwall (Cassidy and Le Page 1967:23). There is an instance of its use by a European immigrant in a vivid sequential narrative: "He drink too much whiskey. Bymbye he get sick and puke" (DC).

catch vs. **get**

"Us go beach—catch da tan."

Swimmers and surfers in Hawaii use *catch* in the sense of *get*. Leland reports the word *catchee* in Chinese pidgin meaning 'to get, have, possess, hold', with the example, *My look-see one piecee man catchee chow-chow* 'I saw a man eating' (1904:121). Hall notes *kitčim* in Melanesian pidgin meaning 'take, obtain, get', with the example *kičim kajkaj* 'to get food, to be fed' (1943:104).

chance vs. **turn**

"Your chance or my chance?"

Meaning 'your turn or my turn?', the question is often asked by children in Hawaii. No parallel is known; Hawaiians would say, "Your time or my time?" (SE), and Japanese would say, "Your number or my number?" (DC).

Chee! or Shee! vs. Gee!

A: "Us no can go show!" B: "Chee! Nevah tole me!"

Chee and *shee* are local pronunciations of the American *gee*. Unvoicing of the initial affricate, producing *chee* (and its change to a fricative in *shee*) could have been an influence of the Chinese language (DC).

Christmas tree vs. poinsettia

The red poinsettia, potted and offered for sale in luxuriant bloom in December, is sometimes called the Chtistmas tree by old-timers in the immigrant groups. In Japan and Korea, the poinsettia appears so regularly on American Christmas cards that it is thought of as a kind of Christmas tree and this idea has been transferred to Hawaii (DJL).

close the light and open the light vs. turn out the light and turn on the light

These loan translations have apparently entered Hawaii's English from a language that uses the verbs *close* and *open* for electric switches, just as English uses these verbs for water faucets. Since the Romance languages contain these idioms, we may suspect that the expressions came to Hawaii in the English speech of Puerto Rican or Spanish immigrants. "Close the ears" is often heard for "Stop listening."

clean the yard vs. cut the grass

The yardman may ask politely at the door, "You like I clean ya:d today?" His counterpart on the Mainland would ask, "Shall I cut the grass?" or "Shall I mow the lawn?" Because Filipinos are commonly employed as yardmen in Hawaii, the expression may be a loan translation from one of their languages.

come outside vs. come, become

"You put da taro in da machine an' you say 'hocus-pocus' an' he come outside poi."

A Hawaiian tour-bus driver gave this lively account of the operation of a poi factory. In a different sense, the relatives of a newborn baby sometimes say, "Da baby come outside today." No one has offered a theory as to the source of this phrase.

Cool head main thing vs. **Don't panic!** or **Keep calm**

Q: "Ey, watah pipe wen broke! Wat I mus' do?" A: "Cool head main t'ing."

"Cool head main thing" seems to be a spontaneous Hawaiianism, similar to "Geev um!" Apparently merely a shortening of "A cool head is the main thing," it has lost the linking verb and two articles. As it stands it is an example of the laconic quality of the "local language"—noted especially in the speech of men.

corns vs. **corn on the cob**

"Hot corns for sale!"

This was on a sign at a vegetable stand on Windward Oahu in the 1940s, where youngsters were selling cooked corn on the cob. Taking orders for products of school gardens, secretaries will still often ask the teachers, "Do you want any corns today?" The usual Mainland meaning of *corns* finds little use in the Islands, where sandals, grass slippers, or bare feet are answers to the "corn" problem.

crack seed vs. **cracked seed** or **see mui**

"Crack-Seed Center" is the name of a small but popular store not far from the Manoa campus of the University of Hawaii. There, a great variety of dried and salted plums are sold. One of the many kinds comes with the seeds actually cracked, to give an additional (and greatly liked), bitter taste to the plums. The generic name for the whole complex of delicacies has been taken from that cracked variety. Many Island youngsters use the Chinese words *see mui*, pronouncing them "see moy." Other Chinese treats and their names are discussed in chapter 7.

cut, took vs. the causative form of the verb

"I cut my tonsils," rather than the causative expression, "I had my tonsils removed" or "I had my tonsils out," is probably a loan translation from the Japanese or Korean, where parallel forms are used. Also heard in Hawaii are "I took my picture" and "I took a permanent" (or "I took a perm").

A Japanese or Korean causative predication can be made by a circumlocution, but it is not necessary to make it, as in English, because the same verb structure may denote either direct action by the speaker or indirect action when the speaker has caused an action to be performed by another. *Shashin o toru* means 'to take a picture' or 'to have a picture taken' and *hentosen o toru* means 'to remove tonsils' or 'to have tonsils removed' (DJL).

down vs. to

"We goin' down da country" is heard in Honolulu to announce weekend excursions to rural Oahu. Yet residents of Oahu who go to Hilo sometimes say, "I went up the Island las' week."

In many languages one goes *up* to the city or capital and *down* to the country or provinces. Chinese, Japanese, Korean, and Malay all share this choice (DC).

Easy!

This local word of farewell may be accompanied by special gestures and facial expressions. A speaker of Type V explained its history: "The phrase started as 'Easily, Bla!' and was accompanied by a specific hand motion—blowing on the fingers and then polishing them on the lapel with thumb and small finger extended. It carried the same meaning that the gesture does in American usage, that is, a pat on one's own back to imply 'I can do difficult things easily.' The next stage was the shortening of the expression to *easy* [isi]. (Note the *s*.) The gesture became a waggle of the hand from the wrist, with the thumb and little finger extended. The meaning was expanded to include 'Don't worry about anything.' In saying goodbye, it implied 'Okay, everything will be all right. Take it easy!' " (PPA).

eye-glass vs. spectacles or glasses

"My eye-glass been los'." 'My glasses are lost'.

Eye-glass for 'spectacles' or 'glasses' is a direct translation from the Hawaiian *makaaniani*, in which *maka* is 'eye' and *aniani* is 'glass' (SE). The Chinese, Japanese, and Korean languages support this form (DC). To Koreans and Japanese, *glasses* are a unit and the singular rather than the plural seems appropriate (DJL).

-fellow as a suffix

"Dese two-fellow, man and wife—dere name A'alona."

Spoken by the Type II speaker of chapter 3, the words illustrate an old form that is fast disappearing in Hawaii but may be reflected in the current *-guys* in this glossary. Melanesian pidgin employs *fella*, sometimes in the form *-pela*, added to adjectives as a suffix and classifier:

etpela ten man 'eighty men' (Mihalic 1957, grammar:13). Examples of
-pela attached to pronouns in Melanesian pidgin are: *mipela* 'we' (exclusive) and *you-mipela* 'we' (inclusive). *Onepela Mary* means 'a woman'.

few vs. a few

"Get few house ova deah." 'There are a few houses in the valley'.

The Type II speaker quoted has failed to perceive the slight but important difference that exists between *few* 'not very many', 'hardly any'
and *a few* 'a small number' (but definitely more than the number implied
by *few*). Example in standard speech: "There are a few swimmers on the
beach this morning" (a small number), versus "There are few swimmers
on the beach this morning" (scarcely any at all). Immigrant peoples often
fail to hear the unstressed indefinite article *a*.

find for vs. look for

"Wait, wait—I'm finding for the scissors in this drawer!"

Still heard occasionally in Hawaii, even in the speech of Type IV, as
in the quotation above, the expression seems to point to a link with
Melanesian pidgin. Hall cited this example: *mi faynim faynim, no lukim*
'I searched and searched but didn't see it' (1943:95). Mihalic's dictionary
gives *painim*, verb transitive, 'to look for'; and *lukim*, verb transitive,
'to see'. His example is: *Mi painim, painim, tasol i-no got* 'I looked and
looked for it but did not find it' (1957, dictionary:100).

fire (vb.) vs. burn

"Pele, she no good! She only fire us."

The semantic range of the noun *fire* has been extended to include the
meaning of a verb, 'to burn'. The Hawaiian language provides a direct
parallel, since the noun *ahi* 'fire' is also used as a verb.

for vs. to

"Dat's his business, fo' talk!"

"We don't know what fo' do!"

The use of *for* rather than *to* in the form of the infinitive, often pointed
out as a characteristic of Hawaii's dialect, is attributed to the influence
of the Portuguese *para* (Reinecke and Tokimasa, 1934:125; Knowlton,
1967:234). Pires gives a number of additional examples from the Portuguese (1956:114).

for why vs. **why**

"For why you tell lies?"

The usage was noted by Reinecke and Tokimasa (1934:126), but the Portuguese *para que* means literally 'for what?' A loan translation from the Portuguese and a confusion of the two standard forms *why?* and *what for?* might have brought *for why* into the local dialect.

from before, from when vs. **before, when**

Q: "Ey, you get one new dress?" A: "No, I had 'em from before."

Q: "From when you had 'em?" A: "From long time."

Several time-indicators in local speech are illustrated here, similar to *before-time*, but these particular examples make use of the function word *from* rather than the standard *for:* "for how long?" "for a long time," "for some time." No parallels have been suggested in other languages.

Geev um! vs. **Give 'em the works!** or **Give 'em hell!**

From the cheering sections in Island grandstands, one hears the brief but expressive *"Geev um!"* Dialects tend to shorten, to abbreviate, and to omit grammatical objects. See, as an additional example of brevity, "That one get" in the following entry.

get vs. **have**

Q: "Whose car get room?" A: "That one get."

The questioner was the student chairman of a picnic committee (Type IV speech), asking for a ride for one of the members of his committee.

Get used for *have* is strongly reminiscent of the Hawaiian language, in which there is no verb meaning specifically 'to have' (SE). For *have*, the verb employed is usually *loaʻa*, defined as 'to find, to get, to acquire'. *Loaʻa iāia ʻelima kaʻa* would be translated literally 'He gets five cars', although it is translated 'He has five cars'. Also from Hawaiian is the following conversation:

Q: *Loaʻa iāʻoe ka pāpale?* 'Get you the hat?' that is, 'Have you the hat?' A: *Loaʻa.* 'Get.'

The Portuguese language is suggested as an influence by Knowlton (1967:235) and by Reinecke and Tokimasa (1934:124). Pires provides examples, showing that the Portuguese *ter* embraces the meanings of the English *get, have,* and forms of *be* (1956:153, 156, 161).

get down vs. **get out of**

"We drove his car and when we came to Kukuihaele, we all get down and walk."

Some Asian languages have this idiom. Korean *naerida* and Japanese *oriru,* meaning 'to go (come) down' are used for getting out of a car and getting off a bus (DJL).

glass cup vs. **drinking glass, water glass, glass**

Glass cup has been used widely for *glass* or *water glass* in Hawaii until quite recently. It could have come to Hawaii with immigrants from the East or West. The Portuguese word *copo* entered the Japanese language in Japan as the loanword *koppu* meaning 'drinking glass', as it does in Portuguese. This could easily have been brought to Hawaii with Japanese, Korean, or Portuguese immigrants. One definition of the word *glass* in *A New English-Korean Dictionary* (1964), is 'a cup made of glass'. The water glass is a relatively recent introduction to Korea and Japan and the combination *glass cup* is no doubt a loan translation in English of the name given the new culture item in the Asian languages (DJL).

go, goin' vs. standard auxiliaries for future tense

"I go make one dress."

This sentence, from the tape recording of speech of Type II, illustrates the use of the locally developed auxiliary *go* to express the future tense. (The complete "set" of auxiliaries is: *stay* to express the present progressive, *been* or *wen* for past and present perfect, and *go* or *goin'* to express the future.) "When I graduate high school, I goin' be one nurse" is an example of the next stage of the progression toward the fully developed future tense, *going to be.*

go for broke vs. **make the greatest effort, go all-out**

As the motto of the famous 442nd Regimental Combat Team during World War II, *go for broke* is the most widely known of all Hawaiianisms. With the meaning 'make the extreme effort', 'shoot the works', it has been frequently quoted. An article by Alf Pratte, featuring this motto, appeared in the *Honolulu Star-Bulletin,* Island Edition, May 15, 1968.

-guys vs. **and his (her) pals**

"We goin' meet Jane-guys at the movie."

Heard in the nonstandard speech of Types III and IV, *-guys* is a kind of suffix with the meaning of the word widened to include both female and male persons, that is, 'Jane and her pals'. In standard English the meaning of *guys* is limited to the masculine, as in *guys and dolls. Jane-folks* and *Jane-them* are also heard in the Islands. In the Hawaiian language, *ma* functions in a similar way. *Tita ma* is parallel to *Jane-guys*, while *Papa ma* means 'father and mother' (PPA). Japanese has a suffix *-ra*, used in approximately the same way. The Korean equivalent for the Japanese suffix *-ra* is *-dul* (DJL).

-half vs. and a half

"We stay eight year-half, no?"

The Type I speaker was a plantation laborer of Japanese extraction. Chinese, Japanese, Korean, and other languages have parallels for this usage; for example, *eight year-half* is the literal translation of the Japanese *hachinen-han* and of the Korean *palnyun-ban* (DJL).

In Hawaii today, *dollar-half* and *dollar-quarter* are used by great numbers of dialect speakers, rather than the longer forms, *a dollar and a half* and *a dollar and a quarter*.

hard, 'Ass why hard! vs. It's terrible! Pity me!

"I miss da bus and mus' walk from down Moʻiliʻili—'ass why haːd!"

The speaker in this case was of Type II, but the popular Hawaiianism is heard everywhere, even being imitated by Type V speakers and visitors. It is roughly equivalent to "Too bad!" "It's terrible!" or even to "Auwē!"

humbug vs. troublesome (adj.), nuisance (n.)

Q: "What grade were you in then?" A: "Oh, third grade, when I was a real rascal, humbug boy."

Two things are interesting in this use of *humbug* in Hawaii: that it is an adjective (whereas in standard English it is a noun), and that the meaning is merely 'naughty, bothersome' rather than a more pejorative one involving cheating and deception.

Mother to daughter: "I go crazy when your father stay home! Too much humbug!"

The Type IV mother explained that the father got ashes all over the house, played the radio too loudly, and was a general nuisance. Used thus in the more conventional noun form, the meaning in Hawaii is still a mild one—of a person who is a bother rather than a fraud or an impostor. A. Grove Day (1951) pointed out that *humbug, country jack,* and *rascal,* as used in Hawaii, have an archaic flavor. Hall reported the term in Melanesian pidgin as an intransitive verb with a similar meaning: 'to be lazy, fool around' (1943:100). In the *Oxford English Dictionary* also, one definition of *humbug,* as a verb, is 'to fool around'.

hybolic vs. pompous, bombastic

An adjective developed in Hawaii, used to describe a pompous style of speaking or writing.

A group of university students provided the following examples: "Don't use that kind of hybolic words here!" "Why do you use such hybolic language?" "Sally is hybolic when she meets new people." Possible sources of the word suggested by these students were: high + symbolic; high + faluting [highfalutin]; hyperbolic; a highball drink. Reinecke and Tokimasa suggested (1934:55) that the term was created by syncope from *hyperbolic* 'of, pertaining to, or employing hyperbole or exaggeration'.

inside vs. in, into

"Den you see da *kualele* [falling star] goin' down inside da watah."

This Type II speaker from the island of Niihau was describing a meteor that was apparently falling into the ocean. (*Kualele* is a shortened form of *akulele* 'meteor', literally 'flying god'; see Pukui and Elbert 1957). The Hawaiian *loko* is translated 'in, inside, within' (Pukui and Elbert 1957).

The Japanese *no naka ni* may have been an influence in the selection of *inside* for *in,* particularly among Hawaii's issei and nisei, but not in the case of Hawaiian speakers (DC).

junks vs. junk, things

"I was so shame! All da junks wen fall down from my purse!"

In Hawaii, *junks* is used much more frequently to mean small personal possessions than to mean old automobiles and jalopies (PPA).

Even now, in the 1970s, the use of the pluralizing *s* at the ends of nouns is often unpredictable, if not indiscriminate, and some fascinating observations result. In markets, where local high-school boys often print hasty signs to indicate the prices of fruits and vegetables, a list may read: "Chinese parsley, haole [i.e., Mainland] parsley, mints, radish," whereas the standard replica would read "mint, radishes" (without the luxury of two kinds of parsley). On the fruit counter, signs very often announce "orange, grapefruits," and over the vegetables, "fresh bean" and "cabbages," although only one kind of cabbage is in sight. For those who approach English from an Asian-language background, even from the distance of a generation or two, the puzzle involved in knowing which nouns are "countable" and which are not is far more difficult than the native speaker of English can possibly imagine. Nonstandard forms such as *junks, corns, mails, underwears, sceneries, furnitures,* and *baggages* have become crystallized in dialectal speech—there to remain for all except those youngsters who (by some educational process) get the s-forms sorted out from the no-s forms.

kaukau vs. food, eat

"Come! Get plenty kaukau!" 'Come along, there's plenty of food.'

"When dey go kaukau, anybody crash da party!" 'When they begin to eat, everybody comes in.'

Kaukau passes for a Hawaiian word to many residents of the Islands and to visitors. It is a pidgin term, however, probably the same term as the *chow-chow* of Cantonese pidgin, which also meant 'food' and 'to eat' (Leland 1904:121).

kind, da kine vs. this kind of

Used in innumerable ways, this is one of the most popular of all terms in Hawaii's nonstandard speech. It is a shibboleth—a phrase distinctive of Hawaii's local talk. The following examples show some of its patterns:

Substantive: "Take da kine [broom] and sweep da floor."
Pronoun: Q: "We goin' have one party. I like you come." A: "Where da kine [it] goin' be?"
Adjective: Q: "You think Sam in love wid Alice?" A: "Man, he da kine [crazy] 'bout her!"
Suffix: Q: "Oh, hey! We go show? Get da kine rock music!" A: "Oh, da rock-kine! I like!"
Suffix: "I see the Oahu-kine surfboard and the over-here-kine" [on Kauai].

Rock-kind corresponds to Japanese *to iu mono ka,* where *ka* is an interrogative particle. In *over-here-kind,* the word *kind* corresponds to Japanese *no mono ga* or *wa.* Japanese often has *to iu yō na mono ka* and *kochira no yō na mono ga* or *wa,* where *yō* means 'sort', 'kind', 'like'.

This may well be the origin of *kine* and *da kine*. Even the noun in "Take da kine and sweep da floor" corresponds to an indefinite *mono* or *are* in Japanese (DC).

The *da kine* of Hawaii's local talk often literally translates the Hawaiian word *'ano* meaning 'like' or 'type': *kēia 'ano kanaka* 'this kind of person' or 'da kine kanaka'; *'ano maikai* 'pretty good', 'somewhat good' or 'da kine good' (SE).

lawn-mow, lawn-mower vs. cut, mow

A: (telephoning) "Bumbye I come—lawn-mow da ya:d." B: "Yeah, but I wen lawn-moah [mower] da grass a'ready!"

These two Hawaiian coinages are compound verbs, and somewhat rarer in form than the compounds listed in chapter 8, all of which were nouns or adjectives. Forming compounds in this way is within the English tradition, however, and *to lawn-mow* is roughly parallel with *to housekeep* (composed of goal-noun + verb, resulting in a verb). *To lawn-mower*, however, (with goal-noun + agent-noun, resulting in a verb) goes a little beyond this pattern.

level vs. straight along

"Den you go level da road, eh?"

The Hawaiian woman (the Type II speaker of chapter 3) meant 'straight along the road'. This use of *level* may well have come from a loose translation of the Hawaiian word *pololei*, illustrated in the words of a Molokai cowboy on seeing his first airplane (Judd 1961:140):

Cowboy: "By golly, he *pololei* [level] go, he no go like this [moving his outstretched arms up and down] . . ."
Foreman: "Sure he no go like this?" [moving his arms up and down like a bird in flight].
Cowboy: "No, he *pololei* go."

The Japanese language has a number of words for 'flat', 'level', and 'straight along'. Several overlap in meaning and fail to coincide with the range of the term *level* in English (DC).

like vs. want to, want

Q: "Wat you like me come out heah foah?" A: "I like talk to you."

The use of *like* for *want to* is a characteristic part of Type III teen-age talk in Hawaii, but the substitution can be traced to pidgin English far beyond the Islands. Hall listed *like* in his vocabulary of Melanesian pidgin, giving the examples: *lajk go* 'want to go', *no lajkim kajkaj* 'not wish food', 'not be hungry' (1943:106), and Mihalic listed terms illustrating the same usage and explained them (1957, dictionary:68). Knowlton suggested that the "range of meanings of [Portuguese] *querer* may account for this feature" [use of *like*] (1967:234). The Hawaiian *makemake* means both 'like' and 'want'. No known Polynesian language distinguishes between these two words (SE). Thus the very general use of *like* for *want*, or *want to*, in Hawaii's English is reinforced by a number of linguistic models: pidgin English elsewhere, the Portuguese language, and the Hawaiian language.

local vs. from Hawaii

Servicemen from Hawaii, walking in San Francisco, saw a *nisei* girl and called out to her, "Ey! Local girl!" Although California also has *nisei* girls, the men found that this one was, indeed, from Hawaii. *Local* can mean 'from Hawaii' to traveling residents, even when they are many miles from the Islands.

look-see vs. look

"Ey! I like take one look-see!"

A teen-age Type III speaker made this comment as he went to take his place in front of the telescope at the Pali lookout.

"Look-see-nana" was frequently heard in the 1920s (and earlier) when *haoles* spoke to Hawaiians or Asians. Since the Hawaiian *nānā* means 'to look at, to see', the three words together imply an enthusiastic "Look, look, look!" (OAB).

Look-see was present and conspicuous in Chinese pidgin (Leland 1904:128), and it is one of the terms that may have come to Hawaii from Canton with the early trading ships traveling the Pacific.

mails vs. letters

"Five of the outgoing mails need to have stamps on them."

"Helen, what do you know! You have a mail in the box!"

These examples are from the Type IV speech of two school secretaries discussing the day's departmental mail. The treatment of *mail* as a countable noun is similar to the example given earlier of *corns;* in both, there are humorous overtones.

make vs. become or behave

"My brother just made six years old yesterday."

This way of reporting birthdays is widely used by Types I through IV. It is attributed by Knowlton (1967:234) to the influence of the Portuguese language. In military and academic circles the use of *make* in connection with promotions is growing, for example, "Clark made admiral last week," and "Jones made associate professor this spring." A similar, and common, expression is "He couldn't make it," but the use of *make* in connection with birthdays is still strange to standard English.

"No make like dat!" 'Don't do that!'

Such an expression is heard in the speech of the first three dialect types, and there are many possible influences. Japanese, Chinese, and Korean, like many European languages, have widely differing semantic boundaries for *make* and *do*. Koreans, for example, would say *jalmot hada* 'mistake do', when someone makes a mistake (DJL).

make quick vs. hurry

"Mo' bettah you make quick an' close da light!" 'Hurry up and put out the light!'

Make quick for *hurry* is sometimes heard in the speech of Types I, II, and III. Influences are probably the same as for *make like that*.

meat vs. beef

"No meat today, only pork." 'No beef today.'

This phrase was seen, within the last decade, on a sign in a small restaurant in Honolulu. Several decades ago, *meat* was the general term in Hawaii for 'beef'.

The Japanese and Korean languages both use a generic term for beef alone and give specific names to pork and mutton (DC). On the other hand, some languages of southern China use a general word equivalent to *meat* to mean pork (Ball 1925:246). Native speakers of Hawaiian would never use their word for 'meat' to mean 'beef' since the English word *beef* has been transliterated and naturalized into Hawaiian as *pipi* for many years and is very widely known (SE). The use of *meat* for 'beef' may, therefore, have been a Japanese innovation in Hawaii, reinforced by Korean usage.

minor vs. it's nothing

A: "Ey, no can go show—wen forget my money." B: "Ah, minah! I get plenty foah two."

A popular word with young people, the word means 'of no importance', 'no worry', or 'minor matter'.

more better vs. better

"Leela bitch dreenko, kaukau first, moah betta." 'It's better to have a little bit to drink and some food first.'

The Type I Japanese host urged his *haole* guests to drink and eat before settling down for the rest of the evening (Holt 1965:10). *More better* has strong ties with both Chinese and Melanesian pidgin. Leland cited *my more-betta go 'way* as meaning 'superior' (1904:129). Mihalic noted that the adjective *good* in Melanesian pidgin has three forms of the comparative: *moa gut, moa gutpela,* and *moa beta* (1957, grammar:16).

much vs. many

"I didn't get much good grades las' yeah."

Confusion in the use of *much* and *many* is not limited to the simpler levels of speech but may be heard even in Type IV conversations. This widespread difficulty may result from the very general use of *plenty* in Hawaii's English of the early days to cover the meanings of both 'much' and 'many' ("Me—I get plenty money but he no get plenty pig.") *Plenty* so used was popular in Canton (Leland 1904:131) and in Melanesia (Hall 1943:142–143).

never vs. didn't, haven't, etc.

"I nevah take that picture." 'I didn't take that picture.'

"I nevah sleep today." 'I haven't slept today.'

"He nevah come a'ready." 'He hasn't come yet.'

Never plus the simple form of the verb serves as the negative in a great many expressions in the preterit and present perfect tenses, as illustrated here in the speech of Types II and III. The word, so used, may well be a Hawaiianism, developed in place of the standard negative contractions—*didn't* etc.—which are difficult for Island people to pronounce.

news vs. new things

"Dey dive down, dey go inside [the underwater cave]. Dey come out. Dey tell us all kinds news."

Spoken by a part-Hawaiian woman of Type II, the word *news* seems to mean 'details', 'strange things', 'new things'. The Hawaiian word *nūhou* means 'news' as a noun, but 'strange' as an adjective. The speaker seems to combine these two meanings in her sentence.

. . . no? . . . yeah? vs. . . . isn't it? . . . is it?

"She go take permanent today, no?" 'She's going to have a permanent today, isn't she?'

"He no come today, yeah?" 'He isn't coming today, is he?'

The tag-question words *no* and *yeah*, used with rising intonation and glottal stop, are heard in innumerable nonstandard utterances. They turn a statement into a question as in the standard English examples: "This is Monday, isn't it?" and "It isn't our last chance, is it?" *No* is more commonly used than *yeah*, and this lends weight to the observation of Reinecke and Tokimasa that the tag -*no* merely invites the listener's continued attention and that it is probably the angl_iziced form of the Japanese *ne* 'you know' (1934:128).

no vs. not: no can vs. cannot

"No can open da doah!" 'I can't open the door.'

No, standing before the verb for present-tense negations, is parallel to *never* similarly used for negations in the past tenses. This, one of the earliest of pidgin forms, is still heard in Hawaii, used by speakers of Types I through III, and sometimes in jest for "local language" imitations. It avoids the difficult endings of such standard negative terms as *can't*, *doesn't*, and *don't*. In Cantonese pidgin such constructions as *no savvy* and *no can* were basic. Leland gave a great number of examples such as "no catchee milk for chowchow" (1904:96). Negative constructions in Melanesian pidgin are regularly made with the adverb *no* plus a verb (Hall 1943:28; Mihalic 1957, grammar:42).

The Hawaiian word *'a'ole* covers the meaning of both *no* and *not*. It is probable that no Polynesian language distinguishes these two words (SE). The Portuguese *não* corresponds to both *no* and *not*. As for the position of *no* before the verb, the Chinese language has negative forms preceding the verb, which may reinforce this dialectal construction in Hawaii (DC), and Korean has a construction consisting of a negative prefix plus a verb: *mot ka*, literally, 'unable go' (DJL).

no big thing vs. not important

"Ain't no big thing" came into use from a song popularized by Don Ho, a well-known singer in the Islands. Its meaning is 'nothing to worry about', 'a small matter'.

no more vs. **no, not**

Q: "Were you ever married?" A: "No more!"

The informant had never been married, but used *no more* as an emphatic *no* or *not*, without the connotation 'not any longer' or 'not now'. Of this commonly heard phrase, one informant says, "In stores, it's used by clerks to mean, not that they are sold out of what you're asking for, but that they never had it and probably never will."

The phrase is sometimes accompanied by shrugging the shoulders, raising one or both hands to shoulder height and shaking them from the wrists. Such a set of gestures is a part of the hula accompanying the song "Manuela Boy"—"No mo' fi' cent, no mo' house . . ."

no more nothing vs. **nothing else**

Q: "Why you like go show everyday?" A: "No moah nottin' [nothing] foah do!"

The Hawaiian language does not have a double negative, but nearly all the other tongues spoken in Hawaii could have supported this usage (DC). Early colonial American English itself contained the double negative in standard usage. A parallel expression from the Portuguese is as follows:

Q: "O Senhor sabe alguma coisa?" 'Do you know something, sir?' A: "Não, não sei nada." 'No, I don't know nothing.'

number one vs. **the best, the most**

"Him numba one pilau luna!" 'He is the very worst overseer on the plantation.'

The speaker represents Type I. *Pilau* is a Hawaiian word defined as 'rotten' or 'rottenness' and *number-one pilau* means 'extremely bad'.

Number one is cited by Leland in Cantonese pidgin: *numpa one*, 'first class', 'very' with the example, "Hab got top-side *numpa one* ugly Englishee lawyer. . . ." (1904:130). Hall noted not only *number one* but also *number one too much* in Melanesian pidgin, meaning 'very fine' (1943: 111). The Hawaiian language has *helu 'ekahi* 'number one' and Japanese has *ichiban* with the same meaning.

omission of **of**

Child at a school cafeteria: "I like two scoops rice an' one piece pie."

If the word *to* is most frequently omitted in Hawaii's English, the preposition *of* must be next in frequency of loss. There are many recorded examples, as in the reminiscences of a woman of her arrival at Honolulu's immigration station long ago. Speaking of the death of a fellow passenger, she said: "She no die dat sickness [cholera]. She die some oddah sickness."

Yet there are certain Island patterns in which a superfluous *of* is inserted, showing what is called "hypercorrectness"—the strong desire to speak in the approved way; an example is "Buy one dozen of eggs and one-half dozen of lemons."

on vs. in, at

"I got on the Ford, drove to town, and got off."

The person quoted was a Type IV speaker. In standard American English, one gets *into* and *out of* an automobile but *on* and *off* a bus. In Hawaii, *on* and *off* are sometimes used in connection with both kinds of transportation. The Hawaiian language reinforces the local idiom with such sentences as *Holoholo mea luna o ke ka'a* (in which *luna* is 'on') 'to ride on a car' (SE). Chinese, Japanese, and Korean also have the same expressions for entering and leaving any means of transportation (DC).

"I sat on the table and had my lunch."

The little girl speaking in this example might be a child in almost any public elementary school in Hawaii—a polite child who had actually sat *at* a cafeteria table to eat her lunch.

on top vs. on

"Da policeman come catch you! He take you on top da horse!"

This Type II speaker is quoted in the idiom of the past, when policemen still rode horses. The words are now frequently pronounced "eentop," for example:

"Turn on da radio an' we dance eentop da san' [sand]."

Speakers of Types IV and V sometimes use this phrase for fun or for humorous impersonations, in such sentences as 'I put perfume on top me" and "My madda [mother], she on top welfare."

The Hawaiian word *luna* is sometimes translated 'on top' in pidgin-talk (SE).

one vs. a, each

"I thirsty, an' I drink jus' like one horse."

"Da candy bah cos' fi' cent one." 'The candy bars cost five cents each.'

The use of *one* for *a*, very common in Hawaii, has parallels in all areas of pidgin English. Leland reported it in Canton, "You catchee one piecee wifey?" 'Have you a wife?' (1904:130). In Melanesian pidgin, the suffix *-fellow* is joined to *one* as a classifier, for example, *Mi lukim wanpela man* 'I saw someone' (Mihalic 1957, dictionary:158). The absence of an indefinite article in Chinese, Japanese, and Korean makes the use of *one* a natural choice for immigrants to an English-speaking country. Yet this usage may also be evidence of an earlier contact between the Portuguese language and Cantonese pidgin. Knowlton (1967:234) has pointed out parallels to Portuguese usage, citing Pires (1956:90).

or what vs. or about that

Q: "How many people used to live in Waipio Valley?" A: "Thousand or what."

In this local sense, *or what* is not a question (as in "Do you want this, or what?") but carries the meaning of 'approximately', 'or about that'.

package vs. paper sack

"Gimme one package. I like buy five poun' orange."

The usual meaning of *package* 'a bundle of something', 'a parcel' has been widened in Hawaii to include the flat, unopened paper sack seen in markets. Many speakers continue to call the sack a *package*, however, even after it has been filled with groceries. This semantic shift can be heard in the conversation of speakers of Types I through IV.

pear vs. avocado

As an example of narrowing in meaning, the word *pear* can be heard in Hawaii denoting only the avocado. (To distinguish them, Mainland pears are frequently referred to as *Bartlett pears* because of the trade-mark that is conspicuous on cans of pears in the markets of the Islands.) For the source of this use of *pear*, we should look to the place of origin of the first avocado trees in Hawaii. Cassidy wrote: "When *pear* is used without qualification [in Jamaica], the *avocado* or *alligator* pear is meant; both these words are originally Jamaicanisms" (1961:355). Thus it seems probable that the term *pear* arrived in Hawaii along with the avocado tree, certain varieties possibly directly from Jamaica.

pickaninny vs. small

This widely traveled term came into Cantonese pidgin from the Portuguese language. It was recorded in Hawaii in 1791 by the Spaniard,

Manuel Quimper. Used as an adjective meaning 'small', it was one of the first pidgin-English terms heard by the New England missionaries after their arrival in Hawaii in 1820 (see chapter 7). The word continues to appear in unexpected places, for example, in a glossary of terms used by the Australian aborigines (Baker 1966:318). In its adjectival usage, however, it has disappeared from Hawaii.

pine vs. pineapple

Q: "What did you do in the summer?" A: "Me—I pickin' pines for Dole."

In Hawaii, the word *pine* usually refers to a pineapple rather than to a coniferous tree—a usage which frequently startles, and sometimes confuses, visitors to the Islands. Cassidy and Le Page noted the same usage in Jamaica and explained that the first name for the fruit in English was the Spanish loanword *piña* 'pineapple' (1967:351). This was anglicized as *pine* at about the middle of the seventeenth century (OED, s.v. *piña*).

plenty vs. many

"I get plenny place stay!" 'I have many places to live.'

This Type II speaker makes use of *plenty* as a pluralizing device, using it instead of inflectional endings on nouns. Yet in speech of somewhat further development, when inflections have appeared, *plenty* may still be retained as a colloquial term for 'many', 'lots of', for example, "Da movie had plenty laughs." Knowlton listed the use of *plenty* as one of the identifiable influences of Chinese pidgin on Hawaii's English (1967: 230). Leland (1904:131) listed it as occurring in Canton, and Mihalic (1957, dictionary:249) pointed it out in Melanesian pidgin. *Plenty* has proved to be a popular loanword in many foreign languages. Eastern and southern European immigrants in the mainland United States use the word in the same way that it is used in Hawaii (DC).

poke vs. injection or prick

"I wen go doctah for get my poke." 'I went to the doctor to get my medical injection.'

Children frequently use *poke* for *injection*, and their mothers often say, while sewing, "Da needle wen poke me!"

The influence may be the Hawaiian language, where the verb *hou* means 'to push, thrust, poke, stab, shove, inject, prick' (Pukui and Elbert 1957).

pull down vs. lose weight

"Didn't you pull down while you worked there?"

The origin of this phrase, used commonly in speech of Types III and IV, is apparently unknown.

-quarter vs. and a quarter

"Dis one, two inch-quarter. Dat one, inch-tree-quarter."

As in the case of *-half*, the word *quarter* sometimes becomes a suffix (cf. *-half*). The Japanese, Chinese, and Korean use of *quarter* without the equivalent of *and a* might have been an influence. The strength of the analogy of *dollar-half* probably was an influence also (DC).

rascal vs. mischievous

"In the sixth grade, I was a real, rascal, humbug boy . . ." (cf. *humbug*)

Day pointed out that *rascal* is used in Hawaii as Shakespeare used it—as an adjective (1951:26). This archaic usage is frequently heard in Hawaii, *a rascal child* meaning 'a lively, playful child'.

reach down, hit down vs. arrive at

"When you hit dat road down, de name of dat place is Waimihi—dat's de name of dat place you hit down."

The speaker was a Chinese-Hawaiian woman whose speech was of Type II. Reinecke and Tokimasa noted: "*Down* and *up* are important directives: 'When we reached down, I walked up Honoka'a.' *Down below* has been adopted into the speech of the Hawaiian-Japanese as an adverbial substantive, *danburo*" (1934:126).

The Hawaiian verb *ku*, which means 'to stop, hit, reach, arrive', may well have been a contributing factor to the speaker's choice of words in English. The Hawaiian words *lalo* 'down, downward, beneath' and *luna* 'high, upper, above, up' are in constant use among Hawaiian speakers. All Polynesian and Micronesian languages employ directional terms far more frequently than does English (SE).

refreshments vs. soft drinks

Waiter: (helping with a take-out dinner) "You goin' have refreshments?"

Hostess: "What do you mean?"

Waiter: "Oh, you know—sodas, cold drinks. . . ."

Many local speakers have narrowed the meaning of *refreshments* to 'cold drinks, soda pop, juice' (which may not be fruit juice, but a carbonated drink).

sabe, savvy vs. understand, know how to

Q: "You talk-talk sabe?" A: "Yeah, me talk . . . talk English."

Q: "You too-much sabe ride horse?" A: "Yeah, little bit."

Much used in the plantantion-style pidgin of Type I, the word can still be heard in the conversation of older people. It probably came to Hawaii from Chinese pidgin. Leland recorced *savvy* in the pidgin of Canton and attributed the word to the influence of Portuguese (1904: 132). Mihalic noted *save* in Melanesian pidgin but indicated that the influence was probably the Spanish *saber* (1957, dictionary:125). Hall wrote: "The word *savvy* for 'know', which is perhaps the most widespread of all words in the different kinds of Pidgin English, is a borrowing from its Portuguese predecessor at Canton (Portuguese *saber* 'to know', third person singular *sabe*)" (1955:27).

saimin

"Saimin is a term peculiar to Hawaii. We do not know when or how it was coined. Local Chinese think *saimin* is a Japanese dish; local Japanese think it's a Chinese dish. One thing seems certain: it's a local [Hawaii] dish." These are the words of a Hawaii-born, Japanese-American University of Hawaii professor, Shunzo Sakamaki. He has given much attention to the English and Japanese languages in Hawaii.

The second element of the word, *min*, is easily identified as the Cantonese word for 'noodle', but the first element, *sai*, is more difficult to identify. A plausible interpretation is that *sai* in this term may be a form of the Cantonese word for 'water', and that the literal meaning of *saimin*, then, may be 'water noodles' or 'noodle soup' (see chapter 7, Chinese loanwords).

scare vs. afraid

A: "Ey, run fas' on da bridge!" B: "I scare for go!"

Q: "Are you afraid of the dog?" A: "Me, I no scare!"

Although *scare* is undoubtedly the adjectival use of *scared* minus its final inflection, it (like the *shave* of *shave ice* and the *crack* of *crack seed*), has become a relic form and a localism, used regularly by many speakers and imitated in jest by many more.

shaka, shakka vs. right on! that's great!

A: "Us, we go surf Makaha?" B: "Shaka, bla!"

This term is popular at the moment in Honolulu. Whether it is a recent coinage or the revival of an old form remains to be discovered. It is pronounced with considerable stress on the second syllable: shah-ká.

shame vs. bashful

Q: "Why don't you hold up your hand when the teacher asks a question?" A: "I shame ansa da question." 'I am too bashful, or embarrassed, to try to answer.'

As in the case of *scare*, the uninflected form *shame* has become a localism. In both *I shame* and *I scare*, an important feature may be the lack of the English verb *to be*. Whether this lack in Island English stems from the failure of immigrants to hear the unstressed parts of certain words, particularly of contractions (as the *'m* and *a* of "I'm ashamed"), or whether it is connected with the lack of a verb equivalent to the copula in some of the Asian and Pacific languages, is an unanswered question. The absence of the copula in another language often leads to difficulty in translating from, or into, English,

The Hawaiian term *hilahila* meaning 'embarrassed, shy, ashamed, bashful' may be a contributing influence on the use of the word *shame* in Hawaii's English. Probably all Polynesian languages have one inclusive term for these meanings (SE). The Korean and Japanese equivalents, *bukkurupta* and *hazukashi*, cover the semantic area of both 'ashamed' and 'bashful' (DJL).

shave ice vs. shaved ice

Shave ice is a fistful of joy to children—a paper cone filled with finely crushed (shaved) ice and generously doused with sweetened and colored water.

To pronounce *shaved ice* in standard English, a speaker must utter the two-consonant medial cluster -*vd*-, and to pronounce *cracked seed* he must master a three-consonant medial combination -*kts*-. The consonants most often lost from these clusters are the two alveolar stops *d* and *t*, sounds which are especially unstable in the speech of persons with a foreign-language background.

Even where English is the native language, the same alveolar stops are frequently lost from the ends of words. For example, the word *ice cream* began its existence as *iced cream* in 1688 in England (OED, s.v. *ice-cream*). The *ed* ending was dropped after 1769 and the form *ice-cream* became established in England, according to the Craigie-Hulbert *Dictionary of American English.*

down-side, top-side vs. below, above, on top of

Q: "Where does the family live?" A: "Down-side da mill."

Words compounded with *side* as the second element have been noted by Reinecke and Tokimasa (1934:127) and by Knowlton (1967:230). This pattern of compounding goes back to Cantonese-pidgin days, when *top-side, bottom-side,* and *allo-side* 'around' were commonly heard in the China ports. Leland noted that *-side* qualified adverbs and prepositions (1904:133). Hall cited examples in Melanesian pidgin, such as *halfside belong house* 'the side of the house' and *long halfside* 'on one side, over there, over here, opposite' (1943:99). A word equivalent to *side* in Japanese or Korean could be suffixed to almost any noun or adjective. In the case of Japanese, *no* meaning 'of' is often inserted between the noun and *gawa,* the equivalent of *-side* (DC).

That the influence might have been nautical and American or British is suggested by an entry in the *Random House Dictionary* (1967), which lists *topside* used adverbially, with the example "He left the engine room and went topside."

slangs vs. slang words

"The reason this student was classified as a pidgin speaker was because of her phrases or slangs which the writer felt were characteristic of the local slangs."

Written by a college senior who is a speaker of Type IV English, this sentence illustrates the use of the term *slangs* even by those whose speech is approaching standard American English. In a final examination, five of seventeen University of Hawaii sophomores used the form *slangs* meaning 'slang words'. The word must take its place, along with *corns* and *mails,* as a Hawaiianism.

sleep late vs. go to bed late

Q: "Why are you so tired this morning?" A: "Because I slept late last night."

In this local, Island sense, "sleeping late" means getting *less* sleep than usual because of going to bed late. In the standard English sense we might hear:

A: "How rested you look today!" B: "That's because I slept late this morning."

Here, *slept late* means 'remained asleep longer' and hence 'had a longer night's sleep than usual'. The slight and tantalizing difference may have come about because of a loan translation into the English from Japanese or Korean. In English a person must differentiate between 'going to bed' and 'going to sleep' (falling asleep or *being* asleep). This differentiation is possible but not necessary in Japanese where *Watakushi wa osoku nemutta (nemashita)* means 'I went to bed late' and *Watakushi wa sanji-kan nemutta (nemashita)* means 'I slept three hours', the verb *nemutta (nemashita)* serving for both meanings. In Korean, *jada* is the equivalent for both 'to sleep' and 'to go to bed'; its range of meaning is similar to that of the Japanese verb *nemuru* (DJL).

small-little vs. small

"The wind called *konalani* came from the small-little island out there."

"That was when my children were small-little boys."

These Type IV speakers demonstrate the redundant compound adjective *small-little*, widely used in Hawaii. It is reminiscent of the *little-tiny* of colloquial American speech.

soft vs. careful, gentle

"Make soft! Get eggs in dat basket!" 'Be careful! There are eggs in that basket!'

There are more than fifty Hawaiian words meaning *soft*, some with very slight differences in denotation. For example, *nahenahe* may mean not only 'soft' but also 'gentle-mannered' (Pukui and Elbert 1964, s.v. *soft*).

some vs. very

"Da party was *some* good, boy!"

Some good, uttered with an especially wide 2–3–1 falling intonation pattern, is said to be characteristic of the island of Maui, but the phrase is heard on the other islands also. On the Mainland, there are innumerable occurrences of similar phrases, for example, "That was *some* party!" The difference is that in the Mainland usage, *some* modifies a noun ("That's *some* dress you have on!") while in Hawaii, *some* often modifies an adjective ("some neat," "some nice"). In addition, the phrase in Hawaii has a wider upward rise in pitch and downward drop than in standard English.

sore vs. aching, sensitive

"My sistah—she like one aspirin. Get sore head." 'My sister wants an aspirin because she has a headache.'

Particularly in rural areas, a headache may be called a *sore head*. The Hawaiian word *'eha* has a cluster of meanings, among them 'hurt, sore, aching, painful'. It is understandable that children in Hawaii might choose *sore* as an inclusive term for painful areas.

spark vs. see

"Wen I spahk him, I jus' . . . *Auwē!*" 'When I catch sight of that good-looking fellow, I just think,"''Oh, dear! Alas!"' '

To spark is used with the meaning 'to glimpse', 'to catch sight of'. Some informants believe that the original word might have been *spot*. Further than that, the term has not been identified.

stay vs. forms of to be

"Where you stay go?" 'Where are you going?'

"What you stay eat?" 'What are you eating?'

Stay, a locally developed auxiliary used with the simple form of a verb, is employed by some speakers of Types I, II, and III to express the present progressive tense, and occasionally to indicate habitual action. The *stay* form is abandoned as standard means of forming verb tenses are acquired. Reinecke and Tokimasa attributed *stay* to the Portuguese *estar* (1934:123), and Knowlton took a similar view (1967: 234). *Stay* was not cited in Cantonese pidgin by Leland. Mihalic listed *stop* rather than *stay* as the auxiliary used to express the present progressive tense in Melanesian pidgin (1957, grammar:30).

Because of the similarity in the use of *stay* and *stop* as auxiliaries for the present progressive, it does not seem impossible that the Melanesian form *stop* might have been known at one time in Hawaii (through contacts during the whaling days), and that later it might have been replaced by *stay*.

step vs. step on

"Hurry! Step da bug!" 'Hurry and step on the bug!'

The Hawaiian verbs *hehi* and *'e'ehi* may have had an influence in this local form. In both instances the meaning is 'to stamp, tread, step on'.

In Hawaii, the use of *step* for *step on* is heard more often from children than from adults and more often on the outer islands than in Honolulu.

stop vs. remain

Q: "Is Sammy there?" A: "He no stop." 'He isn't here.'

Formerly *stop* was much used as a verb meaning 'to remain, to be present', but today it is heard only occasionally in the speech of Types I and II, and then more often as the negative *no stop* than otherwise. Hall listed a similar use of *stop* in the Sepik River region of New Guinea, again with the meaning 'remain, be' (1943:118). Mihalic described the use of *stop* in the Wewak area of Melanesia as an auxiliary to express the present progressive tense, in a manner similar to *stay* in Hawaii's dialect (cf. *stay*).

stuff, stuffs vs. thing, things

"When da stuff fly back, da man know da log was bad." 'When the bird flew back again, the man knew that the log was worm-eaten.'

Stuff appearing in this way is always used after an antecedent—*bird* in this example. It thus functions as a pronoun. The usage may have some connection with the Hawaiian word *mea*, meaning 'thing, person'. *Stuffs* is often used by Island children in the sense of 'things', for example, "I learned a lot of stuffs at school today."

suck wind, suck vs. go hungry, go without

A: "No moah samwitch. I hungry!" B: "You suck win' den!"

A: "No can go beach. Gotta help my fadda." B: "You suck!"

Popular with younger speakers, the phrases are thought to mean "You eat the wind," "You lose out." The second could be a bit of slang from the Mainland equal to "You're stuck" or "You're a sucker."

talk vs. tell

"Us—we goin' talk story tonight."

Talk story is heard even on college campuses in Hawaii; it is not a disappearing form but is fixed in popular speech—often, of course, as a part of the conscious and nostalgic fun-language of young adults. *Talk* and *tell* are a pair of words with tantalizing likenesses and differences that help to make still more elusive the "almost imperceptible line" at some points between Type IV and Type V speech.

Talk story may reflect the influence of the Hawaiian language, where the single verb *'olelo* can mean 'say, tell, talk, speak' (SE). Far away from Hawaii, Daniel J. Crowley has noted the phrase in the Bahamas and has used it in the title of his folklore study, *I Could Talk Old-Story Good* (1966:127).

tell vs. repeat or say

"That's when they tell, *'Ai ka manō pua ka wiliwili.'* " 'That's when they say, "When the *wiliwili* blooms, the sharks bite." '

Tell and *say* present the same problems of differentiation as do the pair *talk* and *tell*. *Say* or *repeat* seem more appropriate than *tell* for the example above because "When the *wiliwili* blooms . . ." is a wise saying, a bit of folklore repeated.

Tell used for *say* is illustrated in the conversation between the two girls in chapter 4. GB, trying to find out what time the party is to be, says:

"My mada [mother] goin' tell [say]: 'Wat kine pa:ty *dis* goin' be? No more time?' "

The use of *tell* for *say* may result from the influence of the Hawaiian word *'olelo*, mentioned earlier, which may mean 'say, tell, talk, speak' (cf. *talk*).

That's OK, That's all right vs. Thank you, No, thank you

Q: "Would you like some mangoes?" A: " 'Ass OK. Ouah house get plenny." 'Thank you, but we have lots of them.'

Q: "You like I carry you' books?" A: " 'Ass awri'." 'No, thank you.'

That's all right (or *OK*) seems to be a local substitute for 'thank you' just as *try* is an occasional substitute for 'please'. An additional word or phrase may be added to communicate the full meaning. The American *OK* has become firmly fixed at all levels of the local language.

the pretty, the good vs. the pretty flower, the good cookie, etc.

A (seeing a bright red rose): "Oh, da pretty!" B (being treated to fresh cookies): "Oh, da good!"

In *Patterns of English*, Paul Roberts explains that the word *the*, a structure word or determiner, always patterns with a noun. It operates as a signal that a noun is coming (1956:31). *The pretty, the good, the big* are innovative, therefore, and nonstandard in that the structure word, *the*, patterns with an adjective.

It is quite possible that "Oh, the pretty!" derives from the Hawaiian phrase *Auwē ka nani!*, in which *ka* is 'the' and *nani* is 'pretty'. Translated literally the phrase means "Oh, the pretty!" and more freely, "Oh, how pretty!" (SE). Reinecke and Tokimasa pointed out this usage but did not link it with the Hawaiian language (1934:126). Knowlton (1967:235) cited Pires, who gave a parallel phrase from dialectal Portuguese.

-them vs. and her friends, and others

Q: "You go library wid Alice-dem?" 'Are you going . . . with Alice and her pals?' A: "Yeah, I go wid dem."

A proper noun is here linked to a pronoun in an expression similar to the noun-plus-noun illustrated by *Jane-guys*. In both cases the suffix changes a singular concept into a plural one, but it does more—it adds the implication 'Alice and her crowd' or 'Jane and her friends'. As used by speakers of Types I to IV, the combination may mean a group containing boys as well as girls (cf. *-guys*). The expression may be a development of the suffix *-fellow*, heard long ago in Hawaii and currently used in Melanesian pidgin (cf. *-fellow*). A parallel use of *-them* as a suffix in Jamaica was discussed by Cassidy (1961:52).

throw out vs. throw up

"Poor baby—he trow out his milk." 'The poor baby threw up his milk.'

A probable loan translation from the Japanese, reinforced by Korean usage, the term *throw out* may have come into existence in Hawaii from the influence of the Japanese compound verb *hakidasu*, which combines the meanings 'to vomit' and 'to spew out'. The single verb *haku* (*haki*) is often used with the same meanings (DJL).

till vs. to, as far as

"We had a road from Hilo till up here." 'There was a road from Hilo to this place.'

In standard usage, *till* means 'to the time of, up to, until'. In Hawaii's speech, *till* is sometimes used as a preposition to indicate space or distance, as in the example above. One of the immediate influences seems to be the Hawaiian language, in which the phrase *a hiki i ka muliwai* means 'till the river', that is, 'to the river' (Pukui and Elbert 1957, s.v. *hiki*). Japanese, Chinese, Korean, Malayan, and many other languages do not distinguish between space and time in all their prepositions and preposition equivalents (DC). Japanese *made* and Korean *kkaji* are expressions used in designating both space and time (DJL).

Till is also heard occasionally in Hawaii in the sense of 'while'. An advertisement for fruit on sale at a market in Honolulu read: "Good till the supply lasts" (PPA).

-time vs. at the time when, at the time of

"Me boy-time, I don' know too much." 'When I was a boy, I didn't know very much.'

"Me thirty-six-year-old-time, my bradda *make*." 'When I was thirty-six years old, my brother died.'

Frequently, at the beginning of an utterance, a noun or phrase plus the word *time*, in the speech of Type I, serves to give the meaning 'at the time of'. Mrs. Kim, the Type I speaker in this book, used a number of such expressions (e.g., chapter 2, utterance 18).

This method of expressing a temporal idea is used by the Chinese, Japanese, Korean, and many other languages (DC). Korean *ttae* and Japanese *toki* (the literal meaning of which is 'time'), are the equivalents of 'when' (DJL). The Hawaiian language also has parallel forms, using the word *wā* 'period of time': *wā li'ili'i* 'childhood, little time'; *wā u'i* 'youth, beautiful time, vigorous time'; *wā kahiko* 'ancient time' (SE).

tired for vs. too tired to or too bored to

"Big pond you know, tired for swim!" 'It was such a big pond that it made swimmers feel too tired to swim across it.'

Used by some speakers in Types I to IV, the phrase *tired for* has become a localism. A child will sometimes say, "Oh, tired for go school!" early in the morning, showing boredom rather than fatigue, in the sense of 'I'm tired of school'. Parallels for this usage have not been suggested.

omission of to

"Us—we like go show tonight." 'We want to go to the show.'

In the speech of Types I, II, and III, the omission of the word *to* is very frequent both as the introductory word of an infinitive and as a preposition. Both kinds of omission were illustrated many times in the speech of Mrs. Akana (chapter 3).

Knowlton noted that *"to* is often dropped before an infinitive" and cited a parallel Portuguese example (1967:234). No writer whose work has come to hand, however, has pointed out how much greater is the incidence of omission of the preposition *to* than of any other preposition in Hawaii's English.

too much vs. very much or very many

Q: "Long time befoah, you firs' come Hawaii, fish too much?" 'When you first came to Hawaii, were there a great many fish?' A: "Yeah, any place, too much fish." 'Yes, everywhere there were lots of fish.'

The Hawaiian language does not distinguish between 'too much' and 'very much'; both can be expressed by *nui loa* (SE). The expression *too much* meaning 'very much' and 'very many' has long been a recognized part of pidgin English elsewhere. Leland entered it in his word lists as *too-muchee*, defining it as 'very, excessive', with the illustration, "You too-muchee hanson" 'You are very good-looking' (1904:135). Mihalic included the term in phonetic spelling as *tumas* with the definitions 'too much; very, very much'. One of his examples was *plenti tumas*, 'more than enough' (1957, dictionary:155).

try vs. please

A: "Will you have anything else?" B: "Yeah, try pass da rice." 'Yes, please pass the rice.'

Try is sometimes heard, in the speech of Types I through IV, as a polite form, replacing "if you please." Reinecke and Tokimasa described its use in this way: *"Try* has become an auxiliary of the imperative, a trifle less polite than *please:* 'Mr. Reinecke, try read this page' " (1934: 123).

The influence may have its source in Asia, since Chinese, Japanese, and Korean have a similar idiom (DC). In Korean, *please* is usually accompanied by *try; jom mogo poayo*, literally "please try eat," means 'please eat' (DJL).

used to to vs. used to, accustomed to

Q: "Aren't you tired after driving this old bus?" A: "No, I'm used to to this work."

Probably a true Hawaiianism, this expression can be heard most often in the speech of Type IV. The combination *used + to* [yuzd + tə] unites into one form, the [z] of *used* becoming unvoiced to [s] and the [d] to [t].

The final sound of *used* and the initial sound of *to* fall together and the result is [yústə]. The perception of this combination as a single word is so strong that another *to* is often added, in Hawaii, producing [yústə tù] 'used to to'.

The first part of this Hawaiianism, [yústə], is reminiscent of stories written in dialectal American English on the Mainland, where it has been spelled *yoosta* or even *yooster* (DC). No Mainland example has been found, however, for the addition of an extra *to*, to produce a parallel for Hawaii's *used to to*.

wait a while vs. wait a minute, just a second

A: (telephone conversation) "May I speak to Mr. Jones?" B: "Wait a while." 'Wait a minute.'

In American English, a difference is made between *wait a minute* or its variant, *just a second*, and *wait a while*, meaning a longer period of waiting than is normal in the usual telephone call. A nurse at a Honolulu hospital may say "Wait a while" to a patient, yet bring the needed object almost instantly. This may be a parallel to the Hawaiian *kali iki* 'wait a little', used for both long and short periods of waiting (SE).

waste-time vs. boring, useless

Q: "How do you like that course?" A: "Man, dat one real waste-time class!" 'That class is really boring.'

Waste-time is used as an adjective to label distasteful, dull, uninteresting, or useless things (or people). It may be patterned on the Hawaiian expression *ho'opaumanawa* which has exactly the same meaning (Pukui and Elbert 1957, s.v. *-paumanawa*).

wen + verb vs. standard preterit and present perfect tenses

"I wen go from Kaiser Hospital wid da ambulance." 'I went from Kaiser Hospital in an ambulance.' (preterit)

"You wen see da kine flying saucer plenty time in da movie?" 'You have seen flying saucers many times in the movies?' (present perfect)

This use of *wen*, heard in the speech of Types I, II, and III, is an alternate form of *been*, listed earlier in this glossary. There is a parallel form in Jamaican creole, of which Cassidy has written: "Other labials are interchanged in a few individual words: *been*, usually /ben/, sometimes becomes *min*, sometimes *wen*" (1961:40). Cassidy attributes both *been* and *wen* to earlier forms of dialectal English. A complete entry occurs in *A Dictionary of Jamaican English* (Cassidy and Le Page 1967:467).

what vs. that

"Eat all what you can!" 'Eat all you can!'

"They have the pork . . . all what they want." 'They have all the pork that they want.'

What often substitutes for *that* as a relative pronoun in the speech of Types I, II, and III. Knowlton cited a parallel form in Pires' Portuguese handbook (Knowlton 1967:234).

Wassa madda you? Assa madda you? vs. What's the matter with you?

"Assa madda you las' night? You no come see mamma!"

In this popular local song *assa madda you* appeared for the first time in writing although it had long been well known in the speech of Types I, II, and III. Bernhard Hormann, the sociologist, wrote: "It is clear that each variety of speech has subvarieties. The plantation or creole pidgin varies somewhat according to the ancestral language of the speakers. So the Chinese say, 'Assa malla you?' and the Japanese, 'Assa madda you?' " (1960:11).

wile vs. be angry, punish

"My fadda goin' wile me wen he fin' out were I been go!" 'My father is going to be furious and punish me when he finds out where I've been.'

Sometimes heard in the speech of Types II and III, the word *wile* has been interpreted by some observers to be the adjective *wild* 'angry, furious' and hence to be used as a verb: *He will wild me.* However, *wile* is probably an entirely different word. Reinecke and Tokimasa (1934) noted that William Churchill had included *wail* in the glossary of *Beach-La-Mar: The Jargon of Trade Speech of the Western Pacific.* Neither Hall nor Mihalic report the word as a verb, but a similar use of *wile* as a verb meaning 'to drive, to chase' was noted in Jamaican English by Cassidy and Le Page, with the example: "Dah sell scissors an' fine teet' comb/ Till police wile dem way." (1967:478).

The verb *whale* has an informal meaning 'to strike as if to produce wales or stripes, to flog, to beat'. One observer has ventured a guess that this word, in the nonstandard pronunciation of British and Australian seamen of the Western Pacific, with its substitution of [aɪ] for [eɪ], might have set a pattern for *wile*: "I'll wile you" versus "I'll wale you."

word order in certain questions

Q: "I no get da money. Wat I can do?"

Q: "W'ere I can find da teachah?"

In questions beginning with *what* and *where* (and in some instances with other interrogatives in *wh*), speakers of Types I through III often use the word order of declarative sentences rather than the normal, reversed position of subject and auxiliary. This trait was attributed to the influence of the Portuguese language by Reinecke and Tokimasa (1934: 128) and was listed again with a Portuguese parallel by Knowlton (1967:234).

. . . yeah? vs. **. . . is it?**

Yeah? and *no?* are used at the ends of statements, to form questions. See the entry for *no?*

Chapter 10 **Analysis of the Glossary**

The one hundred thirty terms included in the glossary (chapter 9) were studied to identify possible influences from foreign-language sources or parallels in languages other than English. All entries were traced in dictionaries and word lists of languages known to have been in contact with Hawaii, and were then submitted to a group of language specialists for additional screening—an informal panel that included persons knowledgeable in the Hawaiian, Chinese, Japanese, and Korean languages and in the nonstandard speech of Hawaii. Special knowledge of the influence of the Portuguese language on Island English was readily available in the published research of John E. Reinecke and Edgar C. Knowlton, Jr. Pertinent information gathered from these various sources was recorded as a part of the entry for each of the glossary items.

It was inevitable, of course, that certain entries should show possible influence from more than one language or dialect but, for the purposes of this study, each item had to be assigned to a single category. The decision as to which category should receive an item was made with two criteria in mind: (1) which of the languages had had the more extensive or widespread contact, and (2) which had had the earlier contact. For example, in regard to the omission of the linking verb in Hawaii's nonstandard English, the influence of either Hawaiian or Chinese might be suspected, since both lack the linking verb. The influence of Hawaiian was judged to have been more pervasive, because it was spoken in all parts of the kingdom from the time when the New England missionaries first began teaching English in the 1820s and on through most of the century, affecting the language of all Island learners of English. The Hawaiian language was an earlier influence in point of time also, because Chinese was not heard extensively enough to interfere with English speech until the end of the century or later.

The next early influence, after that of the Hawaiian language itself, must have come from Cantonese and Melanesian pidgin expressions brought informally to the Islands by visiting crews of ships plying the Pacific as part of the lively trade in furs, sandalwood, whale oil, and whalebone. Young Hawaiians often signed on the ships as sailors, taking an active part in the growing Pacific commerce; these men returned to Hawaii using bits of pidgin English, to be envied and imitated at home, for there was no attempt to restrain pidgin in those days and, as Leland has pointed out (1904:3), it was the very symbol of business, travel, and excitement.

Such infiltration of pidgin terms continued for many decades before the mass immigrations of plantation workers began with the Chinese in 1876, followed by the Portuguese, Japanese, Puerto Ricans, Spanish, Koreans, and Filipinos. These groups made their impacts in differing degrees, according to the intensity of the language interference and according to the time of the contact. Special circumstances must be considered; for example, as Knowlton has suggested, the Portuguese influence must have been greater than the Chinese, even though the Portuguese began arriving a little later than the Chinese, because they migrated in families, intending to remain, and

in the late nineteenth century, in the schools of Hawaii when English was being taught as *the* language [of instruction], the two groups comprising the bulk of the school population were the Hawaiians and the Portuguese. They outnumbered the British and the Americans. The Chinese and Japanese, though forming a large proportion of the population, in early days migrated almost entirely as unaccompanied adult males. [1967:236]

When we attempt to weigh the comparative influences of the Hawaiian and Portuguese languages, however, we must recall that English was actually learned by large numbers of Hawaiian people decades before the Portuguese arrived and before English became the official language of instruction in the public schools. Kuykendall tells us that there was, for example, a "craze for the learning of English" among the Hawaiians in the late 1840s and early 1850s (1938:365). A first language invariably influences the learning of a second one, in pronunciation, grammar, or syntax, and dialectal features resulting from the interference of the first language, Hawaiian, were almost certainly already fixed in the nonstandard English speech current in the Islands long before Portuguese and Hawaiian children sat side by side in the classrooms of the 1890s. Since Hawaiian children by that time had learned some English outside the schoolroom, the Portuguese children may well have absorbed many dialectal traits from their Hawaiian classmates, at the same time spreading features of their own language. Thus the glossary expression, "Oh, the pretty!" was judged more likely to have resulted from the parallel Hawaiian "Auwē ka nani!" than from the Portuguese parallel cited by Knowlton (1967:235) and by Reinecke and Tokimasa (1934:126).

Following such reasoning, an entry with two or more possible influences was placed in the category deemed most likely and most appropriate. Of the total of one hundred thirty entries, seventy-nine fell into groups having parallel forms in one of four categories: (1) pidgin or creole languages from other areas than Hawaii, (2) the Hawaiian language, (3) the Portuguese language, or (4) one of the Asian languages (Chinese, Japanese, or Korean). The fifty-one terms remaining were placed in a category called "Hawaiianisms"—expressions assumed to have sprung from the total cosmopolitan culture of the Islands, itself the source of innovative expressions, for example, the "go for broke" of World War II. A few items included may be archaisms retained in Hawaii—*rascal* and *humbug* used as adjectives, for example. The appearance of an entry in the category called "Hawaiianisms" does not mean that it is considered without any doubt to be a locally created form. Other specialists in various languages and dialects may trace the origins of these expressions further, and may transfer some of them to different groups or explain them in other ways.

Scholars of Asian languages will be startled to see that entries attributed to the influence of the Chinese, Japanese, and Korean languages have been grouped together. This admittedly is a fault. A particular need of the study was for the assistance of a native speaker of Cantonese who had lived many years in Hawaii and could see the subtle influence of Cantonese on Hawaii's English in the years following the great migrations from China. Such a person was not found. The fact that Japanese and Korean are often discussed together in this book does not mean that these languages are thought to be similar in structure, but rather that similarities have been found in the semantic range of a few common words (that is, in the meanings included in basic words), and slight differences in the semantic coverage of parallel basic words in English—a factor that may be responsible for slight incongruities in loan translations into English (see *sleep late* in the glossary).

The final groupings are presented in tables 4–8 and a summary of the analysis is given in table 9.

TABLE 4   Island Expressions with Parallels in Pidgin or Creole Elsewhere

DIALECTAL FORM	STANDARD ENGLISH
been	auxiliary to show past tense
before	'formerly'
broke	'torn'
bumbye	'in the future'
catch	'get'
-fellow (suffix)	'person'
find for	'hunt for'
kaukau	'food', 'to eat'
look-see	'look'
more better	'better'
much	'many'
no, no can	'not', 'cannot'
number one	'the best'
one	'a'
pear	'avocado'
pickaninny (adj.)	'small'
pine	'pineapple'
plenty	'very', 'much', 'many'
sabe, savvy	'know', 'know how to'
-side (suffix)	'in the direction of'
stop, no stop	'is here', 'is not here'
talk story	'tell stories'
-them (suffix)	'and the others'
-time (suffix)	'at the time of'
too much	'very', 'very much', 'very many'
wen	auxiliary to show past time
wile	'to scold', 'drive away'

The results of the glossary study suggest that the Hawaiian language, especially through the process of loan translation, has had a far-reaching influence upon Hawaii's English speech. This would be expected, as the predictable effect of the indigenous language of the land. It was predictable, also, that the Asian languages, spoken by such vast numbers of plantation workers, should have made their impact on the English of the Islands during the time when that English speech was still unstable in the Islands. Those languages, even though they were brought into contact with English later than were Hawaiian and Portuguese, had a significant influence upon its use.

To some readers, the most surprising indication of the study will be that so many of the entries (more than one-fifth) should be survivals of some form of pidgin—the original Cantonese pidgin of China or the

Melanesian pidgin of the southwest Pacific, brought to the Islands long ago. Linguistic entities—phonetic traits, lexical items, and unique phrases—are often exceedingly long lived. In Europe, dialect traits have persisted in secluded areas for many centuries. It has been little more

TABLE 5 Expressions with Parallels in the Hawaiian Language

DIALECTAL FORM	STANDARD ENGLISH
(be) omission of the copula	'to be'
below of	'below'
come outside	'be born'
da kine	'what-you-may-call-it'
eye glass	'spectacles', 'glasses'
fire	'to burn'
get	'have'
-guys (suffix)	'and the others'
inside (the water)	'in', 'into'
level	'straight along'
news	'details', 'facts'
on (the car, etc.)	'in', 'into', 'at'
on top	'on'
poke	'injection', 'prick'
reach down	'reach', 'arrive'
sore head	'headache', 'sensitive scalp'
step	'step on'
the pretty	'how pretty'
till (the river, etc.)	'to'
wait a while	'wait a minute'

TABLE 6 Expressions with Parallels in the Portuguese Language

DIALECTAL FORM	STANDARD ENGLISH
already	'yet'
close (verb)	'turn off'
for (in infinitive)	'to'
for why	'why'
like	'want', 'want to'
make	'become'
no more nothing	'nothing'
stay (auxiliary)	'am', 'are', 'is'
(to) omission in the infinitive	'to'
what	'that'
word order of certain questions (e.g., "what I can do?")	('what can I do?')

TABLE 7 Expressions with Parallels in Chinese (C), Japanese (J), or Korean (K)

DIALECTAL FORM	STANDARD ENGLISH
alphabet (J, K)	'letter'
anybody (J, K)	'everybody'
attend to (J, K)	'attend'
bed clothes (J)	'pajamas', 'sleeping clothes'
borrow (C, J, K)	'use'
burn firecrackers (C)	'shoot firecrackers', 'shoot off'
chee (C)	'gee'
Christmas tree (J, K)	'poinsettia'
cut one's tonsils (J, K)	'have one's tonsils removed'
down the country; up the city (C, J, K)	'to the country', 'to the city'
get down from; get up into (a car) (J, K)	'get out of', 'get into', 'get in'
glass cup (J, K)	'drinking glass'
-half (suffix) (C, J, K)	'and a half'
meat (J, K)	'beef'
-no? (phrase ending) (J)	'isn't it?'
-quarter (suffix) (C, J, K)	'and a quarter'
saimin (C)	'noodle soup'
sleep late (J, K)	'go to bed late', 'fall asleep late'
throw out (J)	'throw up'
try (J, K)	'please'
-yeah? (as phrase ending) (J)	'is it?'

TABLE 8 Hawaiianisms (Expressions Apparently Unique to Hawaii)

DIALECTAL FORM	STANDARD ENGLISH
across	'across from'
bla	'brother'
blad	'objectionable person'
blast	'good', 'great'
but (at end of phrase)	'though'
chance	'turn'
clean yard	'cut the grass'
cool head main thing	'keep calm'
corns	'corn on the cob'
crack seed	'dried plums', 'cracked seed'
easily	'Take it easy!'
few	'a few'
from before	'before'
geev um	'give them everything'
go (auxiliary)	'shall', 'will', 'am going to'
go for broke	'make the extreme effort'
hard ('ass why hard)	'too bad', 'pity me'
humbug (adj.)	'bothersome' .

TABLE 8 (*Continued*)

DIALECTAL FORM	STANDARD ENGLISH
hybolic	'conceited', 'putting on airs'
junks	'small personal objects'
lawn-mow (verb) lawn-mower	'to cut', 'to mow'
local	'Hawaiian'
a mail	'a letter'
make quick	'be quick'
minor	'unimportant'
never (auxiliary)	'didn't', 'hasn't', 'haven't'
no big thing	'It doesn't matter.'
no more	'no'
(of) omission	'a pound of butter'
or what	'or about that', 'approximately'
package	'empty paper sack'
pull down	'lose weight'
rascal (adj.)	'naughty'
refreshments	'soft drinks'
scare	'afraid'
sha-ka, shahka	'that's good', 'great'
shame	'ashamed'
shave ice	'shaved ice'
slangs	'pidgin English', 'incorrect terms'
small-little	'little'
soft (make soft)	'be careful', 'be quiet'
some good	'very good'
spark	'see'
stuff, stuffs	'it' (pronoun), 'things'
suck wind	'go hungry'
tell	'say'
that's OK	'thank you', 'no, thank you'
tired for	'don't want to', 'too tired to'
used to to	'accustomed to', 'used to'
wassamatta you	'What's the matter with you?'
wasetime, waste-time (adj.)	'of no value', 'unimportant'

than a century, actually, since Cantonese pidgin was used enthusiastically in the China ports and since the days of the fur, sandalwood, and whaling trades when ships stopped regularly in Hawaii, bringing this new "language of business and travel" with them.

As this study makes clear, the effect of the Portuguese language does not equal that of the Hawaiian or the Asian languages—a fact that might have been recognized earlier but for the lack of serious exploration of the influences of those languages, to balance the exhaustive research done by several scholars on Portuguese parallels.

The appearance of about one-half of the glossary terms in a category called "Hawaiianisms"—locally developed words or phrases—should serve as a stimulus for further study. Many of these entries may later be shown to have parallels in one of the foreign languages named, or to have developed from other influences.

TABLE 9   Summary of Glossary Analysis

TABLE	CATEGORY	NUMBER OF ENTRIES	PERCENT OF TOTAL
4	Island terms with parallels in pidgin, neo-pidgin, or creole areas	27	21
5	Terms with parallels in the Hawaiian language	20	15
6	Terms with parallels in Portuguese	11	9
7	Terms with parallels in Chinese, Japanese, or Korean	21	16
8	Hawaiianisms	51	39
	TOTAL	130	100

Chapter 11 **In Conclusion**

Because this book has been written so largely *for* Hawaii and Hawaii's people, it should attempt to answer a question that is persistently heard from local observers: Does pidgin still exist in the Islands? The word pidgin, however, may mean many things to many people and we should examine several meanings of the word, as a review, in part, of statements made earlier in the book.

First, there is the meaning given by sociologists that pidgin is a form of language used in a certain situation. When two persons confronting each other have different native languages that are mutually unintelligible, they sometimes communicate in pidgin. Such a situation produced plantation pidgin in the Islands during the years before and after the turn of the century. That situation has passed with the times. The nearest approach to it today may be the immigrant conversing with a speaker of standard English who pidginizes his own speech to gain rapport and understanding. An example was given in chapter 2.

Second, there is the definition of pidgin English as a dialect greatly reduced in structure as compared with the fully developed language. In this sense, a great deal of pidgin exists in Hawaii today, some of it retained and developed deliberately as a language of youth and peer-group appeal (see chapter 4). Its popular name is "pidgin" although it is more accurately called "Hawaiian creole English."

Third, there is the meaning of pidgin that identifies it with terms brought to the Islands from pidgin and creole areas in other parts of the

167

world. The glossary study has pinpointed twenty-seven terms in this category. The majority of these pidgin nuggets may be heard in the speech of Types I, II, and III with a high frequency of occurrence. Although this nonstandard English, with its admixture of imported pidgin terms, is scientifically termed "creole," it too is almost universally known as "pidgin" to Islanders and visitors.

Thus to the question "Does pidgin exist in Hawaii?" the answer must be given in accordance with the definition of pidgin the inquirer has in mind. In the first sense, as a plantation situation involving large numbers of immigrants and their overseers, the answer is *no*—certainly not as it existed in the late nineteenth century. In the second sense, as a dialect greatly reduced in structure, the answer must be *yes*—it is present and is "pidgin" to the man on the street. In the third sense, as imported expressions from pidgin or creole sources away from the state, the answer again is *yes*—it is abundantly present and is also called "pidgin" by Island people.

A purpose of this book, more significant than dealing with the many meanings of pidgin and its identification in Hawaii, has been to show the element of movement and change from the less completely developed types of English to the more developed ones, and to show that a great deal of Island speech today already falls within the category called here Type V.

This progression is clearly evident to long-time observers. Casual readers of the glossary in this book, however, after seeing the entries "omission of *to*" and "omission of *of*" might conclude that there is a wholesale dropping of the preposition in Island nonstandard speech. Such a conclusion would be far from correct. Prepositions are handled more and more ably, as the years pass, by speakers in the nonstandard categories. Only a few prepositions still stubbornly give difficulty. Progress goes on steadily in the use of these and other structure words and in the manipulation of inflected forms of content words, as well as in the myriad other details of fully developed English.

To the author, whose period of interested observation has covered well over a quarter of a century, the degree of growth within that length of time seems remarkable. Yet the greatest growth has taken place almost explosively within the last ten or fifteen years. The new affluence in the United States has made it possible for many Island families to take their children to the Mainland for occasional trips—there to be exposed to the subtle varieties of the English language from coast to coast in its (more or less) standard forms. This same affluence has also provided the means for sending greater numbers of young people to college, either on the Mainland or at home. New kinds of employment have become available

to Island students in recent years, for example, in businesses that provide contacts with Hawaii's visitors, bringing opportunities to hear standard English from a variety of speakers and to gain ease in its use day after day. In the past, students often learned standard spoken English in the classroom, but then had no opportunity to use it in real, living situations. Furthermore, although the effect of television on language standardization in Hawaii has never been assessed, its influence has surely been very great.

What has just been said about the rapid progression toward standard forms in Hawaii does not apply, of course, to the confirmed local speakers of the "fun-language" of Type III, who practice the ultimate in reduction of language structure. With some, this fun-language can be turned on and off at will. Many others, the habitual users of this neo-pidgin or Hawaiian creole, show an inability (or unwillingness) to change and a hopelessness about language, usually coupled with a total disinterest in occupations that require the use of Type V English. However, the majority of Hawaii's speakers, it is safe to say, are fully aware of the trend toward language standardization and feel a desire to be a part of it.

Nowhere is the change more impressive than in the entering freshman class at the University of Hawaii. Decades ago it was quite usual for freshmen to come to the campus with obvious handicaps in their handling of spoken English, even after the screening process had identified the most deficient ones for special classes. Today, as each autumn comes around, greater numbers of students from local high schools arrive on the campus with an admirable freedom in oral expression and an ease in manner. A quarter of a century ago the ability to handle standard English (and the accompanying self-confidence) came to the few; today it has come with a sudden rush to the many.

The author has most particularly attempted to point out that there are reasonable explanations for the structure of the nonstandard types of Hawaii's English and that divergences can by no means be ascribed simply to "carelessness." There are powerful linguistic influences at work in Hawaii—a meeting point of the great languages of the East and the great languages of the West, and a spot on the globe that has seen, within its narrow confines, an extensive and fascinating contact between those languages.

**Technical
Terms
Defined**

AFFRICATE. A two-part consonant, composed of a stop plus a movement through a fricative position (Gleason 1961:22). The English *ch* begins with a sound similar to /t/ and is released with a sound similar to /š/.

ALLOPHONE. A variety or subtype of a phoneme. The forms of the sound *p* are slightly different in the words *pool* [pʰul] and *spool* [spul]. Each of the two *p* sounds is a different allophone of the phoneme /p/.

ALVEOLAR. Designating the gum ridge (alveolar ridge) just behind the upper front teeth. The term is also used for a consonant articulated at this point, for example, the phoneme /t/.

ALVEOPALATAL. Describing a consonant articulated at a point between the alveolar ridge and the hard palate, for example, the phoneme /č/ in *cheese*.

ASPIRATED. Accompanied by an emission of air at the point of articulation. Example: the aspirated [tʰ] in the word *teach* [tʰič].

ASSIMILATION. In phonetics, the action by which one speech sound is changed to a second sound under the influence of a third sound. In partial assimilation, the second sound becomes more like the third one; in complete assimilation, the second sound becomes identical with the third one.

BILABIAL. Formed with the action of the two lips. The consonants /p/, /b/, and /m/ are bilabial.

CONNECTOR. A general term for such words as *be* and *seem*, for example, in the sentences "John is a man," and "He seems thin." Most English

connectors are verbs (Hockett 1958:196). Also called *linking verb* and *copula*.

CONSONANT CLUSTER. Two or more consonants standing next to each other without an intervening nonconsonant, as in the words wasp and splendid. Also, often called *cluster*.

CONTENT WORDS. In linguistic analyses, all nouns, adjectives, adverbs, and main verbs—words that carry the lexical meaning as opposed to *structure words* that show the grammatical relationships within a sentence. See also *contentives*.

CONTENTIVES. Words, or portions of words which are important for meaning, as opposed to *functors* which are important for indicating grammatical relationships (Hockett 1958:261–264).

CORPUS. A body of material being studied in a particular piece of research; a term used in linguistic analyses.

CREOLE. A pidgin which has become the common language of a multilingual community and hence the language of the cradle to the community's children. The vocabulary of such a language is enlarged with words from the home and school so that it becomes a *creolized pidgin* or a *creole language*.

DENTAL CONSONANT. A consonant articulated at the back of the front teeth. The "dental *t*" is contained in some Asian languages but not in English, which has an alveolar *t*. The dental *t*, however, has become a part of Type III speech in Hawaii, where it adds to the non-English effect of the syllable-timed rhythm.

DIALECT. A variety of a language, distinguished from other varieties by differences in pronunciation, grammar, or vocabulary. As used in this book, the standard dialect of English refers to the socially preferred variety of the language as opposed to nonstandard dialects. The adjective *dialectal*, however, is sometimes used to mean the nonstandard in comparison with the standard, as in the Glossary study of chapter 10.

DIP INTONATION. A characteristic intonation pattern in the Korean language, consisting of a fall of the voice immediately followed by a rise.

EXCRESCENT. Excessive or intrusive, as an excrescent sound. It is often an extra vowel sound not appearing in the spelling of the word.

FLAP. A sound made by touching some part of the tongue very briefly to some point of articulation and bringing it away sharply before the characteristic quality of a stop or affricate can be heard (Francis 1958:88–89). Although the flap is rare in American English, it is heard regularly in a large part of the United States as the pronunciation of the medial consonant in *letter*, *butter*, and similar words.

FORTIS. A speech sound pronounced with muscular tension and strong articulation. Examples in Korean are /pp/ and /ss/. See chapter 2.

FRICATIVE. A consonant produced with audible friction as the breath is forced through a constriction in the vocal passage. Examples are /v/ and /s/.

FUNCTION WORDS. Words that indicate grammatical relationships between parts of a sentence. Examples are prepositions, conjunctions, articles. Another term is *structure words*.

FUNCTOR. In linguistics, any of three kinds of structures: (1) substitutes such as *it* and *all*, (2) markers such as *be* and *and*, (3) inflectional affixes such as -*s* (plural) and -*ed* (past tense). See Hockett 1958:264.

GLIDE. A sound involving the movement of the tongue from one articulatory position to another; for example, in forming the glide [ʊ] in the diphthong [aʊ], the tongue moves from a point near the position for [a] toward the position for [u].

GLOTTAL FRICATIVE. A sound articulated at the vocal cords as they are held in a partially closed position, for example, the consonant /h/, a phoneme of English.

GLOTTAL STOP. A sound articulated as the vocal cords are drawn tightly together; its symbol is /ʔ/. This consonant is one of the phonemes of the Hawaiian language but not of English.

GRAMMATICAL CORE. The part-of-speech system, the grammatical categories, the functors, and the structure patterns of a language (Hockett 1958:265).

HAWAIIANISM. A word or expression unique to the Hawaiian Islands or retained as an archaism there.

HYBRID COMPOUND. A compound word whose elements are derived from different languages.

INFLECTION. An element added to a word to denote a grammatical function, without altering the part of speech, as the -*s* of apple*s*, indicating the plural form. The word is not used in this book to mean an alternation of the pitch or tone of the voice.

INTERDENTAL CONSONANT. A consonant made with the tip of the tongue advanced to the edges of the front teeth. The two *th* sounds, [θ] and [ð], are pronounced as interdental consonants by most native speakers of English.

INTERVOCALIC SOUND. A sound standing between two vowels, as the consonant in *A*da.

INTONATION. The different features of speech melody. Features of intonation are stress, pitch, terminal contours, and juncture; these are the suprasegmental phonemes of English.

JUNCTURE. The way in which sounds succeed each other in connected speech. *Plus* juncture is roughly the same as a momentary *pause*: between /t/ and /r/ there is a break or pause in *night rate*. *Close* juncture

is the lack of pause: between /t/ and /r/ there is no break or pause in *nitrate*.

LABIO-DENTAL. Denoting a consonant sound during the production of which the breath is obstructed by the lower lip against the upper front teeth. There are two labio-dentals in English: /f/ and /v/.

LATERAL. In English, the consonant /l/, during the formation of which the breath carrying the sound escapes over one or both sides of the tongue.

LAX VOWEL. A vowel such as [ɪ] or [ʊ] made without the muscular tension characteristic of tense vowels such as [i] and [u].

LENIS. Articulated with very little muscular tension; weak, soft. Examples in Korean are /p/ and /t/.

LIQUID. The sounds /l/, /r/, and their various allophones.

LOANBLEND. A compound word in which the elements are derived from different languages; also called a hybrid compound.

LOANWORD. A word adopted from another language which has come into widespread use in English. It may have become at least partly anglicized in pronunciation, as in the French word *chauffeur*.

MARKER. In linguistics, a word which acts as a structural marker, or signal. Such words serve less as carriers of meaning and more as indicators of the relationships between other words in the sentence or phrase. Also called *structure words* in this book. An example is the *and* of "boys and girls."

NASAL. Referring to the English consonants /m/, /n/, and /ŋ/. During the formation of these the breath is released through the nasal passage.

NATIVE SPEAKER. A person who speaks a language as his first language or mother tongue.

OBSTRUENTS. The stops, affricates, and spirants or fricatives in contrast to the *sonorants* (vowels, nasals, liquids, and the glides /w/ and /y/).

OFFGLIDE. The second part of a diphthong or complex vowel such as [aʊ].

PEAK. Designating the most prominent element of a syllable in the English language. A syllable of the peak type has a vowel as its center.

PHONEME. An element of a language (consonant, vowel, stress, pitch, etc.) which stands in contrast to every other element in that language. A change of a single phoneme can often make a change of meaning. Examples: pet-bet /pɛt/-/bɛt/ and hit-hat /hɪt/-/hæt/.

PHONEMICIZATION. The analysis of a language and the organization of its many speech sounds into the relatively few significant sounds—that is, the essential sounds used within that language to distinguish meanings.

PHONOLOGY. The study of consonants, vowels, stress, intonation and

juncture; the study of the segmental and suprasegmental phonemes and how they are arranged in a language.

PIDGIN. A reduced, marginal language which has developed under the pressure of practical circumstances in a bilingual situation.

PITCH. The rise and fall of the voice in speech, resembling the changes of the voice in the musical scale.

PLUS JUNCTURE. A break in the flow of the voice in speech, as between many words. See *juncture*.

SEGMENTAL PHONEMES. The consonants, vowels, and glides of a language.

SEMIVOWELS. The sounds /w/ and /y/. These two sounds are also referred to as *glides*.

STOP. A consonant characterized by the complete stopping of the breath at some point in the vocal tract, followed typically by a quick release. An example is [p].

STRESS. One of the suprasegmental phonemes of English. Greater stress on a syllable means the application of greater force or loudness on that syllable.

STRESS-TIMED RHYTHM. The kind of speech rhythm characteristic of English. The length of time it takes to produce an utterance depends roughly upon the number of stresses in it, so that unstressed syllables are sometimes squeezed together and produced very rapidly (Hockett 1958:82).

SUPRASEGMENTAL PHONEMES. The features of stress, pitch, terminal contours, and juncture in a language.

SYLLABLE PEAK. The center or nucleus of a syllable. In English, this is a vowel. See *peak*.

SYLLABLE-TIMED RHYTHM. A kind of speech rhythm in which the stress or force is applied evenly upon each successive syllable in an utterance. Examples of languages with syllable-timed rhythm are Spanish, Japanese, and Korean.

TERMINAL CONTOUR. The direction taken by the voice at the end of a sentence or a portion of a sentence. There are three terminal contours: *falling*, as at the end of a command (Go home!); *rising*, as at the end of a simple question (Are you ready?); and *sustained*, used at pauses within a sentence. These features are sometimes called *clause terminals*.

VELAR. Referring to consonants such as /k/, /g/, and /ŋ/, which are stopped or obstructed by the action of the back of the tongue and the velum.

VOICED. Describing vowels and some consonants to indicate that the vibration of the vocal cords is a part of their composition.

VOICELESS. Describing consonants which do not have the vibration of the vocal cords as a feature of their production.

Bibliography

Andrews, Lorrin. 1922. *A Dictionary of the Hawaiian Language*. Revised by Henry H. Parker. Honolulu: Board of Commissioners of the Public Archives of the Territory of Hawaii.

Bailey, Beryl Loftman. 1966. *Jamaican Creole Syntax*. Cambridge: Cambridge University Press.

Baker, Sidney J. 1966. *The Australian Language*. Sydney: Currawong Publishing Co.

Ball, James Dyer. 1925. *Things Chinese: or Notes Connected with China*. Shanghai, Hongkong, and Singapore: Kelly and Walsh.

Bazore, Katherine. 1940. *Hawaiian and Pacific Foods*. New York: M. Barrows.

Bloch, Bernard, and George L. Trager. 1942. *Outline of Linguistic Analysis*. Baltimore: Waverly Press.

Bloomfield, Morton W., and Leonard Newmark. 1965. *A Linguistic Introduction to the History of English*. New York: Alfred A. Knopf.

Bronstein, Arthur J. 1960. *The Pronunciation of American English*. New York: Appleton-Century-Crofts.

Campbell, Archibald. 1967. *A Voyage Round the World from 1806 to 1812*. (Facsimile reproduction of the third American edition, 1822.) Honolulu: University of Hawaii Press.

Carr, Elizabeth Ball. 1953. "Trends in word compounding in American speech." Ph.D. dissertation, Louisiana State University.

———— 1960. "A recent chapter in the history of the English language in Hawaii." *Social Process in Hawaii* 24:54–62.

———— 1961. "Bilingual speakers in Hawaii today." *Social Process* 25:53–57.

———— 1961. "The fiftieth state: new dimensions for studies in speech." *The Speech Teacher* 10:283–290.

———— 1968. "Pidgin English and dialects in Hawaii." *All about Hawaii: Thrum's Hawaiian Almanac* 90:199–203.

Carro, Andrés, ed. n. d. (ca. 1956). *Iloko-English Dictionary*. Translated, augmented, and revised by Morice Vanoverbergh. Baguio, Philippines: Catholic School Press.

Cassell's Spanish Dictionary. 1966. New York: Funk and Wagnalls.

Cassidy, Frederic G. 1961. *Jamaica Talk: Three Hundred Years of the English Language in Jamaica*. London: Macmillan.

Cassidy, Frederic G., and Robert B. Le Page, eds. 1967. *Dictionary of Jamaican English*. Cambridge: Cambridge University Press.

Ching, Iris. 1967. *Chop! Chop!: Chinese Recipes Simplified*. Honolulu.

Chiu, Chiang Ker, ed. n. d. *A Practical English-Cantonese Dictionary*. Singapore: Lam Yeong Press.

Cho, Sung Shik, Byung Jo Chung, and Pong Shik Kang, eds. 1964. *A New English-Korean Dictionary*. Seoul: Omungak Publishing Co.

Craigie, William, and James R. Hulbert, eds. 1938–1944. *A Dictionary of American English on Historical Principles*. 4 vols. Chicago: University of Chicago Press. (DAE)

Crowley, Daniel J. 1966. *I Could Talk Old-Story Good: Creativity in Bahamian Folklore*. Folklore Studies 17. Berkeley and Los Angeles: University of California Press.

Das, Upendra Kumar, comp. 1945. "Terms used on Hawaiian plantations." Revised. Honolulu: Hawaiian Sugar Planters' Association. Mimeographed.

Day, A. Grove. 1951. "How to talk in Hawaii." *American Speech* 26:18–26.

Department of Speech, University of Hawaii. Results of a questionnaire returned by five hundred students, circa 1950. Mimeographed.

Elbert, Samuel H. 1962. "Symbolism in Hawaiian poetry." *ETC: A Review of General Semantics* 18:389–400.

Ferguson, Charles A. 1968. "Absence of copula in normal speech, baby talk, and pidgins." Paper read at the Conference on the Pidginization and Creolization of Languages, April 10, 1968, at the University of the West Indies, Mona, Jamaica. Mimeographed.

Francis, W. Nelson. 1958. *The Structure of American English*. New York: Ronald Press.

Gleason, H. A., Jr. 1961. *An Introduction to Descriptive Linguistics*. Rev. ed. New York: Holt, Rinehart and Winston.

Hall, Robert A., Jr. 1943. *Melanesian Pidgin English*. Baltimore: Waverly Press.

———— 1955. *Hands Off Pidgin English!* Sydney: Pacific Publications.

Haugen, Einar. 1953. *The Norwegian Language in America: A Study in Bilingual Behavior*. 2 vols. Philadelphia: University of Pennsylvania Press.

Hayakawa, Samuel I. 1962. "Hawaii has it made in Webster's Third." *Honolulu Star-Bulletin*, July 28, 1962.

Hayes, Robert Warren. 1958. "A phonological study of the English speech of selected Japanese speakers in Hawaii." Master's thesis, University of Hawaii.

Hermosisima, Tomas V., ed. 1966. *Bisayan-English-Tagalog Dictionary*. Manila: P. B. Ayuda.

Hervey, Wesley D. 1968. "A history of the adaptations of an orthography for the Hawaiian language." Ph.D. dissertation, University of Oregon.

Hockett, Charles F. 1958. *A Course in Modern Linguistics*. New York: Macmillan.

Holman, Lucia R. 1931. *Journal of Lucia Ruggles Holman*. Bernice P. Bishop Museum. Special Publication no. 17, Honolulu.

Holt, John Dominis. 1965. *Today Ees Sad-dy Night*. Honolulu: Star-Bulletin Printing Co.

Hongo, Bob Nobuyuki. 1958. *Hey, Pineapple!* Tokyo: Kokuseido Press.

Hormann, Bernhard L. 1960. "Hawaii's linguistic situation: a sociological interpretation in the new key." *Social Process in Hawaii* 24:6–31.

Houaiss, Antônio, and Catherine B. Avery, eds. 1964. *The New Appleton Dictionary of the English and Portuguese Languages*. New York: Appleton-Century-Crofts.

Hunter, Gene. 1968. "Fresh approaches to old problems." *Honolulu Advertiser*. August 13, 1968.

Hymes, Dell, ed. 1971. *Pidginization and Creolization of Languages*. Cambridge: Cambridge University Press.

Iwasaki, Tamihei, and Jujiro Kawamura, eds. 1960. *Kenkyusha's New English-Japanese Dictionary on Bilingual Principles*. Tokyo: Kenkyusha.

Judd, Bernice. 1931. "Early days of Waimea, Hawaii." *Hawaiian Historical Society, Fortieth Annual Report*: 16–20. Honolulu.

Judd, Gerrit Parmele, IV. 1961. *Hawaii: An Informal History*. New York: Collier Books.

Kindig, Maita M. 1960. "A phonological study of the English speech of selected speakers of Puerto Rican Spanish in Honolulu." Master's thesis, University of Hawaii.

Knowlton, Edgar C., Jr. 1960. "Portuguese in Hawaii." *Kentucky Foreign Language Quarterly* 7:212–218.

———— 1961. "Hawaii, a linguist's paradise in the Pacific." *The Linguist* 23:266–323.

———— 1967. "Pidgin English and Portuguese." *Proceedings of the Symposium on Historical, Archaeological, and Linguistic Studies on Southern China, S.E. Asia and the Hong Kong Region*. Hong Kong: Hong Kong University Press.

Kuykendall, Ralph Simpson. 1938. *The Hawaiian Kingdom, 1778–1854: Foundation and Transformation*. Honolulu: University of Hawaii. (Reprinted 1968, University of Hawaii Press.)

———— 1953. *The Hawaiian Kingdom, 1854–1874: Twenty Critical Years*. Honolulu: University of Hawaii Press.

———— 1967. *The Hawaiian Kingdom, 1874–1893: The Kalakaua Dynasty*. Honolulu: University of Hawaii Press.

Kuykendall, Ralph Simpson, and A. Grove Day. 1961. *Hawaii, a History: From Polynesian Kingdom to American State*. Rev. ed. Englewood Cliffs, N. J.: Prentice-Hall.

Lasker, Bruno. 1969. *Filipino Immigration to Continental United States and to Hawaii*. New York: Arno Press and the New York Times.

Laycock, Donald C. n. d. *Course in New Guinea (Sepik) Pidgin*. Canberra: Australian National University. Mimeographed.

Leland, Charles G. 1904. *Pidgin-English Sing-Song, or Songs and Stories in the China-English Dialect, with a Vocabulary*. 7th ed. London: Kegan Paul, Trench, Trübner and Co.

Le Page, Robert B., and David De Camp. 1960. *Jamaican Creole: Creole Language Studies I*. London: Macmillan.

Lind, Andrew W. 1960. "Communication: a problem of Island youth." *Social Process in Hawaii* 24:44–53.

———— 1967. *Hawaii's People*. 3rd ed. Honolulu: University of Hawaii Press.

Livermore, Harold V. 1966. *A New History of Portugal*. Cambridge: Cambridge University Press.

Lyons, Curtis J. 1892. "Traces of Spanish influences in the Hawaiian Islands." *Hawaiian Historical Society Papers, no. 2*. Honolulu.

―――― 1963. "How the paniolo came." *Paradise of the Pacific* 75(4):27. Honolulu.

McDavid, Raven I., Jr. 1958. "The dialects of American English." In *The Structure of American English* by W. Nelson Francis, Chap. 9. New York: Ronald Press.

Martin, Samuel E. 1954. *Essential Japanese*. Rutland, Vermont: Charles E. Tuttle.

―――― 1951. "Korean Phonemics." *Language* 27:519–533.

Mathews, Mitford M., ed. 1951. *A Dictionary of Americanisms on Historical Principles*. Chicago: University of Chicago Press.

Meyer, Bernard F., and Theodore F. Wempe, eds. 1947. *The Student's Cantonese-English Dictionary*. 3rd ed. New York: Field Afar Press.

Mihalic, Francis. 1957. *Grammar and Dictionary of Neo-Melanesian*. Techny, Illinois: Mission Press.

Minson, William M. 1952. "The Hawaiian journal of Manuel Quimper." Master's thesis, University of Hawaii.

Morimoto, Patricia Toshie. 1966. "The Hawaiian dialect of English: An aspect of communication during the Second World War." Master's thesis, University of Hawaii.

Nagara, Susumu. 1969. "A bilingual description of some linguistic features of pidgin English used by Japanese immigrants on the plantations of Hawaii: A case study in bilingualism." Ph.D. dissertation, University of Wisconsin.

Oxford English Dictionary. 1933. Oxford: Clarendon Press. (OED)

Panganiban, José Villa, comp. 1966. *Talahuluganang Pilipino-Ingles*. Manila: Kawanihan ng Palimbagan.

Phelan, John Leddy. 1967. *The Hispanization of the Philippines*. Madison: University of Wisconsin Press.

Pires, Mário de Costa. 1956. *Portuguese As It Is Spoken*. 2nd ed. rev. Lisbon: A. M. Teixeira.

Pratte, Alf. 1968. "Go for broke is Hawaiian as hula." *Honolulu Star-Bulletin*, May 15, 1968.

Pukui, Mary Kawena, and Samuel H. Elbert, comps. 1957. *Hawaiian-English Dictionary*. Honolulu: University of Hawaii Press. (Reprinted 1971, Pukui and Elbert, *Hawaiian Dictionary*, University of Hawaii Press.)

―――― 1964. *English-Hawaiian Dictionary*. Honolulu: University of Hawaii Press. (Reprinted 1971, Pukui and Elbert, *Hawaiian Dictionary*, University of Hawaii Press.)

―――― 1966. *Place Names of Hawaii*. Honolulu: University of Hawaii Press.

Quimper, Manuel. 1822. *Islas de Sandwich*. Madrid: E. Aguido.

Reinecke, John E. 1969. *Language and Dialect in Hawaii*. Edited by Stanley M. Tsuzaki. Honolulu: University of Hawaii Press.

Reinecke, John E., and Aiko Tokimasa. 1934. "The English dialect of Hawaii." *American Speech* 9:48–58, 122–131.

Reinecke, John E., and Stanley M. Tsuzaki. 1967. "Hawaiian loanwords in Hawaiian English of the 1930's." *Oceanic Linguistics* 6(2):80–115.

Roberts, Paul. 1956. *Patterns of English*. New York: Harcourt, Brace, and World.

Serjeantson, Mary S. 1961. *A History of Foreign Words in English*. New York: Barnes and Noble.

Shun, Laura Lynn. 1961. "A study of selected bilingual speakers of English in the Hawaiian Islands." Master's thesis, University of Hawaii.

Smith, William Carlson. 1933. "Pidgin English in Hawaii." *American Speech* 8:15–19.

Steinberg, Rafael, and the Editors of Time-Life Books. 1970. *Pacific and Southeast Asian Cooking*. New York: Time-Life Books.

Stewart, C. S. 1970. *Journal of a Residence in the Sandwich Islands*. (Facsimile reproduction of the third edition, 1830.) Honolulu: University of Hawaii Press.

Strevens, Peter, and English Language Services. 1968. *English 901*. Collier-Macmillan English Programme, Book I. London: Collier-Macmillan.

Thomas, Charles K. 1958. *An Introduction to the Phonetics of American English*. 2nd ed. New York: Ronald Press.

Trager, George L., and Henry Lee Smith, Jr. 1957. *An Outline of English Structure*. Washington: American Council of Learned Societies.

Tsuzaki, Stanley M. 1968. "Common Hawaiian words and phrases used in English." *Journal of English Linguistics* 2:78–85.

Vanderslice, Ralph, and Laura Shun Pierson. 1967. "Prosodic features of Hawaiian English." *Quarterly Journal of Speech* 53:156–166.

Webster's New International Dictionary of the English Language. 2nd ed. Unabridged. 1934. Springfield, Mass.: G. and C. Merriam Co. (Webster's Second)

Webster's Third New International Dictionary of the English Language. Unabridged. 1964. Springfield, Mass.: G. and C. Merriam Co. (Webster's Third)

Weinreich, Uriel. 1964. *Languages in Contact: Findings and Problems*. The Hague: Mouton and Co.

Williams, Hermon P., comp. 1929. *Dictionary of English-Ilocano and Ilocano-English*. Revised by Angel B. Guerrero. Manila: Christian Mission.

Wise, Claude M. 1957. *Applied Phonetics*. Englewood Cliffs, N. J.: Prentice-Hall.

Wist, Benjamin O. 1940. *A Century of Public Education in Hawaii: 1840–1940*. Special Publication of *Hawaii Educational Review*. Honolulu: Department of Public Instruction, Territory of Hawaii.

Index to Loanwords

This list includes all loanwords discussed or mentioned in the text (some of them no longer heard in the Islands), but excludes family names and place names.

General Index

Affixes: abstract governing derivational, 29; inflectional, 29, 64
Agreement, grammatical, 65
Akana, Annie Loo: analysis of the speech of, 38–43; interview with, 34–38; Type III speech compared with, 50, 54
Allophones, 22, 32, 39
Alveolar flap, 23
Alveolar lateral, 23
American English. See Standard American English
Andrews, Lorrin, 83
Anthony, Pualani Pung (PPA), 124, 129, 133, 134, 154
Archaisms, 58, 63, 65, 161. See also Relic forms
Articles: definite, 41, 54; indefinite, 41–42, 54. See also Function words; Markers
Assimilation, phonetic, 25, 50
Auxiliaries. See Tense, grammatical
Azores, 5, 53, 95, 96, 97

Bahamian folk speech, 55
Baker, Sidney J., 144
Ball, James Dyer, 138
"Barred *i*," 9 n

Bazore, Katherine, 104
Bidialectal group, 56
Bloomfield, Morton W., 81
Borrowings, linguistic. See Loanblends; Loan translations; Loanwords; Syllable-timed rhythm
British pronunciation, 3, 9 n.1, 12, 58. See also Received standard pronunciation
Bronstein, Arthur J., 8 n, 10
Bushnell, O. A., consultant on Glossary study, 120–166

Calques, 82. See also Loan translations
Campbell, Archibald, 97
Cantonese pidgin. See Pidgin
Carr, Denzel (DC), consultant on Glossary study, 120–166
Case, grammatical, 28
Cassidy, Frederic G., 65, 122, 143, 153, 156
Cassidy, Frederic G., and Robert B. Le Page, 55, 108, 123, 144, 157
Caucasians, 45, 67, 77. See also Haoles
Central Midland pronunciation. See Standard American English
Chinese language, 98, 122, 161, 164. See also Loanwords, Chinese

185